Chinese Philosophy

An Introduction

Ronnie L. Littlejohn

I.B. TAURIS

LONDON · NEW YORK

Published in 2016 by
I.B.Tauris & Co. Ltd
London • New York
www.ibtauris.com

Library of Modern Religion 44

ISBN: 978 1 78453 261 1 (HB)
978 1 78453 262 8 (PB)
eISBN: 978 0 85773 982 7

A full CIP record for this book is available from the British Library
A full CIP record is available from the Library of Congress

Library of Congress Catalog Card Number: available

Typeset by Free Range Book Design & Production Limited
Printed and bound in Great Britain by T.J. International, Padstow, Cornwall

Ronnie L. Littlejohn is Virginia M. Chaney Distinguished Professor of Philosophy and Director of Asian Studies at Belmont University, Nashville, Tennessee. His previous books include *Confucianism: An Introduction* (I.B.Tauris, 2011), *Daoism: An Introduction* (I.B.Tauris, 2009) and *Riding the Wind with Liezi: New Perspectives on the Daoist Classic* (2011).

"This work is a comprehensive and highly analytical presentation of Chinese philosophy from the earliest beginnings to the modern era. Arranged thematically in four parts, covering ontology, epistemology, value theory, and political philosophy, it is both daunting in its scope and amazing in its depth. Each section presents the basic features of the kind of philosophy in question, followed by extensive discussions and translations from relevant Chinese works, creating intrinsic connections between eras and opening a powerful vision of the intricate unfolding of Chinese thought. The book inspires and challenges while engaging and clarifying an established subject in an illuminating new light."

Livia Kohn, Professor Emerita of Religion and East Asian Studies, Boston University

"This is an amazingly well-written and helpful introduction to the topic. Systematically divided into four parts—the ontological, the epistemological, the moral and the political—it explores fundamental questions through which readers may begin to appreciate the specificity of Chinese philosophy as well as its commonality with Western philosophy. The book offers a fascinating treatment, from ancient times to the present day, of well-selected Chinese philosophers, their texts and their doctrines: sometimes in comparison with the most important Western philosophers like Plato, Berkeley, Mill, Whitehead and Wittgenstein. Ronnie Littlejohn has written the best concise introductory book of its kind on the market. It does a great job in orienting undergraduate students; it will similarly prove to be of real value to general readers; and even specialists and experts in the field will gain a good deal from reading it."

Vincent Shen, Lee Chair in Chinese Thought and Culture, University of Toronto

"It is daringly ambitious to try to present in a short monograph an overview of what Chinese philosophy as a whole might bring to world philosophical conversation. Yet within a framework of questions that are recognizably philosophical, as well as global, Professor Littlejohn's refreshing thematic approach introduces readers to how Chinese philosophers of different historical periods—and associated with varied schools of thought—think, and what positions they have adopted on the nature of reality, knowledge, value, and government. Written with admirable clarity and breadth, Littlejohn's book succeeds in communicating the distinctive tenors of Chinese thought and experience. This is an invaluable resource for teaching Chinese philosophy that will interest general readers as well as students and their teachers."

Sor-hoon Tan, Associate Professor of Philosophy, National University of Singapore

"With a talented and discerning brush, this discriminating and at the same time student-friendly work paints a vivid picture of the Chinese philosophical landscape. Its canvas is broad, its execution is elegant; and it is sure to serve as a welcome resource for our deeper understanding of philosophy in a global setting."

Robin R. Wang, Professor of Philosophy, Director of Asian and Pacific Studies, Loyola Marymount University; author of *Yinyang: The Way of Heaven and Earth in Chinese Thought and Culture* (2012)

哲学

Contents

Preface   vii
Introduction   1

Chapter I   Ontology: Questions about the Nature of Reality   7

Chapter II   Epistemology: Questions about the Nature and   63
               Scope of Knowledge

Chapter III   Value Theory: Questions about the Nature and   111
               Application of Morality

Chapter IV   Political Philosophy: Questions about the Nature   169
               and Purpose of Government

Guide to Philosophers and Significant Works   223
Quick Guide to Pronunciation   237
Comparative Chronology of Philosophers   239
Notes   245
References   253
Index   267

哲学

Preface

This introduction to Chinese philosophy is offered as a substantive overview to a vast and far-reaching tradition. If we do indeed mark the beginning of Chinese philosophy at 1500 years BCE and bring it to the present day, it represents the longest continuous heritage of philosophical reflection among human beings. Trying to mention each philosopher in this enduring tradition is an impossible task in an introduction such as this. In fact, even covering every *significant* thinker is not possible. So, by necessity, I have been selective, choosing those philosophers who are most representative of the key contributions Chinese philosophy can make to the conversation of world philosophy. I have not tried to equalize the number of words given to each philosopher. Neither have I tried to choose a thinker to represent every historical period of Chinese philosophy. In fact, I propose no periodization of China's philosophical reflection in this work, since it is an introduction, not a history of Chinese philosophy. I have selected those thinkers who actually advance the conversation of philosophy. Sometimes, this means I have selected several thinkers from roughly the same period, while some historical eras have no representative on a particular question. Likewise, some philosophers make significant contributions on a given topic and contribute almost no real advance in the conversation on others.

I should also say that I have engaged several thinkers who are often not included in an introduction to Chinese philosophy. I have no doubt that a first impression of this work will lead those who know the field of Chinese philosophy rather well to conclude that I have allocated too much space to some thinkers and texts and not enough to others. Consider, for example, that the magnitude of Confucius's influence on

Chinese cultural and intellectual history, and indeed over much of East Asia in general, can hardly be exaggerated. Even today, there is an active and vital reappraisal of Confucianism going on in China and East Asia. However, this is not to say that Confucius is the only philosopher of interest China has produced. Frankly, I also think that, based on the records of his own thought available to us at present, Confucius leaves many fundamental philosophical questions wholly unexplored. Other Chinese thinkers, however, have extremely interesting things to say about them and actually contribute to the overall project of what I would call world philosophy.

Still some readers will insist that all Chinese philosophy is but commentary on Confucius! I am well aware, of course, that Alfred North Whitehead once observed of Western thought that the safest general characterization of the European philosophical tradition is that it consists of a series of footnotes on Plato. However, Whitehead amplified this comment in the following way:

> I do not mean the systematic scheme of thought which scholars have doubtfully extracted from his writings. I allude to the wealth of general ideas scattered through them. His personal endowments, his wide opportunities for experience at a great period of civilization, his inheritance of an intellectual tradition not yet stiffened by excessive systematization, have made his writing an inexhaustible mine of suggestion. (1979: 39)

One could make an argument on the basis of this amplification that all Chinese philosophy is a series of footnotes on Confucius, but such a view does not detract from the often-found uniqueness and contrariness of various Chinese thinkers regarding views that might come from Confucius's own extant remarks.

Since the first half of the twentieth century, philosophers have been dependent largely on the 1953 work of Fung Yulan (1895–1990) for an introduction to Chinese thought. What often goes overlooked, though, is that virtually the entirety of Fung's work can be classified as a history of Chinese philosophy, not a true introduction. Fung's works were complemented and supplemented by those of Wing-tsit Chan (1901–94), including his very significant work of primary materials, *A Sourcebook in Chinese Philosophy* (1963b). In fact, Chan was unquestionably the leading translator of Chinese philosophical texts into English in the first half of the twentieth century. Together both Fung and Chan contributed insights and interpretations to their expositions of Chinese philosophy and their contributions were many, varied and indispensable. Nonetheless, neither of these pioneering scholars tried to provide an overview of Chinese philosophy as it might be understood to address fundamental philosophical questions in a systematic way. This task is the principal objective of this book.

In the years since the publications of Fung and Chan, a great deal of ongoing dialogue, discovery of new texts, greater appreciation for comparative philosophy, and the emergence of new scholars conversant with Chinese philosophy have become factors requiring the need for the introduction to Chinese philosophical thought as a part of world philosophical reflection. This evolving situation has not escaped the notice of scholars. In 1985, Donald Bishop edited a volume of expository and critical essays entitled *Chinese Thought: An Introduction*. This work follows the convention employed when approaching Western philosophy and divides Chinese philosophical history into Ancient, Medieval and Modern periods, even though, in my view, such a demarcation is much less appropriate for Chinese philosophy. In the essays, scholars wrote on key figures from each period. Bishop's volume has the virtues of making an effort to provide a comprehensive snapshot of the most important Chinese philosophers and often offering suggestive and significant critical observations. However, it too is mostly on the model of a history of Chinese philosophy.

Chung-ying Cheng and Nicholas Bunnin edited a set of essays focused on *Contemporary Chinese Philosophy* in 2002. This work is a very fine collection and it serves as a solid introduction to modern Chinese thinkers, rightly noting that what was known about Chinese thought by most Western academics, even so recently as 2002, was confined to the "classical" period. Cheng and Bunnin divided the contemporary period into four stages designed by them to cover "all the major philosophical developments and philosophical positions of Chinese philosophy in the twentieth century" (xiv).

In 2006, Jeeloo Liu published an *Introduction to Chinese Philosophy: From Ancient Philosophy to Chinese Buddhism*. Liu severely restricted the scope of her introduction by considering only those philosophers through roughly the ninth century. Accordingly, her introduction can give the impression that nothing of significance has been done philosophically in China since the classical period, or certainly since the Tang dynasty, although, of course, Liu does not believe this. For many, there is a concern even more significant than the limited historical scope of Liu's book. A characteristic feature of this work is that it introduces thinkers by means of the methodology of Western analytic philosophical tradition. This kind of methodology tends to understand philosophical inquiry as limited to argument, logical distinction and preference for the empirically verifiable. Often analytic thinkers do not consider "philosophical" any form of discourse that cannot be put into an argument form, with premises and conclusions. Consequently, in an effort to demonstrate to Western readers that Chinese philosophy is real philosophy as defined in this way, Liu recasts passages from Chinese philosophical texts into arguments of the sort consistent with what analytic thinkers expect and value. I firmly believe Liu is right that many Chinese philosophers did make arguments, although I would claim they did so very rarely in the form that analytic philosophers would regard as normative for philosophical inquiry. Chinese philosophers often prefer analogy, appeal to historical allusions and metaphor in their way of doing philosophy. To so consistently force Chinese philosophy into the analytic model as Liu does may overlook the philosophical merits that emerge only if the method of the Chinese thinker is retained. Of course, this is not to say that Liu is not a skillful and well-informed interpreter of Chinese philosophy. She certainly is. Likewise, there are merits to sometimes exposing the argument of a Chinese thinker in such an explicit way. In this present work, I have endeavored to bring forward the argument structure employed when it is clearly intended by the Chinese philosopher, but I have also not tried to force a philosopher to make an argument of a certain form when he does not. Moreover, I have ambitiously taken on the project of considering philosophers up to the present in our overview, rather than so dramatically limiting the material historically as Liu did.

In 2008, two books of significance to an introduction of Chinese philosophy appeared. One of these was Karyn Lai's *An Introduction to Chinese Philosophy*. Lai, just as Liu had done, limited her introduction to cover only the period from the origins of Chinese philosophy to the emergence of Chan Buddhism (*c*.700–800). Lai writes a strong introduction to the period she chooses; however, she makes no effort to talk about the contemporary philosophic scene in China and more attention to the concepts, themes or aspects Western philosophy and Chinese philosophy both engage could have been included. When she does reference Western scholars, she is almost always concerned with their readings of a Chinese philosopher or text and not with a direct comparison between a claim made in the West and one put forward in China. The second work of importance to our project that came out in English in 2008 was Bo Mou's *A History of Chinese Philosophy*. This work is in the Routledge History of World Philosophies series and it is not a monograph. Mou devotes the chapters to various movements or periods and assigns them to individual contributors. While having many merits, this work really cannot serve readership in the English-speaking world as an introduction to Chinese philosophy principally because the philosophical issues that each contributor has picked out of a Chinese school of thought to become the focus of the chapter depend on the general philosophical perspective, knowledge, scope, intellectual interests and academic tastes of that author. This means that the component essays, while generally carefully researched and critically valuable, lack the flow and continuity needed for an actual introduction to the span of Chinese philosophy. Also, individual contributors generally do not engage other essays in the collection and the general editor does not provide coherent narratives to connect the contributions into a unified story. Of course, I realize this is not the purpose of the work. As a sourcebook for an author writing an introduction, Mou's work is of great value.

Now, having provided a brief survey of the range of works published in English in roughly the last 30 years, one thing is clear. Even though a number of these works present themselves as introductions to Chinese philosophy, they are all characteristically histories. But I suggest that for the person wishing to bring Chinese sources and philosophers into a coherent conversation about humanity's fundamental questions, these works typically spend too much time on the nature and structure of Chinese texts, historical events and internecine debates among Sinologists and specialists in Chinese philosophy to provide a thoroughly usable and ready-at-hand look at how the most dominant minds in China formulated approaches and answers to life's most basic questions.

In the present work, my purpose is to help the reader understand how Chinese philosophers approach philosophical questions and what positions they take. In doing so, I fully acknowledge my debt to all those persons whose works I have mentioned above and to my teachers and colleagues who have labored to help me become a better philosopher.

哲学

Introduction

Philosophy is sometimes thought of exclusively in terms of a philosophical movement or method of approaching fundamental questions associated with a prominent philosopher. For example, we can speak of Platonism, Aristotelianism, Confucianism, Epicureanism, Cartesianism, Kantianism and Hegelianism. At other times, the method used to approach fundamental questions, and even for regarding which questions are fundamental, becomes identified with philosophy itself. This happens when we speak of methodologies *as though* they exhausted the nature of philosophy: Empiricism, Rationalism, Idealism, Positivism, Existentialism, Phenomenology or Pragmatism. But I do not find either of these approaches particularly helpful as ways to introduce what sort of activity philosophy is.

Sometimes we can learn about an intellectual discipline just by looking at the content it addresses. We need not puzzle about the primary content of *literature, French, mathematics* or *accounting*. Unfortunately, this is somewhat less true about philosophy. The word *philosophy* comes from the Greek *philosophia* (φιλοσοφία), literally "love of wisdom"; this is certainly a project in which Chinese thinkers have been as seriously engaged as have Western ones. Still, at first sight this does not tell us much definitively about philosophy's subject mattter.

Actually, the best way to expose how philosophers love wisdom is to look at the kind of questions that concern them. If I ask a student, "What do you want to do when you graduate?" She may certainly answer in a completely nonphilosophical way. There is nothing about this question that requires a philosophical sort of answer. She may simply say, "be a doctor." I may go on to inquire, "How do you get to be a doctor?" Again, a reply may be given that is not philosophical. But suppose I ask, "Will it make you happy to be a doctor?" This sounds more like a philosophical question, although I suppose it could also be a psychological one. But if I inquire, "What is happiness, anyway?" then I have moved to the level of a philosophical question.

What is it that makes the last question a philosophical one? It is a fundamental question about human life and the universe that cannot be resolved by empirical means alone. Indeed, philosophers sometimes understand their work to be distinguishing those claims that are decidable empirically and those that are not. Traditionally, fundamental questions have been categorized as those having to do with epistemology (questions about the nature and scope of knowledge), ontology (questions about the nature of reality), morality (questions about values and value judgments), logic, personal identity, meaning of life (including questions about religion) and a host of topics known as "philosophy of ..." (e.g., philosophy of politics [political philosophy], philosophy of language or philosophy of psychology).

Fundamental questions occur as often to Chinese thinkers as they do to Westerners. It is not cultural ethnocentrism or intellectual imperialism to recognize them, sometimes in very interesting forms, in Chinese philosophical history. For example, some Chinese thinkers are as occupied with questions of epistemology (how we know something is true and the scope and range of our knowledge) as are some Western philosophers. Of course, this no more means that every Chinese philosopher stresses epistemology as a principal concern than it does that all Western philosophers do so. Moreover, Chinese philosophers often approach questions of epistemology differently and provide answers to them that very much set them apart from those offered by Western thinkers. This is one reason why Chinese Philosophy should be introduced into the conversation of world philosophical reflection.

Bertrand Russell, a significant Western philosopher of the twentieth century who visited China, held that the value of philosophy is, in fact, to be sought largely in the very uncertainty of its answers (1912: "The Value of Philosophy"). He argued that the person who has no tincture of philosophy goes through life imprisoned in the prejudices derived from common sense or from the habitual beliefs and convictions that have grown up in the mind without the co-operation or consent of deliberate reason and reflection. To such a person the world tends to become obvious; common objects rouse no questions. However, as soon as one begins to philosophize, on the contrary, one finds that even the most everyday things give rise to questions of wonder and puzzlement. Philosophy, though unable to tell us with certainty the true answer to all the questions it raises, is able to suggest many possibilities that enlarge our thoughts and free them from the tyranny of mere custom. Thus, while diminishing our feeling of certainty as to what things are, philosophy greatly increases our knowledge as to what they may be; it removes the somewhat arrogant dogmatism of those who have never traveled into the region of liberating doubt, and it keeps alive our sense of wonder by showing familiar things in an unfamiliar aspect. We will see that studying how Chinese philosophers have engaged these questions provides vibrant intellectual stimulation.

Elmer Sprague once wrote that philosophy is like the measles. It must be caught from someone who is already infected. He held that to learn to philosophize, one must try his luck arguing with a real philosopher (Sprague 1962: 3). Another way of saying this is to follow Ludwig Wittgenstein's observation that philosophy is not a specific theory or content, it is an activity. It is with this exciting activity that I hope to infect the reader in the chapters that follow.

Four chapters make up this book, each taking up in a broad sense the positions of Chinese philosophers on one set of fundamental questions. Chapter I deals with a set of questions in the category known as *ontology*. *Ontology* is derived from two Greek words: *ontis*, meaning "being" or "reality," "that which is"; and *logos*, meaning "the study of" or "the knowledge of." Sometimes, ontology is also called metaphysics, referring to what can be known about reality beyond that which physics or science tells us. I choose not to use this term because to speak of *meta*physics already implies there is something that is beyond what can be known through the empirical world and Chinese philosophers never framed the problem of reality in such a manner. Some ontological questions are these:

- What is reality composed of/made of?
- Is reality of a single type of thing (monism), two types of things (e.g., minds and bodies; matter and spirit; as in dualism), or many types of things (pluralism)?
- Is reality composed of only transient things or are there enduring, even eternal and universal, components to it?

- Is reality actually as it appears to us or is it something different from what we think it is (the question of appearance versus reality)?
- Does reality have a meaning, is it guided by a mind or intelligence to occur as it does, or does it follow some internal pattern of its own nature, "purposing" of its own accord, or do humans attach meaning or purpose to reality that it does not have in itself?

Chapter II is occupied with fundamental questions that can be gathered under the concept of *epistemology*. Again, as with the term ontology, *epistemology* has an origin in the Greek language. *Epistemis* means "knowledge," and so epistemology is the study of knowledge. Some epistemological questions are these:

- What is it "to know"?
- Can we actually *know* something to be true, or do we only *believe* things to be true (the issue of scepticism)?
- Are all claims to know something of the same sort or justified in the same way?
- What are the tools we use to know something (e.g., reason, experience/senses, etc.)?
- Are we born knowing some things are true?
- Is there a limit to what we can know?
- Are there laws of thinking that must be followed to obtain knowledge?

Chapter III concerns philosophical questions of morality and value. Some fundamental questions addressed by Chinese philosophers in this chapter are these:

- How should we live?
- What is the ultimate purpose of our lives (to pursue happiness or pleasure, obey moral rules, please others or higher beings, or follow our own interests)?
- What is the origin of our morality (do we invent it and agree to it, is it inborn or part of our nature, or is it given by a higher being or intelligence)?
- What really makes something good or right to do (is it the

consequences of the action, doing our duties or going by our passionate feelings)?

- Is morality universally applicable to all persons or is it relative to its culture or to the individual?
- What is most basic and important in morality: the actions we do or the sort of persons we are?

Chapter IV undertakes to explore those fundamental questions related to the creation of society and government. Some of these are the following:

- What is the natural state of humans prior to government and law (are they free, equal and independent or social and interdependent; are they inevitably in conflict or do they live in innocent bliss)?
- From where does government arise (a contract between persons, the recognized superiority of some persons to lead or is it the decree of a higher power)?
- What are human laws and from where do they come (do we arrive at them by participatory exchange of views, or do they derive from the nature of reality, or are they codifications of the lives of exemplary persons or are they decrees of powerful/rulers or a divine being)?
- What is the best form of government?
- Are there checks and balances on government/rulers?
- Is revolt against the ruler or government ever justified?
- What is the proper balance between governmental authority and individual liberty of expression and thought?
- What is the role and responsibility of government to implement justice and how should it do it (in distributing goods, for example, are there rules of entitlement, fairness, equality of opportunity)?

While I have followed a rather standard procedure of grouping philosophical questions into four groups, it is quite obvious that how one answers a question in one category very often requires or presupposes an answer in some other. I hope the reader will bear in mind, then, the interdependence of the materials in each chapter. In fact, I wish to encourage further investigation of the connections between claims made in one chapter and those in another, whether these are made by the same philosopher or by different ones. To the extent that this happens, I will have been successful not only in introducing the responses and answers of Chinese philosophers to fundamental questions but also in contributing in some measure to infecting the reader with the wonder and joy of philosophical inquiry itself.

Before we begin our study, a few comments about the ways I have treated important Chinese philosophical terms are in order. Chinese, of course, is written in characters or graphs and the current Romanization used by Westerners to know how to pronounce the graphs is called *pinyin*. I use *pinyin* rather than the graphs themselves for ease of reading. However, in some cases this can be confusing and I also include the graph in such instances. For example, the *pinyin* "*li*" can have two quite distinct major philosophical uses. One is to refer to propriety in relationships, rules, even morality (*li* 禮) and the other is for the Principle(s) structuring reality (*li* 理). I will use the characters when I feel that confusion over which use of *li* is being meant might occur. I adopt the same practice for *qi* (氣) as the primordial substance of which all things are made and *qi* (器) as used for individual "concrete objects." Also, when the Chinese *tian* 天 is used as a nominative for a supreme agent I use the capital "Heaven." When it is used with *di* for earth (*tiandi* 天地), in order to indicate everything that is, the world, or reality, I use "heaven and earth" in lower case. When speaking of the philosophical system of interacting correlative elemental phases of *qi* (氣) that actualize into the real things of reality, I use capitals (i.e., Five Phases). When speaking of the elements themselves, I use lower case. In other instances of the use of Chinese characters I do so for clarification only. When reading the text, one may assume that the uses of a given Chinese term are the same as the character given, unless I interrupt the text by inserting another character for the same *pinyin*. Although it has been my practice in previous works to include a glossary of *pinyin* words and provide their Chinese graphs, space did not allow for such a table in this work.

CHAPTER I

哲学

Ontology: Questions about the Nature of Reality

Introduction

This chapter deals with a set of questions in the category known as *ontology. Ontology* comes from two Greek words *ontis*, meaning "being" or "reality," "that which is" and *logos*, meaning "the study of" or "the knowledge of." Though ontology is sometimes called metaphysics, referring to what can be known about reality beyond what physics or science tells us, I choose not to use this term because it implies that there is something that is beyond what can be known through science or empirical data. *Meta*physics is often taken to deal with that which transcends or is beyond natural phenomenon. While we shall see that some Chinese philosophers suggest in their ontologies that there may be aspects of reality beyond the way things appear to us, generally speaking, all Chinese ontologies start and finish with what they regard as natural, even if sometimes the objects and phenomena produced by natural forces are not accessible by the limited range of human sensory powers (i.e., sight, hearing, touch, etc.).

We might make a distinction between ontology and cosmology:

- ontology is the set of philosophical positions concerned with the nature and operation of reality;
- cosmology is focused more specifically on the observable movements and processes of the phenomena of the universe.

While ontology concerns itself with the general nature of the entities, qualities and relationships that compose and constitute reality, cosmology occupies itself with making empirical assertions about existence.

The notable contemporary philosopher Chung-ying Cheng prefers using the term *onto-cosmology* of Chinese thought about the nature of reality because he feels it is more accurate than the division of these two approaches as is done in the West.[1] However, for our purposes, we will continue to refer to Chinese ontology, even if as we work our way through the texts and views of Chinese philosophers, we will notice that Cheng's term does indeed capture much of the Chinese approach to questions of reality.

This chapter deals with the following questions:

- What is reality composed of/made of?
- Is reality of a single type of thing (monism), two types of things (i.e., "dualism": minds and bodies; matter and spirit; nature and supernature), or many types of things (pluralism)?
- Is reality composed of only transient, impermanent things, or are there enduring, or even eternal and universal components in its composition?
- Is reality actually as it appears to us or is it something different in its true nature from what we are most directly aware of?
- Does reality have a meaning, is it "purposing" or is it guided by a mind or intelligence to process as it does?
- Does it follow some internal pattern of its own nature, or is it the case that humans attach and invent meaning and impose it on reality, although it is devoid of purpose in itself?

The Formation of the Early Chinese Worldview

The ontology of early Chinese thought comes down to us through a number of philosophical texts that are not traceable to any single author. Included among those covered in this section are the "Great Commentary" (*Da Zhuan*) to the *Classic of Changes* (*Yijing*), the *Commentary of Zuo* (*Zuozhuan*) and the "Great Plan" (*Hong Fan*) section of the *Classic of History* (*Shujing*).

The "Great Commentary" to the *Classic of Changes* (*Yijing*)

The *Classic of Changes* (*Yijing*) is the name for a complete edited work that includes two parts. One part is a quite ancient manual of divination known simply as the *Changes* (*Yi*), or more correctly, as the *Zhouyi*. It is a handbook traceable to the period and practices of the Western Zhou dynasty as is indicated, among other features, by its use of language expressions found on the bronzes of that period (*c.*1046–771 BCE). The other part of the *Classic of Changes* is a set of seven commentaries attached to it. Three of the commentaries are composed of two sections each. Accordingly, taken as a whole, the commentary set making up this second part of the *Classic of Changes* is known as "The Ten Wings" (*Shiyi*).

One of these ten commentaries to the *Classic of Changes* (*Yijing*) is known by the various titles of the "Great Commentary" (*Dazhuan*) or "Appended Statements" (*Xici*). The "Great Commentary" is arguably the most important single text available to us for an understanding of the earliest Chinese ontology. The *Classic of Changes* as a whole is much less valuable to us as philosophers. There are reasons to date some material in the "Great Commentary" into the Han dynasty (206 BCE–222 CE), but I include it as a statement of the early Chinese worldview because the passages I have selected are consistent with a much earlier period and they also lack the overt connections to Han syncretism that we see in the overwriting of classical works during that period, especially with regard to the ontology of the Five Phases (*wuxing*).

The "Great Commentary" sketches out the early Chinese worldview that was basic to all of China's philosophical systems for over two millennia. It also introduces the fundamental philosophical vocabulary of Chinese ontology that has been employed by Chinese thinkers up to the modern period.

What Western philosophy calls *reality*, the philosophers who created the "Great Commentary" generally called by the compound "heaven and earth (*tiandi*)." As for the process of reality's change, they used the term *Dao* (道). While there are many uses of the term *dao* in classical Chinese, Western English-language translators have most often used "way," or "the Way." This text frequently employs the term *Dao* as a nominative and portrays it as operating according to patterns (*tian wen*) or Principle(s) *li* (理).

The Chinese thinkers who created the ontology of the "Great Commentary" observed both change and continuity in reality. They thought of reality as composed of one sort of fundamental substance that was a kind of pure energy they called *qi* (氣). Here is how the

"Great Commentary" uses these fundamental ontological concepts in relation to each other:

> The *Yi* [i.e., the *Classic of Changes*] being aligned with heaven and earth, can wholly set forth the *dao* of heaven and earth. The *Yi* looks up to observe the patterns of heaven (*tianwen* 天文), and looks down to examine the principle(s) (*li* 理) of earth. Thus,
>
> > it knows the causes of darkness and light, origin and ends;
> > it comprehends the meaning of birth and death,
> > it perceives how seminal *qi* forms into things.
> > Now *yin* 陰, now *yang* 陽 move and this is *dao*
> >
> > ("Great Commentary," Part I, 4, 5).

In these passages, the author makes use of a robust philosophical vocabulary. Reality (heaven and earth) is *qi* (氣) substance in constant process, but its changes are not arbitrary, chaotic or haphazard. The term used to capture this order is *Dao*, which is used for the "way" or "path" that the changing processes of reality follow. This path reveals Principles (*li* 理) that are evident to one who reflects on the *Dao*. The *dao* of *qi* gives rise of itself to forces that move it: it is self-moving, according to its internal dynamics of *yin* and *yang*.

The "Great Commentary" not only makes the philosophical claim that all reality is in process but also that there are patterns to its changes. By tradition, a thinker of antiquity named Fu Xi originally developed a system of eight symbols called trigrams to express these patterns. These trigrams had three lines or rows. An unbroken line was used to indicate the *yang* forces operative in change and a broken line represented *yin* forces. According to one interpretation, the first two lines represent *yin* and *yang* and the third represents the relation of the previous two lines standing for reality's creative advance. Taken in this way, there are eight possible figures. Thus, in Chinese, this set of eight is called the Eight Trigrams (*bagua*).

In a commentary appended to the *Classic of Changes* entitled "Discussion of the Trigrams" (*shuogua*), the trigrams are also used as explanatory devices for the emergence of families, seasons, directions, colors and various animals. There is no philosophical justification offered in the commentary for these associations, and we should attribute them to the practitioners who sought to provide more concrete interpretations for the use of the trigrams for the purpose of divination of the future. What is worth noting philosophically is that this elaborate system is rooted in the belief that as *qi* is in process, it is so according to patterns and not by mere chance.

If we look in the *Zhouyi* section (i.e., the actual divination text) of the *Classic of Changes*, we notice not merely Eight Trigrams, but 64 hexagrams. There are various traditions about how these emerged. One is that when it came to applying the Eight Trigrams to human experiences and decisions, practitioners ran into the problem that they could not distinguish the inner and outer aspects of changing human events or what we might think of as the subjective inner feeling and the objective outer event (Cheng 2009b: 76). In order to talk about these aspects of change, the practitioners who were the source of the *Zhouyi* stacked the Eight Trigrams, using the lower trigram to stand for the inner aspects of the process that is occurring and the upper to represent the outer aspects. When this procedure was followed, the total number of possible configurations of the Eight Trigrams became the 64 hexagrams of the current *Zhouyi* text.[2] Accordingly, in the *Zhouyi* divination manual, two hexagrams expressing the patterns of reality are called Qian and Kun. The "Great Commentary" offers this observation on these two hexagrams:

> The *dao* of Qian (i.e., heaven) forms maleness (i.e., *yang*),
> The *dao* of Kun (i.e., earth) forms femaleness (i.e., *yin*).
> Qian (heaven) births the Great Beginning,
> Kun (earth) brings things to completion.
> Qian (heaven) directs with spontaneity,
> Kun (earth) responds with simplicity.
>
> ("Great Commentary," Part I, 1)

The substance that is "*dao*ing" or "pathing" along is *qi*. *Qi* is a multi-phasal phenomenon, sometimes manifesting with properties of what we might call in the West "matter" and sometimes existing in a state that Westerners would call "spirit." *Qi* is moved by pushes and pulls of its internal opposing forces, *yin* and *yang*. These processes of reality give shape to every object whatever.[3]

The result of its process is goodness:
   It [the process of *qi* moving by *yin* and *yang*] achieves completion

as the nature of something (*xing* 性) …

Products-producing-products is [the reality] described by *yi* [i.e., the *Classic of Changes*]

All that *yin* and *yang* do not define [into a visible object form or thing] is called spirit.

("Great Commentary," Part I, 5)

The general philosophical term for the process of reality we have been describing is *correlative ontology*.

Correlation is itself the central concept of the ontological theory of early Chinese philosophy. *Yin* and *yang* may be mutually supportive, or the one may be transforming the other, balancing it, compensating for it, enhancing it or furthering something new in relation to the other. The relationship of *yin* and *yang* may be creative and productive, lead to harmony and stability or deconstruct the present phenomenon and open the way to something new. Even so, *yin* and *yang* are not equivalent to good/evil, and they possess no mentality or intentionality by which they plan or direct reality and they are regarded as natural forces.

Generally speaking, the more *yin* predominates in a process, the more it is associated with the earth, femininity, passivity, suppleness, warmth and darkness. The more *yang* dominates, the more we should associate the process with heaven, masculinity, aggressiveness, rigidity, coldness and light. As Chinese ontology developed, these forces were said to proceed from formless *qi*.

Yin and *yang* are not kinds of things in addition to *qi*. *Yin* and *yang* are not things, not even spiritual things. To take them in this way is to make what philosophers call a "category mistake."[4] It is an error of the sort we make if we nominalize a word like *creeps* (e.g., "He gives me the creeps") and believe that there is some real substance named by the word *creeps* that someone has given to us in the same way that one might give us a piece of candy. Another way of saying this is that language about *yin* and *yang* is nonreferential. These terms are not names that point or correspond to an object in the way that *candy* does.

When reading about traditional Chinese medicine which makes extensive use of the concepts of *yin* and *yang*, we must be careful to remember this fact. To say that one is sick because she has too much *yang* does not refer to some overabundance of a quantity of some substance called *yang*, even if it resembles grammatically the statement,

"There is too much water in your bucket." Nonetheless, even though *yin* and *yang* are nonreferential, they still have an important use in the ontology of early China. They are concepts in Chinese ontology used as explanatory devices for what makes *qi* take the variant forms that constitute reality.

We could summarize the ontology of the "Great Commentary" in the following way. Reality is in process emerging, stabilizing, passing away, renewing and recreating itself all the time. While reality consists of one underlying substance, *qi* is not equivalent to "matter" but neither is it "spirit." The closest analogue to Western philosophy is the term *energy*. *Qi* takes many forms as it is moved by the forces of *yin* and *yang*. How things appear to us is really the way they are; we are not living some dream or illusion. There are tables, chairs, cows, etc. And yet, there is an element of the appearance/reality distinction in Chinese philosophy since many things appear to us to be static and fixed, unchangeable, but they are not. Everything is in process and changing. In fact, the primal existing substance of reality (*qi*) is in process: it is not some eternal, unchanging, perfect thing, such as we see in Greek philosophy's idea of the "unmoved mover" or the concept of God, who is sheer perfection and, thus, cannot change.

So, how can we explain how the universe began in terms of early Chinese ontology? In Chinese thought the formless *qi* has eternally been *dao*ing. Taken as a whole, *qi* as moved by *yin* and *yang* is the explanation for the emergence of what we call material objects. In Western philosophy, the characteristic approach is to think of material things as natural kinds that have different defining essences that make them what they are (i.e., a chair, a cat, a tree). These defining essences are called "the nature" of something. But in early Chinese ontology, there is change as well as continuity and endurance. The characteristic configuration of *qi* that something is *dao*ing (i.e., actualizing) sets it apart from other things. The distinctive correlation of *yin* and *yang* is an explanation that does the philosophical work of the Western concept of *essence*. Accordingly, Chinese philosophers were able to identify kinds and categories of things without recourse to an ontology in which there is a pluralism of substances or essences.

Chinese philosophers inheriting the ontology of the "Great Commentary" continue to use the concept of "nature" (*xing* 性) (e.g., of a horse or a human), but it does not refer or name some underlying essence or unique substance that makes something what it is. "Nature" is a way of talking about the manner of actualized *qi* correlation that sets some specific object apart from the correlations of other things. This may partially explain why an understanding of the early Chinese worldview is sometimes quite a challenge for a Westerner. In Western philosophy an acorn, peach, tree, horse, human all differ because their underlying substantive nature varies; whereas in Chinese philosophy their different natures are temporary phasal combinations of *qi* energy that makes them what they are.

Nonessentialist Ontological Thinking in the West

Even in Western philosophy, there are thinkers who criticize the substance or essence ontology. Among them we should include Heraclitus, David Hume, William James, Alfred North Whitehead and Ludwig Wittgenstein. Here is an illustration from William James of how we can be misled and mystified by our language into thinking of reality as a set of fixed natural kind objects:

> The low thermometer today, for instance, is supposed to come from something called the "climate". Climate is really only the name for a certain group of days, but it is treated as if it lay behind the day, and in general we placed the name, as if it were a being, behind the facts it is the name of. But the phenomenal properties of things do not inhere in anything. They adhere, or cohere, rather, with each other, and the notion of a substance inaccessible to us, which that we think accounts for such cohesion by supporting it, as cement might support pieces of a mosaic, must be abandoned. The fact of the bare cohesion its self is all the notion of the substance signifies. Beyond that fact is nothing. (James 2000: 42)

Let us take all this one further step. In Western philosophy, thinkers habitually speak of material objects and often become involved in debates about whether material things are different from minds. Such philosophical quandaries result from the idea that there is a substance called matter that underlies and gives rise to our experiences such as color, roughness/smoothness, etc. But in early Chinese ontology, material objects are not made of some substance other than *qi*; they are the particular configurations of *qi* that fall within the range of our sensory powers. When a *qi* configuration actualizes in a certain way, it is experienced as solid, hard, rough, smooth, fluid, of a certain color, etc.

Some phenomena move in ways for which we invent the language of purpose, interest, motivation, will, expectation, intention and the like. In early Chinese thought, this is the explanation for our talk about mental processes, it does not mean that some phenomena have minds (e.g., humans) and others (e.g., worms) do not. It means that the configurations of some phenomena are such that we use mental process language to talk about behaviors they exhibit (i.e., "he did that intentionally"). Seeing reality in this way was part of the genius of the creators of the "Great Commentary."

What we dare not overlook in this philosophy is that pattern is not imposed from outside the process, say by a transcendent mind. Novelty, creativity and pattern arise from the internal processes of reality itself. The "Great Commentary" gives us a world of possibility and change, but also of order and pattern. It is a reality full of forces expressed as *yin* and *yang*, but also alterable by human effort and, indeed, by the actions of other sentient beings as well.

The Five Phase (*wuxing*) Ontology

From the time of the beginning of the Zhou dynasty (1045 BCE) to the beginning of the Han dynasty (206 BCE), a number of Chinese texts were compiled. These are known now as the Five Classics (*wujing*), and they became enshrined as texts in the educational system of China for hundreds of years. They are: *Shijing* (*Classic of Poetry*), *Shujing* (*Classic of History*), *Liji* (*Record of Ritual*), *Yijing* (*Classic of Changes*) and *Chunqiu* (*Spring and Autumn Annals*) with its commentary, *Zuozhuan* (*Chronicles of Zuo*). As we have these texts now, they all have materials drawn from a long span of intellectual history. Some may well reflect the concerns and contexts of later (more in the Han dynasty period, 206 BCE–220 CE) rather than earlier (more in the Zhou dynasty, 1056–256 BCE) periods. Despite the uncertain dating of some remarks, the texts do contain a substantial amount of material that is traceable to the early period of Chinese ontology. Some texts from these works are important because they set out the early formation of what is known as the Five Phase ontology.

The Five Phase ontology refers to a conceptual scheme that is found in traditional Chinese thought. The five phases are wood (*mu*), fire (*huo*), earth (*tu*), metal (*jin*) and water (*shui*). They are regarded as dynamic, interdependent modes or aspects of the universe's ongoing existence and actualization. All objects of reality are some combination and interdependent correlation of these five phases of *qi*. Although this fivefold scheme resembles ancient Greek discourse about the four elements (earth, air, fire and water) from which all things are made, these Chinese elements are really phases being expressed by ever-changing *qi* substance, while the Greek elements typically are regarded as unchanging kinds of differing substances. Prior to the Han dynasty, the Five Phase ontology functioned less as a school of thought and more simply as a way of describing the natural processes hidden from ordinary view. During the period of the Han dynasty, Five Phase thought became a distinct philosophical tradition (*jia*, "family" or "school"). Since that time, the Five Phase system has become ever more complicated, and it has been used to explain not only natural phenomena but also aesthetic principles, historical events, political structures, social norms and in medical diagnosis and treatment of illness.

Chronicles of Zuo (c.389 BCE)

This text is a record of occurrences of the Spring and Autumn Period (*Chunqiu Shi Dai*) from *c*.771 to 468 BCE, the authorship of which is traditionally ascribed to a court writer in the State of Lu about the time of Confucius named Zuo Qiuming. The text is arranged as comments on the reigns of various marquises and dukes, and it was likely completed in its original form no later than 389 BCE, although even in the passages below, some philosophical ideas in this text, including its emphases on the Five Phase system, may date into the early Han dynasty.

Remarking on the seventh year of the reign of Duke Wen (626–609 BCE) the *Chronicles of Zuo* (*Zuozhuan*) says: "Water, fire, metal, wood, earth, and grains are called the six natural resources (*liu fu*, or 'six treasures')." In this passage, the character *fu* is used for the treasures of nature, the natural resources for life. This list of six such resources contains the five phases as we have just mentioned them, but with the addition of the grains. In comments on the 27th year of the reign of Duke Xiang (590–573 BCE) the text says: "Heaven has given birth to the five materials (*wu cai*) that supply humankind's requirements, and the people use them all. Not one of them can be dispensed with."

In its remarks on the first year of Duke Zhao's rule (541–510 BCE), the text says, Heaven generates the five tastes (*wu wei*—sour, sweet, salty, bitter and acrid), five colors (*wu se*—green, yellow, black, red and white) and five sounds (*wu sheng*). In the passage on Duke Zhao's 25th year, tastes, colors and sounds are said to be a result of the five phases (*wuxing*) and are not presented as existing as primordial substances on their own. The five phases are understood to be expressions of Heaven's Principle(s) (*li* 理) for ordering reality and the character for patterns is the same one later used for the energy meridian lines in the body traced by practitioners of the traditional Chinese medical art of acupuncture, suggesting that the five phases are to reality as these meridians are to our bodies.

The *Chronicles of Zuo* does not provide an account of how the five phases correlate with each other or intermingle to create objects such as we see in later works of Chinese ontology. Instead, it moves away from a naturalist explanation and postulates Five Officials (*wu guan*) who are each associated with one of the five phases and exercise their wills in order to arrange them into phenomenal reality. For example, in the material on the Duke of Zhao's 29th year, the question is posed, "Why are there no more dragons?" The answer given for the absence of dragons is that each of the five phases is directed by its own official, but if an official neglects his task or if persons on earth distort or mismanage the five phases, animals that depend on the order of these patterns will hide or stop reproducing correctly. Thus, the species will disappear. These officials are presented as spirits or deities who require veneration and offerings to be made to them. The text gives the name of each official and the element over which he has charge.

The "Great Plan" in the *Classic of History*

The "Great Plan" (*Hong Fan*) section of the *Classic of History* is constructed in the style of a dialogue between King Wu and a sage. In this material, Wu states that human relationships and government must follow the patterns (*li* 理) of Heaven, but he wonders how humans may grasp these patterns fully. The sage tells him that whenever the five phases are in disorder, the constant Principles (*li*) of Heaven will disappear and chaos will follow. So, in speaking of the nine divisions of the "Great Plan" by which Heaven orders reality, the text says,

> the first is called "using the five phases (*wuxing*)"; the second, "giving serious attention to the five (personal) matters/relationships (*wushi*)"; the third, "employing conscientious devotion to the eight (objects of) government (*ba zheng*)"; the fourth, "making harmonious use of the five [aspects of] time (*wuji*)"; the fifth, "establishing and using royal perfection (*huang ji*)"; the sixth, "being discriminating in the use of the three virtues (*san de*)"; the seventh, "the intelligent examination of doubts (*jiyi*)"; the eighth, "the thoughtful use of the various evidence (*shuzheng*)"; the ninth, "the guiding use of the five happinesses,[5] and authority over the six sufferings"[6] (*Classic of History*, "Great Plan" 2.2).

In what follows, the *Classic of History* breaks down each of these nine divisions of Heaven's "Great Plan." With respect to the first of Heaven's ways of ordering all things, it gives this explanation:

> First of the five phases is water; the second is fire; the third, wood; the fourth, metal; and the fifth, earth. (The propensity of) water is to soak and descend; of fire, to blaze up; of wood, to be capable of bending and straightening; of metal, to melt and reform; while (that of) earth is seen in seed-sowing and in-gathering. That which soaks and descends becomes salt; that which blazes and ascends becomes bitter; that which is crooked and straight becomes sour; that which yields and changes becomes acrid; and from seed-sowing and in-gathering comes sweetness." (Ibid., 2.3)

For the first time in Chinese ontology, each of the five phases has its natural pattern more fully explained: water moistens and descends (*run xia*); fire blazes up (*yan shang*); wood bends and straightens (*qu zhi*); metal melts and reforms (*cong ge*); earth receives and gives (*jia se*), such as through seeds and crops.

As the "Great Plan" develops the other divisions of Heaven's work, the correlational mechanisms of the system become more obvious. The five phases are tied to the five tastes: that which moistens and descends produces saltiness; that which blazes up produces bitterness;

that which bends and straightens produces sourness; that which yields and reforms produces pungency; that which seeds and gives crops produces sweetness. Then, in the subsequent paragraphs, the five phases are correlated to the five ways or powers of a human being: appearance, speech, sight, hearing and thinking.

The "Great Plan" does not spell out how the correlations work, it only asserts that they exist. It is made clear, though, that if humans do not behave in the proper manner, they throw the five phases out of harmonious operation, illness and weakness arise in the body and disorder shows up in nature and the human world of history (ibid., 2.1).

Lao-Zhuang (c.350–139 BCE) Daoist Ontology

To speak collectively of "Lao-Zhuang" tradition is to identify a set of philosophical sentiments and positions in common between the two classical works of emergent Daoism in Chinese intellectual history: the *Daodejing* and the *Zhuangzi*. Both the *Daodejing* associated with Laozi and the Zhuangzi ascribed to Zhuang Zhou (369–289 BCE) are composite works not written by a single author. Throughout the classical period, there were many lineages of teachers and disciples, as well as multiple oral and written versions of transmitted materials that came together to form these texts. So, there was no unified, coherent school called Daoism in the classical period, but the term Lao-Zhuang can be used to capture the family resemblances between philosophical lineages and their transmitted teachings. In what follows, I have isolated some of these teachings on the fundamental questions of ontology.

We have already noticed in our survey of the earliest Chinese ontologies that reality (i.e., "heaven and earth") is in constant process, but the changes are not arbitrary, chaotic, haphazard or by mere chance. The Chinese term used to capture the order reality exhibits is *dao*, which literally means the "way" or "path" that the changing processes of reality follow. In this process, there are patterns and principles that are evident to one who reflects on the *dao*. The *dao* of *qi* (the energy that composes all things) gives rise of itself to forces that move it. So, it is self-moving, according to the dynamic energies of *yin* and *yang*.

The term *dao* is one of the most important concepts in the *Daodejing* (*DDJ*).[7] Sometimes it is used as a noun (i.e., "the *Dao*") and other times as a verb (i.e., "*dao*ing"). This is the way it changes meanings in the opening lines of Chapter 1.

> The *Dao* that can be expressed in words (*dao*ed) is not the eternal [constant] *Dao*.
> The name that can be named is not the eternal name. (*DDJ*, 1)

Many passages in the *Daodejing* take the position that the nature of the *Dao* cannot be put into words and that *Dao* is misrepresented if we try to give it a name (e.g., Reality, God, Nature, etc.). In talking about the inability to explain *Dao* and the inherent inaccuracy of putting a name to it, the masters whose teachings are embodied in the *Daodejing* were pointing both to its numinosity and ineffability and to the limitations of human language. But the *Daodejing* continues to recognize some need to talk about *Dao* and its role in an understanding of reality.

> There is a thing chaotic yet perfect, which arose before heaven and earth.
> Silent and indistinct, it stands alone and unchanging,
> Moving it is tireless,
> We can take it as the mother of heaven and earth.
> I do not know its name.
> I have styled it "the Way" (*Dao*). (*DDJ*, 25)

According to the *Daodejing*, the *Dao* has a sort of power in itself from which all things have come.

> *Dao* produces the One;
> The One gives birth to two,
> Two produces three.
> Three produces all things (*wanwu* 萬物).
> All things shoulder *yin* and hold on to *yang*, and by blending these *qi* they attain harmony. (*DDJ*, 42)

In this brief statement of creation in the *Daodejing*, the text puts *Dao* prior to the first thing as a formless blank that produces instantiated things that continue in process to expand by *yin* and *yang* into all the objects that populate and furnish reality.

There is a stated confidence expressed in the *Daodejing*, Chapter 4, that the process of *Dao* is at a minimum benign and Chapter 56 puts the matter more strongly.

> *Dao* is like an empty vessel;
> No one could ever fill it up
> Vast and deep!
> It seems to be the ancestor of all things (*wanwu*).
> It blunts their sharp edges;
> Untangles their knots;
> Softens their glare;
> Merges with their dust,
> Deep and clear!
> It seems to be there.
> I do not know whose child it is;
> It is the image of what was before the Supreme Spirit (*di* 帝)![8]

Actually the text goes beyond the idea of *Dao*'s process as value-neutral. Chapter 37 says, "*Dao* does nothing (*wu-wei* 無為) yet nothing is left undone." *Wu-wei* means effortless, spontaneous, non-intentional, non-deliberative action. In other words, *Dao* is not working by a design through some intelligence. It is acting spontaneously, but it is not leaving loose ends or causing problems, disorder or confusion. In fact, it is untangling knots that humans create (see above), blunting the sharp edges caused by those that are resisting or moving contrary to *Dao* and that cut, injure and harm, etc. In a very close association of *Dao* with Heaven (*tian*), the text says,

> Who knows why Heaven dislikes what it does?
> Even sages regard this as a difficult question.
> *Dao* does not contend, but it is good at victory;
> Does not speak but is good at responding;
> Does not call but things come of their own accord to it;
> Is not anxious but is good at fulfilling plans.
> Heaven's net is vast;
> Its mesh is loose, but it misses nothing. (*DDJ*, 73)

> The *dao* of Heaven, isn't it like the stretching of a bow?
> What is high it presses down;

What is low it lifts up.

It takes from what has excess;

It augments what is deficient.

The *dao* of Heaven takes from what has excess and augments what is
   deficient.

The *dao* of human beings is not like this.

It takes from the deficient and offers it up to those with excess.
   (*DDJ*, 77)

The *dao* of Heaven plays no favorites;

It is always on the side of the good. (*DDJ*, 79)

The *dao* of Heaven is to benefit and not harm. (*DDJ*, 81)

When we look closely at the *Daodejing*'s remarks about Heaven, they
make it clear that a critical move is made in Chinese ontology by
thinkers in this tradition. Heaven's movements (i.e., its *dao*) are life-
furthering and full of benefit, but they are without deliberation or plan.

   In the following sections of the *Zhuangzi* anthology of emergent
Daoism, these matters of ontology are expressed in a literary way.

Ziqi said, "The Great Clod belches out breath and its name is wind.
So long as it doesn't come forth, nothing happens. But when it does,
then ten thousand hollows begin crying wildly. Can't you hear them,
long drawn out? In the mountain forests that lash and sway, there are
huge trees a hundred spans around with hollows and openings like
noses, like mouths, like ears, like jugs, like cups, like mortars, like rifts,
like ruts. They roar like waves, whistle like arrows, screech, gasp, cry,
wail, moan and howl, those in the lead calling out yeee! those behind
calling out yuuu! In a gentle breeze they answer faintly, but in a full gale
the chorus is gigantic. And when the fierce wind has passed on, then
all the hollows are empty again. Have you never seen the tossing and
trembling that goes on?" Ziyou said, "By the piping of earth, then, you
mean simply [the sound of] these hollows, and by the piping of man
[the sound of] flutes and whistles. But may I ask about the piping of
Heaven?" Ziqi said, "Blowing on the ten thousand things in a different
way, so that each can be itself all take what they want for themselves, but
who [actually] makes the sound?" ... This comes close to the matter.
Although I do not know what makes them the way they are. It would

seem as though they have some True Master (*zhen di* 真宰), and yet I find no trace of him. He can act—that is certain. Yet I cannot see his form. He has identity but no form. (*Zhuangzi* 2; Watson 1968: 36–7)

Chapter Six in *Zhuangzi* likewise shows a clear affinity with the philosophical positions advocated in the *Daodejing* with respect to *Dao*.

> *Dao* has its reality and its signs but is without action (*wu-wei*) or form. … It is its own source, its own root. Before heaven and earth existed it was there, firm from ancient times. It gave spirit to the numinal beings and to God (*shen gui shen di* 神鬼神帝); it gave birth to heaven and earth. It exists beyond the highest point, and yet you cannot call it lofty; it exists beneath the limit of the six directions, and yet you cannot call it deep. It was born before heaven and earth, and yet you cannot say how long it has been there; it is earlier than the earliest time, and yet you cannot call it ancient. (Ibid., 6: 81, my change)

The point being made in this passage is that the *Dao* is beyond our language because language inevitably uses categories such as space and time. We cannot say *Dao* is in any space or that it has any temporal description. As such, *Dao* functions as what philosophers call a "limiting concept." The concept itself marks the point at which reason and language are exhausted. We cannot ask when *Dao* began because time does not apply to it. Nor can we speculate about where it exists. Daoists recognized that when reason tries to cognize the ultimate nature of reality, it is always tripped up by its own categories (e.g., space, time and causality).

The *Zhuangzi* does not make any explicit reference to the Five Phase ontology we have seen expressed in the "Great Plan" chapter of the *Classic of History*. Nevertheless, it is clear that the thinkers in the earliest Lao-Zhuang tradition were committed to the view that change and process were the most fundamental ontological principles of reality.

> Master Si, Master Yu, Master Li and Master Lai were all four talking together … There was no disagreement in their hearts and so the four of them became friends … Suddenly Master Lai grew ill. Gasping and wheezing, he lay at the point of death. His wife and children gathered round in a circle and began to cry. Master Li, who had come

to ask how he was, said, "Shoo! Get back! Don't disturb the process of change!" Then he leaned against the doorway and talked to Master Lai. "How marvelous the Creator (*zaohua* 造化) is! What is he going to make of you next? Where is he going to send you? Will he make you into a rat's liver? Will he make you into a bug's arm?" Master Lai said, "A child, obeying his father and mother, goes wherever he is told, east or west, south or north. And the *yin* and *yang*—how much more are they to a man than father or mother! Now that they have brought me to the verge of death, if I should refuse to obey them, how perverse I would be! What fault is it of theirs? The Great Clod burdens me with form, labors me with life, eases me in old age and rests me in death. So if I think well of my life, for the same reason I must think well of my death. When a skilled smith is casting metal, if the metal should leap up and say, "I insist upon being made into a Mo-ye [i.e., the greatest of all swords]!" he would surely regard it as very inauspicious metal indeed. Now, having had the audacity to take on human form once, if I should say, "I don't want to be anything but a man! Nothing but a man!" the Creator would surely regard me as a most inauspicious sort of person. So now I think of heaven and earth as a great forge, and the Creator as a skilled smith. Where could he send me that would not be all right? I will go off to sleep peacefully, and then with a start I will wake up." (Ibid., 83–4)

Just whether all Daoist masters believed there was a Creator who controls the process of the transformation of things as does a great smith tending a giant forge is impossible to know. However, *Zhuangzi*, Chapter 14 begins with a series of questions.

Does heaven turn? Does the earth sit still? Do sun and moon compete for a place to shine? Who masterminds all this? Who pulls the strings? Who, resting inactive himself, gives the push that makes it go this way? I wonder if there is some mechanism that works it and won't let it stop? I wonder if it just rolls and turns and can't bring itself to a halt? Do the clouds make the rain, or does the rain make the clouds? Who puffs them up, who showers them down like this? Who, resting inactive himself, stirs up all this lascivious joy? The winds rise in the north, blowing now west, now east, whirling up to wander on high. Whose breaths and exhalations are they? Who, resting inactive himself, huffs and puffs them about like this? (Ibid., 154)

The *Daodejing* suggests in a number of places that some direct experience with the virtuous power (*de* 德) belonging to *Dao* is possible. When this occurs, the sense of some presence is unmistakable. In Chapter 21, the *Daodejing* speaks of this awareness by using the Chinese characters (*huang hu* 恍惚), sometimes translated as "shadowy and indistinct" or "vague and elusive." We might associate this experience with the term "mystical" although there is no such term in the text itself.

> The form of profound virtue (*kongde*) comes from the *dao* alone
> As for *Dao*'s nature
> it is *huang hu*
> *Hu! Huang!*
> There is an image within it.
> *Huang! Hu!*
> There is something within it.
> Deep! Mysterious!
> Within is numinal energy (*jing* 精).
> This numinal energy is undeniably real,
> Within this [i.e., the experience] lies its own proof.

From this passage, we get the clear sense that the person who is its source has had some awareness of a presence he associates with *Dao*. Yet, there is no attempt to prove that such a thing is possible by means of the sort of reasoned argument we value in philosophy. Instead, there is an appeal only to the immediacy of the experience itself. In fact, the text insists, "Those who know do not talk [about it]; those who talk [about it] do not know" (ibid., 56). When the *Daodejing* speaks of there being an "image" in *Dao* it actually does not mean that we can "picture" some being or thing in our minds that corresponds to the *Dao*. In Chapter 14 the text says very directly that *Dao* is the "formless form," "the image of no thing." In that same chapter, *Dao* is associated with the adjectives invisible, rarefied and subtle. The text likens *Dao* to the "inner sanctum" (*ao* 奧)[9] of all things (*wanwu*) (ibid., 62).

Just what puts one into a position to have this experience is not explained in any comprehensive way in either the *Daodejing* or the *Zhuangzi*. However, in the portion of the *Zhuangzi* anthology traceable to Zhuang Zhou's disciples, we find this passage:

Confucius went to call on Lao Dan [i.e., Laozi]. Lao Dan had just finished washing his hair and had spread it over his shoulders to dry. Utterly motionless, he did not even seem to be human. Confucius, hidden from sight, stood waiting, and then after some time presented himself and exclaimed, "Did my eyes play tricks on me, or was that really true? A moment ago, Sir, your form and body seemed stiff as an old dead tree, as though you had forgotten things, taken leave of men, and were standing in solitude itself." Lao Dan said, "I was letting my mind wander to the Beginning of things." ... Confucius said, "I would like to hear by what means this may be accomplished." [Lao Dan replied] "... In this world, all the living things come together in One, and if you can find that One and become identical with it, then your four limbs and hundred joints will become dust and sweepings; life and death, beginning and end will be mere day and night, and nothing whatever can confound you ..." (*Zhuangzi* 21; Watson 1968: 224–5)

Correlative Cosmologies in the Han Period: *Yinyang* and *Wuxing* Heuristics

According to the historian Sima Tan (*c*.110 BCE), there existed a school of teaching during the "Spring and Autumn" (770–481 BCE) and "Warring States" (403–221 BCE) periods that bore the name of *yinyang*. He lists this *yinyang* school alongside other schools such as the Confucian, Mohist, Legalist and Daoist. He says this school focused on divination and explored the patterns of heaven and earth. This school almost certainly had its antecedents in the *Zhouyi* and was likely a theoretical and heuristic extension of many of the practices associated with that text.

By the Han dynasty (202 BCE–220 CE), *yinyang* thought was associated with the standardization of the Five Phase correlative cosmology associated with the work of Zou Yan (*c*.305–240 BCE). The synthesis of Confucianism, *yinyang* and the Five Phase explanatory philosophies is evident in the writings of the scholar Dong Zhongshu (179–104 BCE) and exhibited in his volume, *Luxuriant Dew of the Spring and Autumn Annals* (*Chunqiu fanlu*). The *Masters of Huainan* (*Huainanzi)* is also a primary representative text for correlative cosmology with large sections of its Chapters 2, 3, 7 and 20 depending heavily on this ontology for the cogency of the work's argument about Heaven's relation to human activity. *Masters of Huainan*, however, tends to blend Daoist sensibilities with *yinyang* and the Five Phase system.

Masters of Huainan (Huainanzi) (c.139 BCE)

According to his biography in the *Book of the Early Han* (*Hanshu*, 44.2145) Liu An, the king of Huainan (in modern Anhui province), a man of wide-ranging interests from natural philosophy to rhetoric and poetry, and uncle of Han Emperor Wu, gathered a large number of philosophers, scholars and practitioners of esoteric techniques to Huainan in the period 160–140 BCE. They were supported in the creation of written works synthesizing their views. The *Masters of Huainan* (i.e., *Huainanzi*) was a product of this interchange of ideas. Some traditions say the work was written collectively by the "Eight Gentlemen" (*bagong*) of Huainan and that Liu An was its General Editor.[10] The *Masters of Huainan* is more than a text simply gathering this and that point of view. It is an attempt to present and offer a unified truth about reality, the human being and moral and political order.

For the compilers of *Masters of Huainan* everything in heaven and earth (reality) is unified. There is no dualism such as between the natural and supernatural or objects and the patterned structures that give them coherence. Neither did the editors believe that seeing reality as meaningful is a subjective imposition of humans. Instead, identifying the presence of purpose and meaning in the course of reality is equivalent to recognizing the principles that reality has in and of itself, and that are the basis for the philosophical conclusion that all real things adhere and function in harmony. In turn, the myriad things (*wanwu*) can serve as objects of human knowledge because persons are able to identify these underlying patterns for natural and social order.

However, reality is not guided by a Being with a mind and intention. Reality "daoes" spontaneously but, in doing so, it displays patterns and purposes. If humans also act spontaneously (i.e., in *wu-wei*), they will be directed by "the *dao* of heaven and earth" and live in harmony and with an efficacy that fulfills their lives. When humans fall away from this normative natural process and allow rationality or passion to displace spontaneity, disruption and destruction follow.

We can recognize immediately from this summary the similarities between this account of *Masters of Huainan* ontology and the Lao-Zhuang views set out earlier. This is no mistake. In fact, *Masters of Huainan* is often understood as giving priority to Daoist beliefs, especially those known as the "Yellow Emperor" sentiments in the *Zhuangzi* (Chapters 11, 12, 13, 14, 15, 16, 18, 19).[11]

> As for the Way (*Dao*):
> It covers heaven and upholds earth.
>> It extends the four directions
>> and divides the eight end points (i.e. eight spatial relations).
>> So high, it cannot be reached.
>> So deep, it cannot be fathomed
>> It embraces and infolds heaven and earth
>> It endows and bestows the formless.
>> …
>> It is dark but able to brighten.
>> It is supple but able to strengthen.
>> It is pliant but able to become firm.
>> It stretches out the four binding cords[12] and restrains *yin* and *yang*.
>> …
>> Mountains are high because of it.
>> Abysses are deep because of it.
>> Beasts can run because of it.
>> Birds can fly because of it.
>> The sun and moon are bright because of it.
>> The stars and timekeepers move because of it.
> (Major et al. 2010: 1.1)

> Of old, in the time before there was heaven and earth:
>> there were only images and no forms.
>> All was obscure and dark,
>>> vague and unclear,
>>> shapeless and formless,
>> and no one knows its gateway.
> There were two spirits, born in murkiness, one that established heaven and the other that constructed earth. (Ibid., 7.1)

Here *Masters of Huainan* is telling us that in the beginning of all beginnings, there was only shapeless, formless darkness and where that came from (what its "gateway" is), no one knows. It birthed two forces (spirits), one established heaven (i.e., it was *yang*) and the other earth (i.e., it was *yin*).

The text continues with philosophical doctrines about the origin of reality in this way.

> The two August Lords of high antiquity
>> grasped the handles of the Way (*Dao*)
>> and so were established in the center.
> Their spirits mysteriously roamed together with all transformations
>> and thereby pacified the four directions.
> Hence, they could revolve like heaven and stand still like earth,
>> cycle round and round without stopping,
>> flowing ceaselessly like water,
>> they ended and began together with all things.
> As winds arose and clouds formed, there was no event to which they did not respond.
>> As thunder rumbled and rain descended, to all they responded without end.
>> Ghosts departed and spirits entered.
>> Dragons arose and phoenixes alighted.
>> Like the potter's wheel turning, like the wheel hub spinning, they circled round and round.
>> Both carved and polished, they returned to the unhewn (*pu* 撲).
>> They acted non-actively (*wu-wei*) and were united with the Way (*Dao*).
>> They acted non-actively (*wu-wei*) and were suffused by its Potency (*de* 德). (Ibid.,1.2)
>
> …
>
> The *qi* of heaven beginning to descend;
> The *qi* of earth beginning to ascend;
> *Yin* and *yang* mixing and meeting;
>> mutually roaming freely and racing to fill the interstices of time and space,
>> enveloping [virtuous] potency (*de*) and engulfing harmony;
>> densely intermingling;

desiring to connect with things but not yet having formed
boundaries and bodies. (Ibid., 2.1)

In *Masters of Huainan*, each creature has its natural propensity that is
not received from the outside, but is the internal endowment given
it by the structure of its five phases. Creatures act from this structure,
instinctively. But the *Masters of Huainan* makes a shift in explanation
about just how things were made, and it is a distinction in the nature
of *qi*. Representing an anthology of many divergent streams of thought,
the work brings into its characterizations of *qi* the concepts of "heavy"
and "light" as well as "clear" and "bright" and "turbid" or "muddy" *qi*.

When heaven and earth were yet unformed, all was
    ascending and flying,
    diving and delving.
Thus it was called the Grand Inception (*taishi* 太始).
    The Grand Inception produced the Nebulous Void.
    The Nebulous Void produced space-time (i.e., the cosmic process,
    yu zhou 宇宙);
    Space-time produced the original *qi*.
A [membrane divided] the original *qi*.
    That which was pure and bright spread out to form heaven;
    that which was heavy and turbid congealed to form earth.
    It is easy for that which is pure and subtle to converge
    but difficult for the heavy and turbid to congeal.
Therefore
    Heaven was completed first;
    Earth was fixed afterward.
    The conjoined [propensities] of heaven and earth produced *yin*
    and *yang*.
    The scattered [propensities] of the four seasons created the myriad
    things.
    …
When *yin* and *yang* rub against each other, their interaction produces
    thunder.
    …
    When the *yang qi* prevails, it scatters to make rain and dew;
    When the *yin qi*, prevails, it freezes to make frost and snow.
                                                    (Ibid., 3.1)

It is just one more step in this ontology to extrapolations made about the connection between the fundamental components of reality and the lives of human persons.

> Joy and anger are aberrations from the Way (*Dao*); worry and grief are losses of virtuous potency (*de*).
> Likes and dislikes are excesses of the mind; lusts and desires are hindrances to nature.
> Violent anger ruins the *yin*;
> Extreme joy collapses the *yang*.
> The suppression of vital energy (*qi*) brings on dumbness; fear and terror bring on madness. (Ibid., 1.14)
>
> …
>
> Sadness and enjoyment are aberrations of virtuous potency (*de*),
> Pleasure and anger are excesses of the Way (*Dao*);
> Fondness and resentment are the fetters of the mind.
>
> Therefore, it is said [that sages]
> "In their life, act in accord with Heaven; and their death, transform with other
> things.
> In tranquillity, share the virtuous potency (*de*) of the *yin*;
> In activity, share the surge of the *yang*."
> Being calm and limitless, their quintessential spirit (*jingshen* 精神) is not dissipated amid external things, and the world naturally submits to them. (Ibid., 7.6)

In these passages, the *Masters of Huainan* is teaching the correlational relationship between robust *qi* and human emotions and even moral dispositions. The emotional states of worry and sadness are caused by deficiencies of the *Dao's* virtuous power known as *de*.

If we draw out the implications of these teachings, we can conclude that the compilers of this text held that one way of living an emotionally and morally healthy life was to enhance *qi* energy, rather than to strengthen something called the will, as we might find in Western thought. This means that there is an inexorable relationship between health and morality, a philosophical connection rather foreign to Western thinking.

When the chest and belly are replete and lusts and desires are eliminated, then the ears and eyes are clear, and hearing and vision are acute. ... When fluctuating attention is done away with and the circulation is not awry, then the quintessential spirit is abundant, and the vital energy (*qi*) is not dispersed. When the quintessential spirit is abundant and the vital energy is not dispersed, then you are functioning according to underlying patterns (*li* 理) [of reality]. When you function according to underlying patterns, you attain [calm stillness]. When you attain [calm stillness], you develop penetrating awareness. When you develop penetrating awareness, you become spiritlike (*shen* 神).

(Major et al. 2011: 7.3, my brackets)

The ontology of the *Masters of Huainan* expresses the interconnectedness of all phenomena in reality. One chapter is entitled "Heavenly Patterns" (*Tianwen* 天文). The primary argument of the chapter is that human life and natural events when tied to Heaven's regularities make a unified whole. In *Masters of Huainan*, we see that the cosmology of the five phases (*wu xing*) has matured into a totalizing interpretive model. Everything in the universe is situated in a dynamic cycle of the relations of the five phases that are constantly changing in their configurations, producing and reconfiguring all phenomena and events. Planets are related to colors that are tied to political dynasties that are connected to persons' actions (see Major et al. 2010: 8.9, 10).

Speaking of the Five Thearchs and the Three Kings (Yao, Shun, and Yu) "looking downward, they observed earth's patterns in order to devise standards and measures. They investigated the suitability of mountains and plains, rivers and water meadows, rich and poor land, and high and low areas ... Thereupon they clarified and outlined the [respective] natures of metal, wood, water, fire and earth in order to establish the affection [that should prevail] between fathers and sons to protect the family. They distinguish the high and low sounds of the five tones and the numerology of the mutual production of the six double pitch-pipe notes in order to establish the rightness [that should prevail] between rulers and ministers so as to perfect the state. They studied the successive order of the four seasons in order to establish the propriety [that should prevail] between elders and the young so as to perfect bureaucratic rank." (Ibid., 20.11)

Han thinkers used the Five Phase system to account for an ordered sequence or cycle of change in reality's process. For example, in the "mutual production" (*xiangsheng*) series, wood produced fire, fire produced earth, earth produced metal, metal produced water and water produced wood. In the "mutual conquest" (*xiangke*) series, wood conquered earth, metal conquered wood, fire conquered metal, water conquered fire and earth conquered water. Applied to the rise and fall of ruling dynasties, if a dynasty's emblem was water, one might anticipate it being overcome by a dynasty whose emblem was earth. This schema was appropriated politically as the Han dynasty was thought to rule under the red phase of fire, and by the time of the year 184, their most formidable revolutionary challengers, the Yellow Turbans, employed this ideology in recruiting for their movement. They attempted to exploit the ideas that red would be conquered by yellow and fire by water, the Five Phase phases associated with their movement.

The Five Phase ontology of change is, of course, nonfalsifiable. Trying to use empirical data to prove or disprove it, even on the very broad definition of empiricism that the ontology allows in itself, is philosophically futile. One cannot really specify the results that will follow from adhering to this worldview with any precision.[13] Attempts to measure anticipated results, when not actualized, are explained away or interpreted into an ever more complex physics.

As a heuristic, the Five Phase system may call forth many different responses. One obvious reaction is to choose to accept the entire model and commit oneself to master its processes and even manipulate them to one's own advantage. This was the approach taken by what were called the "masters of techniques" (*fangshi*). We know that a great many of such persons were assembled in Huainan at the time of the formation of the *Masters of Huainan* text. Some of their approaches undoubtedly found their way into the text. But another response to the Five Phase ontology also found its way into the work.

> I live within the world, yet I am also a thing in it. I do not know whether the things of the world are complete because of me or whether only without me are things not incomplete. However, I am also a thing and things relate to things. A thing is related to other things [by this underlying unity], so why must we be things to [i.e., objectify] one another? Even though this may be so, what gain is there

in its [*Dao*] giving me life; what loss is there in its taking my life away? Because what fashions and transforms us treats me as an unfired brick, I have no way to defy it. How do I know that to practice acupuncture and moxibustion and to desire life is not a delusion and to seek death by strangulation is not a blessing? Perhaps life is just servitude, and death is a respite from this toil. The world is vast: who understands it? It gives me life, but not because I intentionally seek it. It takes my life away, but not because I intentionally seek an end. Desire life, but do not strive for it. Detest death, but do not refuse it.

...

The way in which what fashions and transforms us takes hold of things can be compared with the way the potter moulds his clay. The earth that he has taken hold of and made into bowls and pots is no different from the earth before it had been taken from the ground. The earth that remains after he has made the vessels and then smashed them to pieces and thoroughly soaked them with water so that they return to their cause is no different from the earth that had been in the bowls and pots that had existed earlier. (Ibid., 7.5, my brackets)

Buddhist Ontologies

The founder of Buddhism was Siddhartha Gautama, who is believed to have lived in the sixth century BCE in India. Although the time of his birth and death are uncertain, most modern scholars still date his lifetime between 563 and 483 BCE, even if recent research points to a date about a century later. *Buddha* is not Siddhartha's personal name. It is a title coming from the Sanskrit *budh* meaning "to wake up," and it honors his experience as one who has awakened to the true nature of reality and his own being. He is also known as Shakyamuni, meaning "monk of the Shakya clan." His teachings and those transmitted by his students cluster around a set of basic philosophical ideas that intertwine ontological, epistemological and moral concepts. Central among these are the Four Noble Truths: the impermanence of all things, the interdependency of causes, the karmic effects and consequences of deeds and the cessation of the ego as nirvana. These concepts tend to reoccur and even define Buddhism wherever it may be found in all its forms.[14]

The Four Noble Truths

The First Noble Truth states that "Life is Dukkha." *Dukkha* is most often translated as "suffering" and it is by this "truth" that Buddhism teaches that the basic human problem is suffering. But *dukkha* literally means "cares and troubles" (Rahula 1974: 99–106). It means that in life we have troubles and cares. Try as we may, we cannot make people turn out right, do right, etc. We encounter problems, things and people who are unpleasant and when life seems to be going well, it does not last or it is not pleasant in the way we thought it would be.

The Second Noble Truth represents the Buddhist explanation for the cause of *dukkha* (suffering). Why is it that our lives are unsatisfactory? The Buddhist answer is that the problem is within us not out in the world or in something that someone else does. Our lives are unsatisfactory because of *Tanha*. *Tanha* is usually translated as "desire," and its root meaning is traceable to "thirst." Our desires cause suffering and they must be extinguished. Not merely our "evil" desires must be eradicated, but even desires for things we might call "good." Such desires are still desires and they can cause us to suffer (ibid., 95–7). It is desire itself, rather than mere desire for evil that is the cause of our cares and troubles.

The Third Noble Truth claims that cessation of desire occurs when our attachments to things and others are cut off. One way to describe this is through the concept of "nirvana," which can be understood to mean "blowing out a flame." So, by extinguishing the fire of "tanha" (desire) "dukkha" will cease. There is then no more unsatisfactoriness in life. It is this state of being which is known as "nirvana." Nirvana is not a place such as Heaven, but a serenity that arises from the detachment from those things we desire. The last attachment to be severed is the most difficult of all. It is the attachment to the self. Our clinging to the idea that we *are* or *have* a self that endures through time and even beyond death must be abandoned if we are to be free from suffering.

The Fourth Noble Truth names the way(s) to detachment the Eightfold Path. The Eightfold Path is the method one uses in order to extinguish attachment and blow out the fire of desire. It is called the Middle Way, because the path is the middle between indulgence and ascetic renunciation. It is Right View, Right Intention, Right Speech,

Right Action, Right Livelihood, Right Effort, Right Mindfulness and Right Concentration. Although the means to nirvana is characterized as eightfold, Buddhist thinkers describe its width as like the edge of a razor. It can be talked about, but it is easy to get off of it. The eight "Rights" of the path are pursued more or less simultaneously and not in a hierarchy and, taken together, the eight factors mutually support each other and what helps one individual most may be of lesser value to another person.

Buddhism is a massive world system of thought and practice with a complexity of expression that is rivaled only by Christianity and Islam. Its diversity and multiple schools and branches often reflect finely grained nuances and internecine conflicts between teachers and school lineages over a staggering array of questions. Different Buddhist schools offer divergent philosophical answers to ontological questions such as these:

- If the individual self is impermanent, just what is it?
- If reality appears to be made up of fixed and concrete things, but this is not how things truly are, then what are they and why do we think of them as concrete?
- How are our perceptions of things interrelated?
- What causes our perceptions and sensations? (See Kalupahana 1976: 29–31, 44, 51–2, 84, 153–61.)

China did not escape the diversity of Buddhist philosophical schools and their respective answers to these questions, although Leon Hurvitz has shown convincingly that for quite some time Chinese thinkers did not realize that the Buddhist texts coming from India represented different schools of thought and so they tried quite unsuccessfully to harmonize them into a coherent and single philosophical system (Hurvita 1999). Gradually, Chinese thinkers also created some distinctively Chinese Buddhist approaches to these questions and even began some schools that were indigenous to China, several of which made significant contributions to ontological reflections in the history of Chinese philosophy.

Tiantai Buddhism

Unlike earlier schools of Chinese Buddhism, the Tiantai School (*Tiantai zong*) was entirely of Chinese origin. Tiantai grew and flourished as a Buddhist school under its fourth patriarch, Zhiyi (538–97), who asserted that the *Lotus Sutra* (i.e., *The Sutra of the Lotus Blossom of the Subtle Dharma, Miaofa Lianhua Jing*) contained the supreme teaching of Buddhism. The school derives its name from the Tiantai Mountain that served as its most important monastic community and the one at which Zhiyi studied. The most distinctive ontological claim of Tiantai is that there is only one reality, which is both the phenomenal existence of our everyday experience and nirvana itself. There is no transcendent dimension or place that exists apart from the reality we can and do experience in the here and now.

This is a significant divergence from early Buddhist teachings in India that drew a sharp demarcation between the phenomenal world of experience and the world of nirvana, often conceived of in popular thought as some supernatural location. Still, substantial effort is made by Tiantai principal thinkers to dissolve the incompatibility between their views and the two-world ontology that characterizes popular or lay Buddhist beliefs.

In Tiantai the one reality is ultimately empty. The reason all things are empty is that everything is being produced and exists as it is through an indefinite number of interdependent causes. Nothing has its own nature or essence that underlies or enables it to exist apart from the interplay of all the causes which create it. Accordingly, all things have only tentative existence and they are impermanent (Hurvitz 1999: 444).

Humans and other beings with consciousness experience phenomenal reality as various forms of pain and suffering, happiness and contentment and even possibly realize overwhelming enlightenment and peace. In fact, Tiantai writings describe ten ways of existing in reality, but these do not reflect any interest in the kinds of extrapolations offered in the other Chinese ontologies, such as *qi, dao, yin* and *yang*, or an elaborate Five Phase system.

**The Ten Ways of Existing in Reality According to
Tiantai Buddhism**

1.   Hell Beings

2.   Hungry Ghosts

3.   Beasts (i.e., beings of animal nature)

4.   Asuras (demons)

5.   Human Beings

6.   Gods or celestial creatures

7.   Voice-Hearers (Skravakas)

8.   Self-enlightened Ones (Pratyekabuddhas)

9.   Bodhisattvas

10. Buddhas

The first four of the ten ways of existing are characterized by suffering and at least three of them are associated with pain and disorder brought on by evil, immoral living. Other ways of existing in reality are related closely to moral life and attachments to others and to the objects of reality. Tiantai teachers used the category of Voice-Hearers to describe those who have achieved nirvana (i.e., enlightenment) and are freed from their attachments. Dwelling in nirvana, they do not occupy some other place in the universe; they exist here and now in a different state of consciousness gained by hearing and following the teachings of others. They exist in reality in a different way than do the unenlightened. The Self-enlightened Ones gained this state of consciousness on their own, not by following the teachings of others, and they exist in a state of detachment from others and phenomenal things. They are not focused on the condition of others, nor do they desire to help them reach enlightenment. But the Bodhisattvas grasp nirvana as release from attachment and suffering, and yet they engage in this life out of compassion for others, in order to help them find nirvana as well. Finally, Buddhas move in this life in a way that can only be characterized as existing in nirvana itself and in a form of isolation from others different from a Bodhisattva.

In Tiantai ontology, the reality that the Hell Beings inhabit is the same reality in which the Buddhas live. There is no supernatural boundary between these ways of existing or transcendent place to which some go (e.g., Heaven), while others dwell elsewhere (Hell). Living and working next to us may be one who is a Hell Being or a Bodhisattva or even a Buddha. The goal is not to depart this world and go into some other reality which transcends it. There is no other reality except this one; reality is one. An individual who is experiencing pain or punishment for his misdeeds or desires need not wait for death to go to hell; he is a Hell Being right now. Getting clear on this teaching helps us correctly understand the meaning of Zhiyi's statement that, "one thought contains three thousand worlds." Our thoughts, as well as our actions, may propel us to exist in reality in many ways, but this is not the same as saying that our thought is the *substance* of the world (Liu 2008: 283). A single thought can make our experience that of a Hell Being or that of a Buddha, but thought (idea) is not all that exists in reality.

On the way of living as Buddha, the *Lotus Sutra* text regarded as the chief philosophical source of the Tiantai school does not teach that persons can become supernatural beings but reports the following instead:

> After Buddha had finished bringing great benefit to living beings, he passed into extinction. After his correct law and counterfeit law had ended, another Buddha appeared in the same land. ... This process continued until twenty thousand million Buddhas had appeared one after the other, all being the same name (Watson 2002: 110).

Here we see the basis for Tiantai's view that everyone has the capacity to live in reality as a Buddha and when this is done, the person lives in "the Buddha-realm." The Buddha is not the creator of the world. Buddha is not a supernatural being or some type of being which we may become who is other than what we are in substance. We will be extinct, just as all the other Buddhas before us. This is the nature of reality; the only reality that there is. The Buddha-realm is not some other place in reality or a different reality. It is existing in a particular way within the one reality that is all there is. Zhiyi writes,

> To keep away from the mundane dharmas [concrete things] and
> yet seek the ultimate Truth [elsewhere] is similar to avoiding this
> Emptiness and seeking Emptiness elsewhere. The mundane dharmas
> are themselves the ultimate Dharma [i.e., Ultimate Reality]. There is
> no need to forsake the mundane and adhere to the sacred.
>
> (Quoted in Ng 1993: 166)

Tiantai does not deny physical reality. It is no Idealism. It is a form of
ontological realism, confident that there exist manifold concrete things.
Likewise, as the major interpreter of Tiantai, Zhiyi is not interested in
speculation about the actual substance of reality itself. He insists, "We
do not say that the mind exists first and the dharmas [bodies, objects]
come to be later; nor do we say that dharmas exist first while the mind
comes to be later." (Liu 2006: 285)

Consciousness-only (*Wei-shi*) Buddhism

Xuanzang (*c.*596–664) was a Chinese Buddhist monk, scholar, traveler
and translator in the early Tang dynasty. He spent more than ten years
traveling and studying in India. When he returned to Chang'an (Xi'an),
he brought back 657 Buddhist texts and devoted the remainder of
his life to a translation school he established in that city. Xuanzang's
creation in China of the Consciousness-only School of Buddhism
(*Weishi zong*) was greatly influenced by the writings of the Indian
Yogacara master, Vasubandhu (Chinese name, Shi Qin). Xuanzang
wrote an extensive commentary in ten volumes on Vasubandhu's
text *Thirty Stanzas of Consciousness-Only*, entitled *A Treatise on the
Establishment of Consciousness-Only* (*Cheng Wei-shi Lun*), and used it to
set out his own views of this tradition of Buddhist teaching.

The central ontological tenet of Consciousness-only Buddhism
is that nothing exists but consciousness. Of course, this is in direct
conflict with early Chinese *qi* ontology since, as we have noted, *qi*
is an energy that may produce consciousness but is not itself a form
of consciousness. According to Consciousness-only philosophy, we
experience a flow of ideas that we also call perceptions. But these ideas
or perceptions are not caused by concrete or material things external
to us and which continue to exist whether we are conscious of them
or not. In philosophical language, the ontology of Consciousness-
only is called *Idealism*. The objects of our mental experience occur

in particular times, ways and places, giving us the idea of an ordered reality (Fung 1953: II, 321–3). Yet, there are no objects external to our minds which produce our ideas. Accordingly, all objects of our experience are empty, because they have no substance other than as objects of our consciousness.

When we are born, that is to say, when we come into awareness, our experience is not funded by an encounter with objects in a world external to us, but by something Xuanzang called the "storehouse consciousness." The storehouse consciousness is a bank of ideal perceptions gathered through all time. Every ideation that has ever occurred has entered into this storehouse. Likewise, every experienced ideation depends on other ideas for its appearance. No dharma or experienced idea exists on its own and any alteration in the way other ideas cause it to exist makes it something different. This is what is called "dependent co-arising" in Consciousness-only philosophy.

Not all consciousnesses experience the same level of development. Some forms of consciousness are higher than others. The ideas experienced by some consciousnesses "perfume" the highest level of consciousness into being. Jeeloo Liu clarifies just what is meant by this claim. "The notion of 'perfume' is unique to the Buddhist theory of causality. Being in a room with bouquets, one's hair will slowly take on the fragrance; walking in the mist, one's clothes will gradually become damp. Analogously, anything that takes place will slowly but surely have a perfuming effect on its agent or later events". (Liu 2006: 215) So, the awareness of certain ideas and their relation to each other can perfume into existence as human consciousness itself, and ever higher forms.

In its original context in India, the Consciousness-only teachings on ontology were direct contradictions to the prevailing Indian physics of reality, according to which all things of concrete reality (*dharmas*) were believed to be constructed from the atoms of earth, water, fire and air. This meant that the traditional Indian explanation for what reality is like was a *materialist* one. Under this description there is nothing that cannot be reduced to physical matter in some combination or another. However, a classical version of the Consciousness-only argument against this Indian atomistic materialism has been stated by Liu quite well.

1. If a single atom is to be combined with other atoms to form objects, then it must have surfaces of contact with other atoms.

2. There are six sides of contacts: up, down, left, right, front, back.
3. Therefore, every basic unit is already a unit of six parts.
4. Therefore, there cannot be a single unit that is not further divisible (that has no parts).
5. Therefore, the very concept of *atom* is unintelligible.

(Ibid., 234)[15]

Regardless of how we might judge the cogency of this argument against the ontology of atomistic materialism, in China the basic theory of reality was built around the element of *qi*, and its energetic forces *yin* and *yang*, which were said to give rise to the five phases from which all things are made. There was no concept of material substance in its Western or Indian philosophical meaning in early Chinese ontology. The five phases are not material; they are phases of *qi* which are experienced in a certain way (i.e., accessible through what we call our senses). Yet, in Chinese ontology, while not being matter, *qi* was a substance external to us that is more than and other than an idea in our minds, keeping Chinese ontologies based on *qi* constructions from collapsing into Idealism. This significant difference in ontology partially explains why Consciousness-only philosophy did not gain much traction in China. The Chinese already had an ontology that seemed functional and was left relatively unassailed by the main arguments against materialism made by Consciousness-only.

There are philosophical difficulties with the Consciousness-only ontology of Idealism. Some of these can be revealed in the following questions:

- If reality is coextensive with my consciousness, why cannot I imagine a world to exist in whatever way I desire?
- Is the "storehouse consciousness" notion adequate to explain why an individual cannot generate ideas of whatever reality he wishes?
- Alternately, if reality is only the ideas of my consciousness, why cannot I simply dispense with a number of ideas that actually do not have the function I think they do (e.g., food relieving hunger, knives causing wounds, clothing keeping me warm)?

- But perhaps most troubling is the question, if reality is my experienced consciousness, on what grounds can I know that there are other minds or other consciousnesses?
- Am I the only mind that exists (this is called *solipsism*)?

Because of its importance, we can consider how it is that Xuanzang handled what is known as "the Other Minds Problem." He deals with this problem in his commentary on Stanza 17 in his *Treatise*. Xuanzang is concerned to make it clear that in speaking of "other" minds, he means to refer to minds that are different than his own.

> If there were only one individual consciousness, how is it that there is a variety of ordinary people, saints, the honored ones and lowly ones, and causes and effects in the ten cardinal directions? Who would then expound teachings to whom? What dharmas could there be? And what goal is there to seek? (Chan 1973: 391–2).

Unfortunately, Xuanzang seems to simply beg the question by assuming what he must prove. If I held that there is only my own consciousness, I could continue to hold a perfectly coherent position by saying that the ordinary people, saints, honored ones and the like are ideas in my consciousness. To assume that they exist independent of me and must be explained is to presume what I have not yet proven. Given Consciousness-only ontology, ideas of these people are no more caused by actual other consciousnesses than is my idea of a pen or desk caused by some object external to me.

A Version of Idealism in Western Philosophy

British philosopher George Berkeley (1685–1783) expressed his Idealist philosophy principally in his works *Treatise Concerning the Principles of Human Knowledge* (1710) and *Three Dialogues between Hylas and Philonous* (1715). In these works, Berkeley sets out the dictum that "to be [exist] is to be perceived." Following this principle, he developed a philosophy of Idealism or Immaterialism according to which the only things that exist are the ideas that we perceive. These are not caused by matter. Some are caused by our own minds but the great majority of them, what we call nature or reality, are given to us by God. God gives these ideas in sequences and in an order that makes us think there are things such as natural laws. But natural laws are simply the patterns of the order in which God gives us our ideas. The hypothesis that there should be some thing made of a substance called "matter" that causes us to have the ideas we do, is therefore unnecessary and, in fact, incoherent. It is incoherent because we talk about matter, but we do not observe it. We observe blossoms, trees and mountains, but not *matter*. Blossoms, trees and mountains are ideas or images before our minds. Thus, we have an ontology of immaterialism or idealism.

Xuanzang's appeal to a theory of the storehouse consciousness will not enable him to avoid either solipsism or the problem of other minds. It will not do so because if there are no other consciousnesses and there are no other sentient things or even objects, the entire notion of a storehouse consciousness is erased also. How would such a consciousness ever come to exist if mine was the only mind?

A further difficulty with Consciousness-only philosophy arises if we grant that there are other consciousnesses. The problem to which I refer is the quandary over just how it is that I could *know* that some other consciousness has the same experience that I do. Xuanzang seems to aggravate this problem with the following remark:

The consciousness is merely like a mirror, in which what seems to be an external sphere appears. It is in this sense that it is called the mind that discriminates another. But it cannot discriminate [another mind] immediately and directly. What it discriminates immediately and directly are its own transformations. (Ibid., 391)

This remark may be interpreted to mean that I never really know another consciousness at all, only those transformations in my own consciousness that appear and recede. If this is true, upon what basis can we believe in other consciousnesses at all? Xuanzang's use of the mirror analogy is also troubling. Mirrors reflect objects, but if reality is the ideas of my consciousness, where are these ideas coming from in order for consciousness to reflect them?

Zhu Xi's Neo-Confucian Views on Reality

In the early eleventh century, a group of interdependent Chinese philosophers began to reconstruct Chinese philosophy by using a new grammar. They sought to merge Confucian thought with Daoist and even Buddhist concepts.[16] While they surely thought of themselves as still Confucian, it is clear to all that they were doing something different and novel with their appropriation of classical Confucian ideas. Accordingly, they are grouped together and called Neo-Confucians. The term Neo-Confucianism was first used by Western scholars for the twelfth-century synthesis that emerged in the Chinese philosophy of Zhu Xi and it was later adopted by Chinese interpreters. The Chinese term for this set of thinkers was *Daoxue* (i.e., Study of *Dao)*. While there is still an ongoing debate about the usefulness of the term Neo-Confucianism, philosophers traditionally assigned to this movement do, in fact, use a similar philosophical vocabulary in their ontologies and interact with each other on their various answers to a similar set of questions about the nature of reality.[17]

Without doubt, Zhu Xi (1130–1200) is the most influential of these thinkers. Indeed, he set the parameters of philosophical conversation on ontology throughout East Asia for over 400 years.[18] Master Zhu's oral teachings to students are preserved in *Conversations of Master Zhu, Arranged Topically* (*Zhuzi yule*, hereafter *Conversations*) (Gardner 1990). Zhu Xi's extensive philosophical work rests on the foundation of his theory of reality. The place to begin in understanding his ontology is quite succinctly stated by him in this way: "Everything that has shape and form is 'concrete existence' *qi* (器). That which constitutes the Principle(s) (*li* 理) of 'concrete existence' is the Way (*Dao)*" (*Collected Writings of Chu Hsi*, 36.14 in Chan 1963b).

We may wonder whether the Chinese term we are translating as Principle(s) (*li* 理) is singular or plural. Actually, Principle(s) is sometimes used as a singular and sometimes as a plural in Zhu Xi's writing. So, I will sometimes translate it as singular and sometimes as plural, depending on my understanding of Zhu's meaning.

We may also be puzzled about just what to include in Principle(s) when Zhu Xi uses this as an ontological concept. Does Principle(s) refer to something like the logical scaffolding of reality (i.e., its shape, causal efficacy, logical relationality or pattern)? Could Principle(s) mean something like the natural laws discoverable by chemistry, physics and the like? Maybe Principle(s) refers to what the Western philosopher Immanuel Kant called the "categories of the mind" (i.e., causality, space, time, etc.), which are neither objects themselves nor in objects themselves, but are our mind's means of ordering and structuring things in order to create a world or a reality. Or, perhaps, Principle(s) means "moral principles or norms" that are universally binding and true for all persons.

The truth is that Zhu Xi sometimes uses Principles in one of these senses and sometimes in another. Those thinkers who react to his ideas and who are discussed below (Wang Yangming and Dai Zhen) also make multiple uses of this concept. So, to speak of "the" meaning of Principle(s) in Zhu Xi or Neo-Confucianism as whole is to start out on the wrong foot. We must let the philosophical text speak for itself in each case, resisting the urge to reduce all uses of the concept of Principle(s) to a singular one.[19]

In Zhu Xi, the Principle(s) of reality "reside" in the Supreme Ultimate (*Taiji tu*). He expresses this claim in the following way:

> The Ultimateless! And yet also the Supreme Ultimate! They [these words] do not mean that it [the Supreme Ultimate] is a concrete something glittering in a glorious manner somewhere. They only mean that in the beginning, when no single concrete object yet existed, there was then nothing but Principle(s) (*li*) … and because these Principle(s) are multiple, therefore concrete objects (in the existing universe) are also multiple.
>
> (*Conversations* 94, 21–2, Fung 1953: II, 535, with my changes)

If we are to pin down the word Principle(s), neither existence (*yu*) nor nonexistence (*wu*) may be attributed to Principle(s) because Zhu Xi holds that before heaven and earth existed, Principle(s) already was (were) as it is (they are) (Blakeley 2004: f. 30).

In his reply to a question from Qiang Yuanqin, Zhu Xi says, "the Principle(s) (*li*) of the myriad things, brought into one whole, constitute the Supreme Ultimate (*Taiji*). The Supreme Ultimate did not originally have this name. It is simply an appellation applied to it" (Blakeley 2004: 94.7, 537). For Zhu Xi, the Supreme Ultimate is not an object, or "concrete something glittering in a glorious manner somewhere." Zhu Xi makes the point that before shapes and things existed, the Supreme Ultimate, from which they came, had the principles of shape and order and so did the objects that come from it.

The Supreme Ultimate possesses all Principles governing the five phases and *yin* and *yang*. When a concrete thing comes into being, it has its own expression of Principle(s). Thinking retrospectively, the Principle(s) for anything that exists were already present in the Supreme Ultimate of the universe. Looking from the point of view of Principles, "although a certain object may not yet exist, the Principles for that object are already there. Thus there are already Principles even when objects do not yet actually exist" (*Collected Writings* 46.26).

Fung Yulan interprets Zhu Xi in this way: "In other words, what we call the invention of a boat or cart is nothing more than the discovery by man of the Principle that pertains to boats or carts, and the conforming to this Principle in order to create an actual boat or cart" (*Conversations* 4.6, Fung 1953: II, 536). In reading Zhu as he does, Fung takes him to mean that there are archetypes for boats and carts of which humans become aware, enabling us to create them. He supports his reading by citing Zhu's comments that the bricks of a porch have within them the Principle that pertains to bricks and the bamboo chair contains the Principle of bamboo chairs (ibid., 535–6).

This reading brings Zhu Xi very close to a theory of archetypes or the much older ontology of Plato's view of the Forms. In Plato, the Forms are the ideal patterns for all things in reality according to which humans "make" chairs, but do not invent them. Chairs we make imitate the "Form" of a chair, which the craftsman is remembering from a pre-existent state prior to coming into this material world. A particular chair participates in the Form of chairness; what makes it a chair in its essence. In fact, Fung Yulan thinks that Zhu Xi's concept of the Supreme Ultimate, which consists in nothing more than the Principles of all things brought together in a single whole, is very much like Plato's Form of the Good that also gathers all the Forms into itself. In his *A Short History of Chinese Philosophy*, Fung actually titles the chapter on Zhu Xi, "The School of Platonic Ideas," pointing to similarities between Zhu's conception of Principle(s) and the doctrine of Forms in the dialogues of Plato.

But Zhu Xi can be read in another way I suggest is more accurate and avoids Fung's overzealous use of a Western mind-set to interpret a Chinese thinker. In my view, Fung's interpretation has created a misunderstanding of Zhu's position. Instead of thinking of Principle(s) as Forms or archetypes for objects, with each thing having its own single Principle, we should not neglect Zhu Xi's comment in *Conversations* 4.10 that animals other than humans do not have a distinctively different Principle(s) from humans, but owing to the configuration of their five phases into the shape (body) they possess, their expression of Principle(s) takes the form it does. In fact, Zhu Xi makes it clear that "each individual thing possesses the entire Supreme Ultimate" or set of Principles (*Conversations* 4.10).

On this reading, Principles are something like categories of order that underlie all that is. There is not an actual Form or archetype for each different existing kind of thing as Fung thinks. When Zhu Xi says that the bricks have within them the Principle(s) pertaining to bricks, he does not mean some archetypal "Form of brick." He means that bricks are bricks because they have the Principles and in their five phase configuration they "brick" (as a gerund or verb that functions here as a noun). Zhu means that five phase configuration that comes together as a brick does so by universal Principles. Accordingly, Fung's translation of *Collected Writings* 46.26 above should be "although a certain object may not yet exist, the Principle(s) for the form in which it *could exist* are already there [in the Supreme Ultimate]."

Regardless of whether I have this right or Fung is correct, we cannot deny that for Zhu Xi Principle(s) do not come from concrete things. They ontologically *enable* concrete configurations (i.e., of the five phases) to yield the myriad things that furnish reality. Zhu expresses such a view with respect to both natural and moral realities. I offer these translations.

> Before the thing exists, there is first its Principle(s). For example, there are the Principle(s) governing (the relationship between) ruler and subject before there is any ruler and subject; there are the Principle(s) governing (the relationship between) father and son before there is any father and son. It cannot be that originally there were no such Principle(s), and that it is only when ruler and subject, father and son, finally come into existence, that the Principle(s) for them was implanted in them. (*Conversations* 95.21)

Zhu Xi says,

> The Supreme Ultimate is thus made up of the Principle(s) governing the five phases (*wuxing*) and the *yin* and *yang*, and so is not something "empty." If it were thus "empty" it would resemble the "nature" (*xing*) of things as termed by the Buddhists ... Buddhists see only the external shell and do not see the many Principle(s) that lie within. (Ibid. 94.2)

More to the point, he responds to questions in the following ways:

> Within the universe there are Principles and *qi* (氣). Principles are the *Dao* that has no shape; they are the source from which things are produced. *Qi* (氣) is what constitutes concrete existence (*qi* 器); it [*qi* (氣)] is what things are made of. Hence men or things, at the moment of their existence, must receive Principles to have a nature (*xing*); they must receive *qi* (氣) to have a concrete form. (*Collected Writings* 58.5)

> Question: In what way are Principles displayed through *qi* (氣)?
> Answer: When *yin* and *yang* and the five phases (*wuxing*) intermingle, but do not lose their proper order and succession, this is due to Principles. But if *qi* (氣) was not there to form objects, Principles would have no expression. (*Conversations* 94.10)

> The transformations of *yang* and the congealings of *yin* thus produce water, fire, wood, metal, and earth. The *yin* and *yang*, which are *qi* (氣), produce the five phases, which are tangible things (*zhi* 質). Among the emergent things of heaven and earth, the five phases come first. The earth is composed of the element earth, with which there is also incorporated some elements of metal and wood. There is nothing in heaven and earth that does not combine the five phases. These seven, the five phases and *yin* and *yang* boil forth and combine with one another to form tangible objects (*zhi*). (Ibid. 94.3)

According to Zhu Xi, the five phases produced by *qi* and Principles (*li*) yield tangible objects (*zhi*).

In 94.3 above, Fung Yulan translates *zhi* as "corporeal matter." But this also creates philosophical confusion. To do this may well suggest to the Western reader that *qi* is something spiritual, whereas the five phases and other objects are material, creating a kind of dualism that Zhu Xi does not intend at all. *Zhi* is not "matter" as though it were some other substance in addition to *qi*. Rather it is the five phase configuration of *qi* that is in our sensory range. That is it: full stop. In Chinese philosophy prior to the eighteenth century, there is no concept of "matter" as a substance that resembles the Western notion of something shaped to produce in us certain perceptions. Certainly we do have experiences of objects, but these are not made of some ontological stuff called matter, they are configurations of the five phases, which are themselves *qi*. To misunderstand this ontological point is to hopelessly confuse any interpretation of Chinese philosophy prior to the modern period.

Zhu Xi embraces the ever-flowing process of change that we have noticed from the beginning of Chinese ontology. He thinks there were other worlds before our present one and that in the future, our reality will reform into something different. "In the same way (the ceaseless alteration of) *yin* and the *yang* constitutes a great closing and opening" (ibid.: 94.2).

We must also consider Zhu Xi's ontology to be a form of *naturalism* rather than *theism*. The Supreme Ultimate (i.e., the sum total of all Principles) is neither like the Form of the Good in Plato, nor God in the Western sense. However, neither is it reducible to, or the product of, the other cosmological operators in Zhu's thought (i.e., *qi*, *yin*, *yang*, the five phases). Donald Blakeley has called this role and function of the Supreme Ultimate "transcendent" and he has argued that it is required and integral to Zhu's ontology (Blakeley 2004).

Blakeley might be right. If we compare Zhu Xi to the Western philosopher Immanuel Kant, Zhu does not say that the Principles that are the Supreme Ultimate are empty, as Kant says of the categories of the mind. While Zhu does say that without *qi*, Principles would have no expression and cannot be spoken of as either existing or not existing, where Blakeley seems right is in noticing that Zhu Xi thinks of Principles as part of the fabric of reality and not merely how our mind functions to order things. This is what Blakeley means by stressing their "transcendence."[20] They order and structure concrete things, but they do not depend on things, nor derive from them.

Wang Yangming (1472–1529)

"The fact is that in my own heart I cannot bear to contradict Master Zhu but I cannot help contradicting him because the Way is the way it is and the Way will not be fully evident if I do not correct him" (Chan 1963: 164). Wang Yangming's stormy career was in large measure due to his opposition to the philosophy of Zhu Xi. He departed from Zhu in both his ontology and epistemology. In fact, in the Ming Dynasty, Wang Yangming became the most deliberative of Zhu Xi's critics.[21]

Wang disagreed with the way Zhu Xi distinguished Principle(s) (*li*) from the concrete things of reality. He sought to bring Principle(s) into the fabric of the nature and workings of the human mind, not in a transcendent Supreme Ultimate. Commenting on the very famous example from the writings of Mencius about how one will naturally come to the aid of a child upon seeing the child about to fall in a well (*Mengzi* 2A6), Wang wrote,

> When I see a child fall into a well [and have a feeling of commiseration], there must be the Principle of commiseration … Is it really in the person of the child or does it emanate from pure knowledge (*liangzhi* 良知) of my mind? What is true here is true of all things and events. From this we know the mistake of dividing the mind and Principle(s) into two. (Chan 1963a: 98–9)

> For the Principle(s) of things are not external to the mind. If one seeks Principles of things outside the mind, there will not be any to be found. And if one neglects the Principles of things and only seeks his mind, what sort of thing would the mind be? The substance of the mind is nature, and nature is identical with Principles. (Ibid., 95)

Wang is often characterized as an Idealist because of his emphasis on the role of the mind in his ontology. As we have seen in our discussion of Consciousness-only Buddhism, Idealism is a philosophical worldview according to which reality consists only of immaterial ideas that we call reality. In Chinese thought, Idealism is an ontology that denies the existence of concrete things made of *qi*. Shu-Shien Liu examines the position that Wang was an Idealist (Liu 2009b: 409–11). He calls attention to two passages from *Instructions for Practical Living* that are often interpreted to mean that Wang thought nothing existed except the mind and that the mind is not a concrete thing.

> The teacher [i.e., Wang Yangming] was roaming in Nanzhen. A friend pointed to flowering trees on a cliff and said: "[You say] there is nothing under Heaven and external to the mind. These flowering trees on the high mountain blossom and drop their blossoms of themselves. What have they to do with my mind?" The teacher said, "Before you look at these flowers, they and your mind are in the state of silent vacancy. As you come to look at them, their colours at once show up clearly. From this you can know that these flowers are not external to your mind."
>
> (Chan 1963a: 222)

The other passage Liu considers is also taken from *Instructions for Practical Living.*

> I said, "the human mind and things form the same body. In the case of one's body, blood and the vital force (*qi* 氣) in fact circulate through it and therefore we can say that they form the same body. In the case of other men, their bodies are different, and in those of animals and plants are even more so. How can they be said to form the same body?"
>
> The teacher [i.e., Wang Yangming] said, "Just look at the matters from the point of view of the subtle incipient activating force of their mutual influence and response. Not only animals and plants, but heaven and earth also form the same body as me. Spiritual beings also form the same body as me."
>
> I asked the teacher kindly to explain.
>
> The teacher said, "Among the things under heaven and on earth which do you consider to be [i.e., epitomize] the mind of heaven and earth?"
>
> "I have heard that 'Man is the mind of heaven and earth.'"
>
> "How does man become mind?"
>
> "Pure knowledge (*liangzhi*) and pure knowledge only."
>
> "We know, then, all that fills heaven and earth is this pure knowledge. It is only because of their physical forms and bodies that men are separated. My pure knowledge is the master of heaven and earth and spiritual beings. If heaven is deprived of my pure knowledge, who is going to look into its height? If earth is deprived of my pure knowledge, who is going to look into its depth? If spiritual beings

are deprived of my pure knowledge, who is going to distinguish their good and evil fortune or the calamities and blessings that they will bring? Separated from my pure knowledge, there will be no heaven, earth, spiritual beings, or myriad things, and separated from those, there would not be my pure knowledge. Thus all is permeated with one material force (*qi*). How can they be separated?"

I asked further, "Heaven, earth, spiritual beings, and the myriad things have existed from great antiquity. Why should it be that if *my* pure knowledge is gone, they all ceased to exist?"

"Consider the dead man. His spirit is drifted away and dispersed. Where are his heaven and earth or the myriad things?"

(Ibid., Section 337)

Considering these two passages together, we can see why an interpreter might think that Wang Yangming is saying that our minds have perceptions or ideas in front of them and that these ideas constitute the content of reality. For example, we may interpret the first passage as saying that reality consists of our ideas of a blossom, tree and mountain. Taken in this way, Wang would be saying that experience is of ideas and not of concrete things, a position similar to the Idealism of Consciousness-only Buddhism.

We may ask, though, whether this is really what Wang Yangming was trying to say. It we look carefully at the first passage, the student reminds Wang that he has taught that nothing exists outside of his mind. The student takes this as an Idealistic remark, but finds such a view objectionable. He insists that blossoms and trees operate without requiring any direction or action of our minds, so they must exist outside of our minds. But, then, we see Wang's point emerge in his reply and if we pay close attention, we will notice that Wang is not an Idealist at all.

Unlike Idealism, Wang does not begin to talk about the cause of our ideas (i.e., perceptions) and whether it is our mind, concrete objects, or God. Instead, he makes his position clear. Before we look at the flowers, they just are what they are in their raw being, they exist as they do in a kind of "vacuity" of order and meaning. But, when we direct our attention (i.e., our mind) to the objects, they become "flowers" and "mountains." That is, they are made a part of a structured and coherent "reality" *by our minds*. Why is this? It is because our minds are inevitably, inherently, innately patterning everything experienced.

Our minds Principle (*li*) (here used as a verb). It is this Principling or ordering that makes a "Universe" or a "Reality." Otherwise, while there are still concrete objects moving around, there is really no "World." Wang is not denying the existence of the concrete things at all, but he is insisting that none of these things are "blossoms," "trees" and "mountains" without the ordering that the mind brings to experience.

If we look at the second passage, Wang says that our bodies are the same type as animals and spiritual beings. What he means is they are made from the five phases of *qi* that compose all things. What distinguishes human beings is the possession of the mind. He closely associates the mind of humankind with the "mind" of heaven and earth. What he means when he says this is that our minds give order and pattern to heaven and earth (i.e., to all that exists). Our minds bring structure such as causality, shape, time, pattern and order as Principles to heaven and earth; and heaven and earth have these as part of themselves. It is in this sense that our minds are one with heaven and earth. These Principles are known to our minds immediately or directly by "pure knowledge" (*liangzhi*). This means that they are not known through the mediation or data from our five senses, by the authority of any book or philosophical teacher, or even by our own deliberation and choice to apply them. They are not derived from previous experience either. Instead, the myriad things are just what they are. When our mind applies "pure knowledge" to things they have height, depth and the like. They become blossoms and trees, etc. So, in both of these passages, Wang holds that our mind is the instrument of world-making, he is not denying the existence of concrete things (*qi* 器) made from the five phases.

There is a fundamental difference, though, in Wang's position and that of Zhu Xi. Wang does not set Principles in a transcendent sense apart from concrete things. In fact, he gives Principles no existence apart from the human mind. If there were no human minds, there would be no "World." Objects would not vanish; but their facticity and brute existence would not be a "World" or a "Universe." Accordingly, Wang says:

> What is called your mind is that which makes seeing, listening, speaking, and moving possible. It is the nature (*xing*) of man; it is the Principles of Heaven (*tianli* 天理) … In its capacity as a master of the body, it is called the mind. Basically the original substance of the mind

is none other than the Principles of Heaven, and is never out of accord with propriety. This is your true self. The true self is the master of the body. If there is no true self, there will be no body. Truly, with the true self, one lives; without it, one dies. (Ibid.)

If we ask how it is that the mind Principles (here used as a verb) to make a world and whether we can know that the world is as we Principle it to be through our minds, Wang's answer is that this cannot be resolved through reason and there is no sense experience of Principles to verify their reality. Instead, he says directly that this Principling activity is what is meant by "pure knowledge" (*liangzhi*). It is direct and immediate, and experienced as cognitive certainty.

Shifting Paradigms in Chinese Ontologies

Dai Zhen (1723–77)

Chung-ying Cheng says that Dai Zhen was responsible for a paradigm shift in Chinese thinking on ontology (Cheng 2009a: 460). Even so, Dai is still making use of the same vocabulary of philosophical concepts that Zhu Xi employed and he is still trying to answer the same ontological questions with them (e.g., How do we account for the differences between appearance and reality? What is the source and basis for the order and structure we find in reality?). Yet, there is a difference in the answers Dai offers, and there are important and worthwhile philosophical distinctions and clarifications he provides.

As a conversational partner with the Neo-Confucians, Dai, like Wang Yangming, is seeking to correct and amplify Zhu Xi's ontology. Dai completely removed the transcendent aspect from Principles (*li*) that was present in Zhu's understanding of the Supreme Ultimate. Making this philosophical move certainly represented a shift from Zhu's understanding. Wang Yangming had also departed from Zhu's understanding of Principle(s) as transcendent by identifying them with the workings of the human mind. Dai differs from Wang Yangming because he considered Principles not to be independent of *qi* but to be a way of talking about its internal order (*tiao*) or pattern (*wen*). He completely naturalized Principle(s), locating them in the concrete existing things of our experience and not in our minds.[22]

> The word Principles (*li*) is the name assigned to the arrangement of
> the parts of anything which gives the whole its distinctive property or
> characteristics, and which can be observed by careful examination and
> analysis of the parts down to the minutest detail. This is why we speak
> of the principle of differentiation (*fenli*). With reference to the substance
> of things, there are such expressions as the Principle(s) governing the
> fibers (*jili*), the Principle(s) governing the arrangement between skin
> and flesh (*couli*), and pattern (*wenli*). When proper differentiation is
> made, there will be order without confusion. This is called order and
> arrangement (*tiaol*).
>
> 　　　　　　　(*Evidential Study* 1.1 in Chin and Freeman 1990: 69)

Dai separates himself from the views of Zhu Xi and Wang Yangming
and locates order and pattern within natural phenomena. To use
Western philosophical terms, we could characterize Dai's thought as
a form of *teleological naturalism*. Order, structure and design are not
imposed on reality by human beings (minds), but neither do they
derive from a transcendent realm that is wholly other than the natural
process itself. Instead, they are a part of the very nature of *qi*. Some
interpreters of Dai explain his position by means of a rather distinctive
Chinese example. A method used to determine the authenticity of a
piece of jade in China is to hold it up to the light and observe whether
veins can be seen in its translucence. If so, the jade is authentic. If not, it
is an imitation, a fake. Accordingly, we may think of Dai as arguing that
qi itself has such striations within and these are Principle(s) (*li*).

Holding such a position required Dai Zhen to explain just how
it is that *qi* can possess Principle (*li*) since *qi* is the actual stuff from
which all things in reality are made. In order to do this, he approaches
the concept of *qi* very analytically. He says for a given object, such as
the human being, *qi* takes a certain tangible form (*pinwu* 品物). This
is the shape of an object, e.g., that form that distinguishes one thing
from another. Moreover, *qi* forms in blood (*xueqi*) and in the "cognitive
mind" (*xinzhi*), which is a combination of intelligence and the senses
(*zhi jue*), giving rise to the natural endowments of thought, feelings and
desires, especially in animals and humans (Cheng 2009a: 462). Animals,
for example, possess blood-*qi* and the intelligence and senses sufficient
to be capable of spontaneous behavior based on the feelings of love of
kinship or like-kind attachment:

in their (birds and beasts) love of those who gave them birth, in the love of what they have given birth to, in the love between male and female, and in not devouring their own kind or biting those they are associated with, they have advanced well beyond cherishing life and fearing death. In one case there is concern only for oneself while in the other case concern is extended to others who are close to one, but in both cases the virtue of humanity (*ren*) is exhibited. Being concerned about oneself is being humane to oneself. To extend the concern for oneself to those who are close to one is being humane to those who are nearby. This is the knowing mind naturally expressing itself.

(*Evidential Study* 1961: 27 in Chin and Freeman 1990: 116)

Dai's point is that the behavior animals are displaying based on kinship or like-kind attachment is the endowment of blood-*qi* and even the rudimentary "cognitive mind" that animals possess. They can recognize similarity between themselves and others or remember which other animal is their mother or in their group. However, it is the more developed version of "cognitive mind" humans are endowed with by *qi* that represents the Principle(s) and guides persons to be able not only to exhibit the behaviors animals are capable of but also gives rise to the power to make rational and moral judgments that extend beyond those of animals. Dai made his position clear when he referred to a famous example in Chinese folklore about filial piety among species.

Moreover, as for the habit of the crow to feed its parents, of the fish hawk to recognize sex distinctions, of the bees and ants to recognize the difference between ruler and subject, of the jackal to sacrifice wild beasts, and of the otter to sacrifice fish, they all seem to be in accordance with what human beings call the virtues of humanity (*ren* 仁) and appropriateness (*yi* 義), yet each is just performing its task by following its nature (*xing*). Man is able to extend his knowing until he has reached perfect understanding, until the virtues of humanity, appropriateness, propriety, and wisdom are all complete in him. Humanity, appropriateness, propriety, and wisdom are none other than the ultimate achievement of understanding and the supreme measure of knowing. (Ibid. 28: 118–19)

Hu Shi (1891–1962): The Shift to Western Ontologies

With the arrival of Western Christian missionaries in the late sixteenth century, China came into sustained contact with Europe, and Chinese intellectuals began to believe that the West had overtaken China in various scientific and technological fields. Accordingly, to facilitate their relations with Chinese officials and literati, the missionaries translated works of Western science and technology as well as Christian texts into Chinese. Between 1582 and 1773, more than 70 missionaries of various nationalities undertook this kind of work.[23] The missionaries were assisted by Chinese collaborators. For example, Xu Guangqi assisted Matteo Ricci when he translated Euclid's *Elements* in 1607. Ricci and Li Zhizao introduced the Chinese to classical Western logic via a Portuguese university-level textbook brought to China in 1625.[24]

In collaboration with the Chinese scholar Li Zhizao (1565–1630), Portuguese missionary Fu Fanji (Francisco Furtado, 1587–1653) translated two Western works into Chinese. They were *Huan you quan* (*On Heaven and Earth*), a translation with scholarly commentaries of Aristotle's *De Coelo et Mundo* (*On the Heavens*), and *Ming li tan* (*Inquiries into the Principles of Names*), a partial free translation of Aristotelian logic. The most general effect of these early translations was that China opened to Western knowledge, especially in science and socio-political theory. Among all these currents of thought, the most dramatic impact was the effect on Chinese ontologies caused by the infusion of Darwinian evolutionary science that greatly influenced Chinese intellectuals, whether or not they found Western moral or social theory credible.

After the first Sino-Japanese War of 1894–5, Yan Fu (1853–1921), who studied in England from 1877 to 1879, became the most influential translator of Western works in China. Although Darwinian evolutionism had been introduced into China prior to Yan Fu's translation of Huxley's *Evolution and Ethics* in 1898 (known in Chinese as *Tianyanlun*, *Theory of Evolution*), Yan's translation really shifted the axis in Chinese ontology toward Western science and a revision of the historic grammar and explanatory devices with which Chinese had operated for over 2,000 years.

This new scientific Western ontology made no use of the traditional Chinese operators, such as *qi*, *yin* and *yang* and the five phases. In contrast to China's correlative physics that valorized harmony and mutual interdependence of natural forces the new Western ontology was a conceptual framework employing the mechanisms of "survival of the fittest," "struggle for adaptation" and "natural selection."

One might think that the infusion of Western scientific evolutionary theory that included empirical observation of competition, transmission of dominant characteristics of cognitive and biological developments would require the complete abandonment of traditional Chinese ontologies and that Yan Fu's translation represented the herald of such change. However, the actual situation was much different.

Shen Tsing Song (Vincent Shen) has done an extensive analysis of Yan Fu's version of Huxley's work, and he argues that Yan did much more than translate *Evolution and Ethics* in some literal way (Shen 2014). According to Shen, Yan Fu transformed Huxley's work by infusing into his translation the Chinese ontological concepts and sentiments in which he was steeped. Yan had the sense that Chinese ontology, going all the way back to the *Yijing*, always made room for creativity, novelty and productivity. Even Daoist ontologies of transformation (*hua* 化) could be interpreted as evolutionary in force. Moreover, the Darwinian notion of environmental adaptation as an explanation for evolution was not totally absent from classical Chinese ontology either. In Neo-Confucian thought, as we have seen, the Great Ultimate was understood to have launched a dynamic process of interaction between movement and tranquillity, first in the forces of *yin* and *yang*, then in the five phases, the combinations of which gave rise to the myriad of things.

While Yan Fu made a remarkable contribution to Chinese philosophy in his translation, he was still quite attached to previous Chinese ontological language and conceptualization. His most important contribution was not the translation itself, but what Shen calls, "the reconstruction of Huxley's discourse to adapt it to the current needs of the Chinese people" (Shen 2014). Shen argues that it was left to Ma Junwu (1881–1940), who translated Darwin's *The Origin of Species* into Chinese (1920), to offer a rendering of the paleontological, geographical, botanic and zoological technical terms into good Chinese (ibid., 16).

It was Hu Shi who completed the shift toward Western ontology. The development of Hu Shi's ontology began with his own reading of Huxley's *Evolution and Ethics*, Darwin's *The Origin of Species* and other works of Western science that Yan and Ma had translated while Hu was studying in Shanghai and he tells of the profound influence these works had on him.

> It was these essays which first violently shocked me out of the comfortable dream that our ancient civilization was self-sufficient and had nothing to learn from the militant and materialistic West except in the weapons of war and vehicles of commerce. They opened to me, as to hundreds of others, an entirely new vision of the world. (Chou 1995: I, 91)

Like many other Chinese intellectuals, Hu Shi looked to the development of science and its methods as the most important contribution Western civilization could make to China. While still a young student in Shanghai, he summarized the changes in his conception of reality and the universe in what he entitled "New Credo." Although it was published in 1923, he continued to hold its views until the end of his life. This text reads as follows:

1. On the basis of our knowledge of astronomy and physics, we should recognize that the world of space is infinitely large.
2. On the basis of our geological and paleontological knowledge, we should recognize that the universe extends over infinite time.
3. On the basis of all our verifiable scientific knowledge, we should recognize that the universe and everything in it follow natural laws of movements in change. So, that is "natural" in the Chinese sense of "being so of its self" and there is no need for the concept of a supernatural Ruler or Creator.
4. On the basis of the biological sciences, we should recognize the terrific wastefulness and brutality in the struggle for existence in the biological world, and consequently the untenability of the hypothesis of a humane Ruler.
5. On the basis of the biological, physiological, and psychological sciences, we should recognize that man is only one species in the animal kingdom and differs from the other species only in degree, but not in kind.
6. On the basis of the knowledge derived from anthropology, sociology, and the biological sciences, we should understand the history and causes of the evolution of living organisms and of human society.

7. On the basis of the biological and psychological sciences, we should recognize that all psychological phenomena could be explained through the law of causality.

8. On the basis of biological and historical knowledge, we should recognize that morality and religion are subject to change, and that the causes of such change can be scientifically studied.

9. On the basis of our newer knowledge of physics and chemistry, we should recognize that matter is full of motion and not static.

10. On the basis of biological, sociological and historical knowledge, we should recognize that the individual self is subject to death and decay. But the sum total of individual achievement, for better or for worse, lives on in the immortality of the Larger Self. That to live for the sake of the species and posterity is religion of the highest kind; and that those religions that seek a future life either in Heaven or in the Pure Land, are selfish religions.

(Hu 1931: 260–3)

What we see in this text is a different sort of naturalism than that of Dai Zhen. Hu's commitment is to the experimental sciences and he represents a turn away from traditional Chinese ontology and its vocabulary. He observed,

In this naturalistic universe, in this universe of infinite space and time, man, the two-handed animal whose average height is about five feet and a half and whose age rarely exceeds a hundred years, is indeed a mere infinitesimal microbe. In this naturalistic universe, where every motion in the heavens has its regular course and every change follows laws of nature, where causality governs man's life and the struggle for existence spurs his activities—in such a universe man has very little freedom indeed. (Chou 1995: I, 99)

Hu Shi's ontology set aside the Chinese grammar of *qi, yin, yang, li, dao* and the five phases. He turned toward a new scientific vocabulary and that moved him away from the belief in a soul with which he was familiar as a child. For Hu, the mind is a particular form of the functioning of the material body, and it cannot exist without the body. He compared the mind to the sharpness of a knife and used the argument that we have never seen any sharpness exist once the knife is destroyed.

Hu thinks reality is potentially entirely understandable by science. It does not possess some transcendent mystery or meaning. But the wonder of the universe is the human being in both its fragility and activity.

CHAPTER II

哲学

Epistemology: Questions about the Nature and Scope of Knowledge

Introduction

This chapter is occupied with fundamental questions that can be gathered under the concept of *epistemology*. As with *ontology*, the term *epistemology* is derived from the Greek language. *Epistemis* means "to know." When combined with *logos*, "the science or study of," we have epistemology, the study of knowledge. These are some of the epistemological questions this chapter will address:

- What is it "to know"?
- Can we *know* something to be true, or do we only *believe* things to be true?
- Are all claims to know something of the same sort or justified in the same way? That is, is knowing 2+2=4 the same type of knowledge as "I know the car won't start because the battery is dead"?
- What are the tools we use to know something (e.g., reason/ logic/argument, experience/senses, etc.)?
- Are we born knowing some things are true?
- Is there a limit to what we can know?
- Are there laws of thinking that must be followed to obtain any kind of knowledge whatever?

When we take up these questions with respect to Chinese philosophy, a serious obstacle greets us in the very beginning. Chad Hansen expresses this barrier clearly:

[C]lassical Chinese philosophers had no concept of truth at all. Of course, for Chinese (philosophers and laymen) the truth of a doctrine did make a difference, and, in general, Chinese did reject false propositions and adopt true ones. However, they did not "use a concept of truth" in philosophizing about what they were doing.

(Hansen 1985: 491)

Of course, not all interpreters agree with Hansen. Chris Fraser, for example, has devoted several studies to Chinese epistemology in the classical period (2013, 2011).

Nonetheless, in traditional Chinese philosophy, epistemology was not an explicitly developed discipline, even if Chinese philosophers since ancient times were interested in problems related to human knowledge and developed some explicit strategies for how we know that a claim is true. While there was no classical Chinese term equivalent to the word *epistemology* in Western philosophy, still Chinese philosophers distinguished different types of knowledge and they engaged in a discussion of standards of evidence and relative probabilities. They identified various sources of knowledge and distinguished belief from knowledge. In all of this, Alexus McLeod thinks Chinese philosophers operated to suggest that they considered truth not to be reducible to a single method or approach but actually plural in its realization as shown in the multiple terms they employed for it, e.g., *ran* (然), *shi* (是), *you* (有), and *shi* (實) (2011: 39). We will explore a number of different approaches to epistemological questions taken in Chinese philosophy.

The *Mozi* and the Later Mohist Debaters (*bianshi*)

Mo Di (a.k.a. Master Mo or Mozi, *c.*470–391 BCE) explored the claim that Heaven ordered reality and that this process can and does override human will and decision. This was known as *ming* (命), typically translated into English as "fate."[1] In his examination of the commonly held belief in *ming*, Mozi was asked by his students to set out the philosophical bases for judging between views on whether there is such a thing as *ming*, and if so, what is its scope and function. In general, Mozi's response to this question serves as a reasonable outline for his theory of a claim's truthfulness and provides a window into his epistemology.

When asked how to distinguish between theories, he answers as follows:

> You must establish standards ... [for the choice between theories] these must have three criteria. What are the three criteria? There is the foundation; there is the source; there is the application. In what is the foundation? The foundation is in the actions of the ancient sage-kings. In what is the source? The source is in the truth of the evidence of the eyes and ears of the common people below. In what is the application? It emanates from government policy and is seen in the benefit to the ordinary people of the state.
>
> (*Mozi* 35.5, Johnston 2010)

These three criteria require some explanation.

The first test for judging between knowledge claims is what we may call an examination of the received belief about the claim. In Mozi's context, this is understood as what the historical records report. It was commonly believed by Chinese thinkers of the classical period that the record of Chinese history known as the *Classic of History* (*Shujing*) was a literal and accurate record of the thoughts and deeds of the sage-kings of Chinese history. Moreover, they believed these actions and thoughts should be regarded as the standard for truth by which to judge claims and proposals made in Mozi's day. Mozi does not propose a critical analysis of these sources; neither does he give evidence of any serious doubt about the records.

A second truth test is what Mozi calls "the evidence of the eyes and ears of the common people." He takes this to mean experiential testimony to the truth of a claim. Mozi offers no further direct amplification of this criterion, but his procedure in applying it shows that he pays attention both to how widespread the testimony is for the truth of a claim and also who is providing the experiential evidence. He is not saying that the sheer number of people who believe something to be true is a criterion for regarding it as true. This would involve him in the error of "truth by majority" and lead him down such epistemological dead ends as "the earth must be flat because everyone believes it is." Likewise, Mozi does not regard a claim to be true simply because someone, regardless of learning or status, reports having had an experience of a certain sort. The way in which he operates demonstrates that Mozi understands the difference between belief and knowledge quite clearly, especially when an appeal to one's experience is the evidence being offered.

The third criterion Mozi offers is what Western philosophers would call a pragmatic test. Essentially Mozi is suggesting that one criteria of the truth of a claim rests in its usefulness in furthering the tasks of life or society, or the benefit of acting as though it were the case.

We may find it interesting that based upon these criteria, Mozi argues that ghosts and spirits exist, as well as that Heaven acts in a way that exhibits volition and will, and there is no fate that determines our present or future situation (see *Mozi* 26–37, Johnston 2010).

We may consider an example of Mozi's application of these three criteria for the justification of a belief by looking at *Mozi* 31's examination of the claim that ghosts and spirits exist. Mozi first considers what is at stake in whether such a belief is true from his point of view:

> Nowadays, those who hold that there are no ghosts say: "Ghosts and spirits certainly do not exist." From morning to evening they teach and instruct the world's people, sowing doubt among its multitudes and causing them to be suspicious and doubtful on the question of whether ghosts and spirits exist or not. This causes disorder in the world. (Ibid., 31.2)

Mozi makes clear why he believes that denying the existence of ghosts and spirits is so destructive:

> The people give themselves to debauchery, cruelty, robbery, disorder, theft and plunder, using weapons, poisons, water and fire to stop innocent travelers on the roads and foot paths, seizing their carts, horses, clothes and furs to further their own benefit. And these things have increased since they began, causing disorder in the world. Why have things come to this? It is because everyone is doubtful and suspicious on the question of whether ghosts and spirits exist or not, and do not clearly understand that ghosts and spirits are able to reward the worthy and punish the wicked. Now if all the people of the world could be brought to believe that ghosts and spirits are able to reward the worthy and punish the wicked, then how could the world be in disorder? (Ibid., 31.1)

Mozi recommends that those who wish to determine the truth of the claim that ghosts and spirits exist should follow his three criteria. First, he challenges sceptics to go and examine those who claim to have witnessed ghosts. He utilizes as evidence the "ears and eyes" of commoners and villagers saying, "from ancient times to the present, since people came into existence, there have been those who have seen ghosts or spirits, or have heard ghost or spirit sounds" (Ibid., 31.3). He goes on to cite notable and respected figures who also report having witnessed ghosts and spirits (Ibid., 31.4, 31.5, 31.6, 31.7, 31.8). This appeal to the testimony of those making empirical observations emphasizes the large number of persons who have had the experiences. It does not focus on any expert or well-placed observer.

Next, Mozi turns to the historical records supporting the received belief that ghosts and spirits exist:

> In ancient times, the sage kings certainly took ghosts and spirits to exist and their service to ghosts and spirits was profound. But they also feared that their descendants of later generations would not be able to know this so they wrote it [the knowledge] on bamboo and silk to transmit it and hand it down to them. But they all feared that [these writings] would decay and be worm-eaten, and be lost and destroyed, so their descendants of later generations would have no record. Therefore, they carved it on [ceremonial] basins, plates and engraved it on metal and stone to be especially sure. (Ibid., 31.11)

Mozi does not seem to notice that such records are based ultimately on the testimony of the ancients and thus they are subject to the same criticisms that are applicable to reports made by those living in his own day.

Finally Mozi offers a pragmatic defence of the importance of continuing to accept as true that ghosts and spirits exist:

> It is right to think that ghosts and spirits are able to reward the worthy and punish the wicked. If this [i.e., acting on this belief] could be established at the outset in the state and among the ten thousand people, it would truly be the way to bring order to the state and benefit to the ten thousand people. If the officials of government departments are not pure and incorruptible, and if the proper separation between men and women is not maintained, ghosts and spirits see it. If people are depraved

and cruel, giving themselves to plunder, disorder, robbery and theft, and use weapons, poisons, water and fire to waylay innocent travelers on the roads, … there are ghosts and spirits who see them …Therefore, the awareness of ghosts and spirits is such that it is not possible to do something in the darkest places … without the awareness of ghosts and spirits certainly knowing it. The punishments of the ghosts and spirits are such that it is not possible [to avoid them]. (31.16, 17)

Mozi's point is that we *ought to act as though it is true* that there are ghosts and spirits who pay attention to the actions of noble and commoner alike because, in continuing to affirm this belief as true, we are much more likely to ensure that all persons will do what is right for fear that the ghosts and spirits might find out about any of their wrongdoing and punish them. However, saying that we ought to act as though something is true is not really an epistemological criterion for truth at all. It may represent a duty we have to preserve social order, but it is certainly possible that order can and has been preserved by persons acting on beliefs later shown to be false.

Mozi's interest in how we know something was further developed in the years following his life by his students and their students. In *Records of the Grand Historian* Sima Tan (d. 110 BCE) identified a group of thinkers as *Mingjia* (School of Names). These thinkers have been variously classified as debaters, rhetoricians, dialecticians, logicians and skeptics. Sima Tan chose the term *mingjia* because one of the main foci of this group was on the connection between names and their corresponding realities. In Western philosophical terminology, this means they were concerned with questions of reference. Actually, though, in the Warring States Period (*c.*475–221 BCE) the name used more generally for thinkers occupied with such questions of language and reality, as well as with other questions of knowledge, was *bianshi* 辯士 (often rendered as "disputers" or "rhetoricians"). The *bianshi* philosophers were well known for their skill in argumentation, making finely grained distinctions between concepts and exposing the flaws in received beliefs and traditional knowledge claims. Accordingly, Karyn Lai seems on target when she writes,

Their [the *bianshi*] ideals and philosophical methods fill an often-perceived gap in Chinese intellectual thought. The debates of the pre-Qin period (before 221 BCE) are represented predominantly—some would say *overrepresented*—by Confucian and Daoist views on ethics and government, while the arguments and analyses of the *bianshi* are neglected. (Lai 2008: 113)

The approaches and arguments of the *bianshi* can be associated with the work of the so-called Later Mohist philosophers. This group of thinkers is known to us largely through the final six chapters of the *Mozi* text (Chapters 40–5) that form an entirely different unit than the earlier sections of the work but are nonetheless considered to stand within the general epistemological tradition first expressed by Mozi himself.[2]

The Chinese term *bian* (辯) is sometimes used for "argument" in the sense of "competition" (i.e., to win one's case), but it can also mean to debate in order to clarify and articulate what is known. This second use predominates in the Later Mohist chapters. The *bianshi*, whose ideas show up in the last chapters of the *Mozi*, employed some important epistemological distinctions such as these:

- what can be affirmed as possible (*ke*) and what cannot be possible (*buke*),
- how items were the same (*tong*) or different (*yi*),
- this thing/truthfully (*shi*) or not this thing/falsely (*fei*), is so (exists) (*ran*) or not so (does not exist) (*buran*).

All this explains the confusing fact that the *bianshi* known for their activity in disputation typically characterized their own work with the homophone, *bian* (辨), which means "discriminate" (i.e., discriminate between concepts, positions, etc.).[3]

In general, the task of identifying the Later Mohist apparatus for approaching problems of epistemology is complicated by the fact that the target chapters in the *Mozi* text are badly mutilated in the surviving manuscripts and moreover they employ a number of unique Chinese characters that are not used elsewhere.[4] The material is set out like this: Chapter 40 states a Canon or definition; Chapter 42 offers the Explanation of that Canon. In his translation of *Mozi*, Johnston (2010) arranges these pairs for Chapters 40 and 42 by calling them "Canons & Explanations A," and he organizes them into 99 pairs. Chapters 41 and 43 are set up in the same manner as "Canons and Explanations B" with 81 pairs. In the examples below, I follow his convention.

Some of these pairs are concerned with the discrimination (*bian*) between moral concepts (e.g., humaneness [Chapter 40, 7], appropriateness [Chapter 40, 8], propriety [Chapter 40, 9], filiality [Chapter 40, 13] and courage [Chapter 40, 20]); others are devoted to the definition of scientific operators (Chapter 40, 21, force), time/duration (Chapter 40, 40), space/extension (Chapter 40, 41), limit (Chapter 40, 42), and movement (Chapter 40, 50).

Here are a few examples of Later Mohist understandings of epistemological concepts:

C: A cause is that which obtains before something comes about.
E: Cause: Where there is a minor cause, the result is not necessarily so; when no minor cause is present, something is necessarily not so ... When there is a major cause, the result is necessarily so. (40 & 42, A1)

C: Consciousness is a capacity, an awareness.
E: Consciousness: With regard to the capacity of consciousness, it refers to conscious certainty. It is like seeing something. (40 & 42, A3)

C: Deliberating is seeking.
E: Deliberating: With regard to deliberating, it is seeking knowledge, but not necessarily finding it. It is like peering. (40 & 42, A4)

C: Knowing is by hearing, explaining, personally experiencing. It is about names, object, correlation and actions.
E: Knowing: Receiving knowledge by second hand is hearing, removing obstructions to knowing is explaining, knowing by observing something oneself is personally experiencing. What something is called by is its name. What is named is the object. The pairing of name and object is the correlation. (40 & 42, A81)

C: Assent does not have just one use.
E: Assent: When both agree, both reject, knowing directly prior to experience, both assert the same claim, both allow the same possibility. These are the five uses of "assent." (40 & 42, A94)

C: Difference: Different categorical classes are not comparable.
E: Difference: Of wood and night, which is longer? Of knowledge and grain, which is the greater? Of the four things (rank, family, good

conduct and price), which is the most valuable? Of the tailed deer and the crane, which is the higher? Of the cicada and the zither, which is the more mournful? (41 & 43, B6)

In these few examples, some significant insights into *bianshi* epistemology as expressed in the Later Mohist texts are evident. A1's canon defining cause seems much too broad, but the explanation is an improvement. In the explanation a distinction seems to be made among a contributing cause (a minor cause that does not necessarily lead to a result, but does contribute to its occurrence), a sufficient cause (a minor cause in the absence of which the result will not occur, but by itself, it will not bring about the result) and a major cause as something that necessarily produces the result or is required in order for the result to occur.[5] The *Mozi* does not offer any epistemological guidelines for determining cause such as those given by John Stuart Mill.

Mill's Methods for Determining Cause

John Stuart Mill (1806–73) was an English philosopher who wrote on a wide range of topics from language and science to political philosophy. In his *Science of Logic* he meant to expand our epistemological capacities in science by identifying five reliable means for the determination of the cause of an event or occurrence. These are as follows:

The Method of Agreement. Suppose a family went out together for a buffet dinner. Upon returning home, all of them started feeling sick and experienced stomach aches. How do you determine the cause of the illness? Mill's rule of agreement says that if in all cases where an effect occurs, there is a single prior factor that the cases have in common, that factor is the cause of the effect. So, make a list of what everyone ate and determine what was eaten by everyone who is ill (i.e., that in which all the cases agree is the cause).

The Method of Difference. Suppose you are the only one in your family who did not fall ill. The only difference between you and the others is that you did not eat oysters. Oysters are probably the cause of the others' illnesses (i.e., the case *not* having the result differs also in not having the cause).

The Joint Method of Agreement and Difference. By identifying the one item that you did not eat (difference) and then determining that all those who are sick did eat the oysters (agreement), the cause is confirmed.

The Method of Concomitant Variation. If across a range of situations that lead to a certain effect, we find a certain property of the effect varying in a factor common to those situations, we can infer that that factor is the cause. If you felt somewhat sick having eaten one oyster, whereas your sister felt not well at all having eaten a few, and your father became critically ill having eaten ten, since the variation in the number of oysters corresponds to variation in the severity of the illness, it would be rational to infer that the illnesses were caused by the oysters.

The Method of Residues. If we have a range of factors as possible causes for an effect and the contributing role of all factors except one can be identified, the remaining factor is the cause of the effect not yet explained. When an airplane crashes, investigators look at the crash site to determine the cause of the crash. Part of the damage to the aircraft could be attributed to its impact with the ground. Another part can be attributed to the wind shear the plane experienced as it fell from the sky. However, some of the damage cannot be accounted for by either of these factors. Investigators examine the remaining results not yet explained and hypothesize that explosives are the cause of them.

A3's canon on consciousness is interesting not because it specifies self-consciousness as this distinguishes persons from other conscious entities, but because it defines consciousness as possessing awareness, being able to experience phenomena, knowing pain or pleasure and the like. Consciousness is regarded as something direct and immediate. That is, if we close our eyes, then open them, the perceptions of our sight are directly impressed on us, it is not in our control not to see when we open our eyes, neither do we need any other instrumentation or mediation by which to see. Of course, we may be mistaken about *what* we see (e.g., is it a sheet in the wind or a ghost), but *that* we see is not something about which we can be mistaken or which we can choose not to do. This is the difference between consciousness as awareness and deliberating and knowing in Later Mohist epistemology.

A4 and A81 deal with deliberation and knowledge. The Later Mohists considered deliberation to be a process, and we know it was one they practiced well. Deliberation is considering options, investigating, exploring and debating. This is the enterprise in which philosophy and science are typically engaged. Often a conclusion is not reached, it is only sought after. In such cases, the explanation compares deliberating to indirect seeing. That is, we are not quite sure what the conclusion is, just as we may be unsure of what we see. We must investigate further, check it out, improve our point of view, rule out possibilities and the like. Is it a sheet blowing in the wind that we see, or is it a ghost? We must inspect, go and look, eliminate competing options.

When deliberation moves to knowledge, Later Mohists thought it followed one of several paths. It came by indirect experience through the testimony of others who knew by their direct experience (e.g., hearing), through explanations that removed the obstacles and uncertainties to knowing what is the case (e.g., by argument) or by direct personal acquaintance with an event, object or person. The most significant factor added to Mozi's original three criteria for justification in the Canon on knowing is *shuo* (i.e., arguing, explaining).

Later Mohists realized that part of the epistemological process required distinguishing categories and classes as B6 above indicates. If these are confused, one may be misled. In classical Western philosophy, Aristotle considered the problem of reasoning about classes or categories in his development of categorical logic in the syllogism in his *Prior Analytics*. In the contemporary period of Western philosophy, Gilbert Ryle demonstrated just how important it is to distinguish categories in his book *The Concept of Mind*.

In B6, Later Mohists are stressing that if we do not recognize that we are using the term *longer* differently when applying it to a piece of wood (i.e., how many centimeters is it compared to another) and to the night (i.e., the night seems interminable because I cannot sleep), we will be misled. This is a point in the logic of language, but it has a great deal to do with epistemology as well. What counts as *longer* with respect to the pieces of wood, what evidence I require to resolve the question about which is longer, is different than the evidence I expect to receive and credit with respect to the length of the night and knowing whether it was true that it was a *long* night.[6] The *bianshi* philosophers of ancient China certainly recognized the importance to epistemology of making such logical distinctions.

Some *bianshi* affiliated with the Jixia Academy between 340 and 284 BCE and became so adept at challenging various worldviews and arguments that they were often criticized, probably because of their skill at exposing weak arguments and superstitious beliefs. The great Confucian philosopher, Xunzi, wrote the following about them:

> They investigate things with extreme acuteness but without any beneficient intent, and they debate matters but provide no useful results. They meddle in many affairs but have few accomplishments, and they cannot be the binding thread of good order. Nevertheless, they can cite evidence for maintaining their views, and they achieve a reasoned order in their explanations, so that it is enough to deceive and confuse the foolish masses. Just such men are Hui Shi and Deng Xi. (*Xunzi*, Chapter 6, Hutton 2014: 41)

The ideas of two of the *bianshi* are known to us through sources about which we have some degree of confidence. They are Hui Shi (307?–210? BCE) and Gongsun Longzi (b. 380? BCE).[7] Most of what we know about Hui Shi, who was likely affiliated with the Jixia Academy, is found in the Daoist text known as the *Zhuangzi*. Hui Shi shows up in nine chapters of the *Zhuangzi*, and he is typically presented as a friendly but misguided interlocutor of Master Zhuang. One passage says that Zhuangzi was accompanying a funeral when he passed by the grave of Hui Shi. Turning to his attendants, he said,

> "There was once a plasterer who, if he got a speck of mud on the tip of his nose no thicker than a fly's wing, would get his friend Carpenter Shi to slice it off for him. Carpenter Shi, whirling his hatchet with a noise like the wind, would accept the assignment and proceed to slice, removing every bit of mud without injury to the nose, while the plasterer just stood there completely unperturbed." Lord Yuan of Song, hearing of this feat, summoned Carpenter Shi and said, "Could you try performing it for me?" But Carpenter Shi replied, "It's true that I was once able to slice like that but the material I worked on has been dead these many years." [Thus, Zhuangzi said] "Since you died, Master Hui, I have had no material to work on. There's no one I can talk to any more."
>
> (*Zhuangzi*, Watson 1968: 269)

In the final chapter (Chapter 33) of the *Zhuangzi* an overview of various schools of Chinese philosophical thought is given. The text says that Hui Shi "wished to make a name for himself by winning arguments; that is why he came to be so unpopular" (ibid., 376). *Zhuangzi* Chapter 33 offers a list of ten paradoxes attributed to Hui Shi and another 21 assigned to the general group of the *bianshi*. These are Hui Shi's ten paradoxes:

> The largest thing has nothing beyond it; it is called the One of largeness. The smallest thing has nothing within it; it is called the One of smallness.
>
> That which has no thickness cannot be piled up; yet it is a thousand li in dimension.
>
> Heaven is as low as earth; mountains and marshes are on the same level.
>
> The sun at noon is the sun setting. The thing born is the thing dying.
>
> Great similarities are different from little similarities; these are called the little similarities and differences. The ten thousand things are all similar and are all different; these are called the great similarities and differences.
>
> The southern region has no limit and yet has a limit.
>
> I set off for Yueh today and came there yesterday.
>
> Linked rings can be separated.
>
> I know the center of the world: it is north of Yen and south of Yueh.
>
> Let love embrace the ten thousand things; Heaven and earth are a single body. (*Zhuangzi* 33, Watson 1968: 374–5)

While these remarks are often interpreted as statements of skepticism, the *Zhuangzi* offers a striking response. It says, "With sayings such as these, Hu Shi tried to introduce a more magnanimous view of the world and to enlighten the rhetoricians" (ibid., 375). Hui Shi's propositions draw attention to the relativity of measurements and the names used for them and also serve as reminders of the limits of language epistemologically.

The Lao-Zhuang Tradition on Knowing the Truth (c.350–139 BCE)

There is much that seems to suggest anti-intellectualism in the *Daodejing*. For example, the text says that sages make sure the people are without knowledge (*DDJ*, 3), those who pursue the *Dao* are cautioned to abandon learning (20), states are difficult to rule because the people "know too much" (65), and the knowledgeable are distinguished from the enlightened Daoist adept (33). However, the *Daodejing* is not actually saying in a literal sense that being ignorant or unlearned is better than having knowledge of the world in which one lives. The text is making a point by exaggeration. It is saying that persons may come to rely so much on human knowledge and its reduction of truth to what reason and sense experience allow as evidence that they may miss the kind of knowledge that is most important.

Daoists surely were not suggesting that the normal pursuit of knowledge and learning were to be set aside and that all people should return to some primitive stage of simple ignorance, not knowing facts of science, technology or history. Interpreted in their context, the statements that seem to suggest anti-intellectualism are part of the Lao-Zhuang insistence that the distinctions and concepts by which reason works are of human design and may *mislead* people about the nature of reality or tangle them in problems they create for themselves. Karen Carr and P. J. Ivanhoe argue that the Lao-Zhuang tradition takes a position they call "antirationalism." In antirationlism, the employment of the powers of reason is seen as useful but not ultimate. Excessive use of reason, for the antirationalist, can "interfere with proper perception, thought, evaluation, and action" (Carr and Ivanhoe 2000: 46). The *Daodejing* says,

> In the pursuit of human learning, one does more each day;
> In the pursuit of the Dao, one does less each day;
> In fact, one does less and less until one acts effortlessly
>   (*wu-wei* 無為). (48)

Zhuangzi, too, sounds a similar opposition to critical inquiry and application of reason and logic as the sole means to truth. Throughout the text, Daoist sage heroes, whether Laozi (a.k.a. Lao Dan) or Zhuangzi, often engage with those committed to disputation and argument (*bian*) showing the flaws in such an approach as the method for achieving oneness with *Dao* and its power (*de*) to live in spontaneous, effortless efficacy (*wu-wei*). In the *Zhuangzi*, the *zhenren* (真人, perfected person) does not love life and hate death, he forgets these distinctions entirely, and delights in the transformations of life even if this sounds contrary to reason (*Zhuangzi* Chapter 6, Watson 1968: 81).

In *Zhuangzi*, there are numerous and sustained attacks upon reliance on reason and discursive argument as methods for arriving at fundamental truth. The people are cautioned not to wear out their brains with distinctions (ibid., 2; 41). The text uses many examples to show that what a person thinks he knows is really relative to context and not absolute (ibid., 2 45; 17; 179–83).

> Let me ask you some questions. If a man sleeps in a damp place, his back aches and he ends up half paralyzed, but is this true of loach? If he lives in a tree, he is terrified and shakes with fright, but is this true of a monkey? Of these three creatures, then, which one *knows* the proper place to live? ... Men claim that Mao Qiang and Li Ji were beautiful, but if fish saw them they would dive to the bottom of the stream, if birds saw them they would fly away, and if deer saw them they would break into a run. Of these four, which *knows* how to fix the standard of beauty for the world? The way I see it, the rules of humaneness (*ren* 仁) and appropriate conduct (*yi* 義) and the paths of right and wrong are all hopelessly snarled and jumbled. How could I know anything by using such discriminations? (Ibid., 2; 46, my change)

This appreciation for the various uses of "to know" may have been one of the most basic agreements between Zhuangzi and Hui Shi. But Zhuangzi warns that skillfulness in argument culminating in winning a point is not equivalent to arriving at truth, a point seemingly directed at Hui Shi and the *bianshi* dialecticians in general.

> Suppose you and I argue (*bian*). If you have beaten me instead of my beating you, then are you necessarily right and am I necessarily wrong? If I have beaten you instead of your beating me, then am I necessarily right and are you necessarily wrong? Is one of us right and the other wrong? Are both of us right or are both of us wrong? If you and I don't know the answer, then other people are bound to be even more in the dark. Whom shall we get to decide what is right? Shall we get someone who agrees with you to decide? But if he already agrees with you, how can he decide fairly? Shall we get someone who agrees with me? But if he already agrees with me, how can he decide? Shall we get someone who disagrees with both of us? But if he already disagrees

with both of us, how can he decide? Shall we get someone who agrees
with both of us? But if he already agrees with both of us, how can he
decide? Obviously, then, neither you nor I nor anyone else can decide
for each other. Shall we wait for still another person? (Ibid., 2; 48)

In this passage, Zhuangzi is calling our attention to the fact that there
is not a "view from nowhere" that is totally impartial. Noting this
epistemological move by Zhuangzi also explains why rhetoricians and
logicians are compared in the *Zhuangzi* to nimble monkeys and rat-
catching dogs (ibid., 12; 132). They are good at rational gymnastics,
but poor at realization of truth. Consider this comment in *Zhuangzi*
Chapter 13:

> Those who spoke of the Great Way in ancient times could count
> to five in sequence and pick out "forms and names," or count to
> nine and discuss "rewards and punishments." But to jump right in
> and talk about "forms and names" is to lack an understanding of the
> source; to jump right in and talk about "rewards and punishments"
> is to lack an understanding of the beginning. Those who stand the
> Way on its head before describing it, who turn it backwards before
> expounding it, may be brought to order by others, but how could
> they be capable of bringing others to order? Those who jump right
> in and talk about "forms and names," "rewards and punishments,"
> have an understanding of the tools for bringing order, but no
> understanding of the way to bring order. They may work for the
> world, but they are not worthy to make the world work for them.
> They are rhetoricians (*bianshi* 辯士), scholars cramped in one
> corner of knowledge. (13; 147–8)

Clearly, the references to "forms and names" in this teaching from the
Zhuangzi should be taken as a criticism of the *bianshi*, the disputers and
rhetoricians who work in the style and methods of the Later Mohists.

So, for all the affection and friendship between them, Zhuangzi
did not approve of the *bianshi* Hui Shi's work as a philosopher. While
he thought Hui Shi's argumentative skills were close to perfection,
he believed that Hui was far away from possessing the knowledge
necessary to be a perfected person (*zhenren*). Hui was always trying
to make truth apparent but Zhuangzi held that truth could not be
made clear in language. The attempt to arrive at truth through the

means of language had led Hui "into the foolishness of the minute quibbling over the meaning of 'hard' and 'white'" (ibid., 2; 42). This is, of course, a reference to the *bianshi* reputation of making logical distinctions about categories and attributes and using them to impress and confound their opponents.

One recorded disputation between Hui Shi and Zhuangzi demonstrates well how Hui tried to employ the techniques of the *bianshi*, whereas Zhuangzi was about making a philosophical claim that was not really approachable by such means.

> Huizi said to Zhuangzi, "Can a man really be without feelings?"
> Zhuangzi: "Yes."
> Huizi: "But a man who has no feelings—how can you call him a man?"
> Zhuangzi: "The Way gave him a face; Heaven gave him a form—why can't you call him a man?"
> Huizi: "But if you have already called him a man, how can he be without feelings?"
> Zhuangzi: "That is not what I mean by feelings. When I talk about having no feelings, I mean that a man does not allow likes or dislikes to get in and do him harm. He just lets things be the way they are and does not try to help life along."
> Huizi: "If he does not try to help life along, then how can he keep himself alive?"
> Zhuangzi: "The Way gave him a face; Heaven gave him a form. He does not let likes or dislikes get in and do him harm. You, now—you treat your spirit like an outsider. You wear out your energy, leaning on a tree and moaning, slumping at your desk and dozing—Heaven picked out a body for you and you use it to gibber about "hard" and "white." (Ibid., 5; 75–6)

In another debate between Zhuangzi and Huizi, Zhuangzi challenges him by saying that there are five schools of thought: the Confucians, Mohists, Yangists, Ping (i.e., Gongsun Long) and himself (Hui Shi). Zhuangzi asks which is right. Hui Shi replies that the others engage him in debate but none has ever proven his views wrong. But Zhuangzi's reply is that such mixed-up debate did little but create grudges and ill will between persons (ibid., 24; 267–8). When challenged by Hui Shi that his words were "useless," Zhuangzi replied in this way:

"A man has to understand the useless before you can talk to him about the useful. The earth is certainly vast and broad, though a man uses no more of it than the area he puts his feet on. If, however, you were to dig away all the earth from around his feet until you reached the Yellow Springs, then would the man still be able to make use of it?" "No, it would be useless," said Huizi. "It is obvious, then," said Zhuangzi, "that the useless has its use." (Ibid., 26; 299)

In the Lao-Zhuang philosophical tradition, the function of these exchanges between Zhuangzi and Huizi is to display the limitations of human reason when trying to approach the Way (*Dao*) itself. Accordingly, while there is always an air of some affection toward Hui Shi in the *Zhuangzi*, its final conclusion leaves little doubt about the tradition's evaluation of his work, and indeed of the debaters/rhetoricians (*bianshi*) in general.

Weak in inner virtue, strong in his concern for external things, he walked a road that was crooked indeed! If we examine Hui Shi's accomplishments from the point of view of the Way of heaven and earth, they seem like the exertions of a mosquito or a gnat of what use are they to other things? True, he still deserves to be regarded as the founder of one school, though I say, if he had only shown greater respect for the Way (*Dao*), he would have come nearer being right. Hui Shi, however, could not seem to find any tranquility for himself in such an approach. Instead he went on tirelessly separating and analyzing the ten thousand things, and in the end was known only for his skill in exposition. What a pity that Hui Shi abused and dissipated his talents without ever really achieving anything! Chasing after the ten thousand things, never turning back, he was like one who tries to shout an echo into silence or to prove that form can outrun shadow. How sad! (Ibid., 33; 377)

Whereas the friendship and disputation between Zhuangzi and Huizi form the background for a rejection of the use of argument and debate in some passages in the *Zhuangzi*, a series of narratives in Chapters 12, 13 and 14 are directed toward the same end by being very critical of Confucius. They usually portray Laozi (Lao Dan) as his teacher and master but likewise demonstrate a criticism of reliance on reason and human knowledge in order to be one with the *Dao*.[8] The following is one such dialogue with Confucius (called by his personal name, Qiu), in which Laozi is made to offer his view of the rhetoricians.

Confucius said to Lao Dan, "Here's a man who works to master the Way as though he were trying to talk down an opponent making the unacceptable acceptable, the not so, so. As the rhetoricians (*bianshi*) say, he can separate 'hard' from 'white' as clearly as though they were dangling from the eaves there. Can a man like this be called a sage?"

Lao Dan said, "A man like this is a drudging slave, a craftsman bound to his calling, wearing out his body, grieving his mind. Because the dog can catch rats, he ends up on a leash. Because of his nimbleness, the monkey is dragged down from the mountain forest. Qiu, I'm going to tell you something—something you could never hear for yourself and something you would never know how to speak of … Forget things, forget Heaven, and be called a forgetter of self. The man who has forgotten self may be said to have entered Heaven." (Ibid., 12; 132)

In the *Zhuangzi*, the power to master life is not an achievement of reason. However, this is not the same as saying that the Lao-Zhuang teachers had no use for reason, sense evidence and logical thought. Truth comes from oneness with the *Dao*, that much seems certain. When realized, one flows in life spontaneously and effortlessly, without thought.

In the Yellow Emperor-Laozi logia of *Zhuangzi*, the Yellow Emperor is held up as a possessor of truth that is portrayed as a "Dark Pearl." When he lost this "Dark Pearl" he sent Knowledge to look for it, then the scientist Li Chu and finally Wrangling Debate but none could find it. Not until he employed Shapeless was it found (ibid., 12; 129). In contrast to others, the "perfected person" (*zhenren*) as understood in the Lao-Zhuang tradition is in possession of the wordless teachings that are oneness with *Dao*. In the Lao-Zhuang tradition, whenever "perfected persons" "get the dao," they become like the figurative numinal powers of the universe: the Big Dipper (*beidou*), the Yellow Emperor (*Huangdi*) and the Queen Mother of the West (*Xiwangmu*) (ibid., 6; 82). They can enter Kunlun (i.e., the Daoist paradise), but none of this transformation comes by the employment of argument and logical analysis (ibid., 6; 87).

Mencius and Analogical Argumentation

The *Records of the Grand Historian* (*Shiji*) provides information about the biography of Mencius (a.k.a. Meng Ke or Master Meng-Mengzi, *c.*372–289 BCE), whose influence was so significant that he became recognized as the most authoritative interpreter of Confucius's teachings in all of Chinese history and was known as "Mengzi the Second Sage" (*Yasheng Mengzi*). Mencius was a defender of Confucianism during the period of the One Hundred Schools (*baijia*) and was quite likely one of the major teachers at the Jixia Academy. Participation in this community created a rich environment of debate. Mencius wrote:

> I am not fond of disputation, … [but] I have no alternative … If the way of Yang [Yangzi, 440?–360? BCE] and Mo [Mozi] does not subside and the way of Confucius does not shine forth, the people will be deceived by heresies and the path of morality will be blocked. … Therefore, I am apprehensive. I wish to safeguard the way of the former sages against the onslaught of Yang and Mo and to banish excessive views. Then advocates of heresies will not be able to arise.
>
> (*Mengzi* 3B9, Lau 2003: 71, 73)

Although it is often said that classical Chinese philosophers did not place a premium on argumentation, this is certainly false as we have seen in our discussion of the *bianshi* and their methods. While finely grained skills of distinctions and technicalities of argument characterized the *bianshi* and also represented the points at which they were most criticized, other classical Chinese philosophers pursued arguments designed to persuade others to adopt certain points of view and change their way of living. Mencius's epistemology may be reconstructed from his criticisms of Mozi and Yangzi who engaged in this form of persuasion.

Mencius made use of analogical reasoning in his criticism of Mozi and Yangzi. This method included both the use of one thing to throw light on another and the use of one proposition known to be true to throw light on another of similar form. Two advantages of this form of argument in the classical period have been identified. One is that an analogy is often as valuable epistemologically when it breaks down as when it works. The second is that analogy is often the only tool available to reason to explore a subject that is obscure or elusive of direct experience.

Mencius and his interlocutors carry on their debates in the *Mengzi* largely through the method of analogy. One example of Mencius's method is his famous exchange with Gaozi recorded in the *Mengzi* 6A1, 2. In 6A1, the exchange reads as follows:

> Gaozi said, "Human nature is like the willow. Appropriate behavior (*yi* 義) is like the cups and bowls. To make benevolence (*ren* 仁) and appropriate behavior out of human nature is like making cups and bowls out of the willow."

Gaozi is saying that it is not the nature of a willow to make cups and bowls. By analogy, then, making humans moral is like the process of making cups and bowls from a willow and cannot be accomplished by relying on human nature. Mencius makes the following reply.

> "Can you," said Mencius, "make cups and bowls by leaving the willow untouched? Or must you mutilate the willow before you can make it into cups and bowls? If you have to mutilate the willow to make it into cups and bowls, then, on your analogy you must also mutilate a man to make him moral. Surely these words of yours would cause all men to consider benevolence (*ren*) and appropriate behavior (*yi*) to be calamities.

Mencius goes straight to the heart of the disanalogy in Gaozi's strategy as he sees it. He wants Gaozi to conclude with him that the downfall of morality would result if there could be no appeal to the inner nature of a person, if each person had to be radically changed and reshaped (mutilated) in order to act morally. The educational and policy implications of such a belief, although unstated, are, in Mencius's view, immediately obvious as calamities.

When evaluating analogical arguments in order to clarify or extend knowledge, some principles are clear. One must first think of the similarities that exist between the two items being compared. How many similarities are there and what is the relevance of the similarities? Next, one must consider what are the differences or dissimilarities between the two things being compared. How many dissimilarities are there and what is the relevance of the dissimilarities? It is possible that a single, highly relevant dissimilarity may render an analogy epistemologically valueless or make it what logicians call a "false analogy."

In his reply to Gaozi, Mencius is pointing to the dissimilarity between how morality is to be fashioned in a person and the method by which cups and bowls must be made from a willow. Mencius insists that if this analogy is taken seriously, then just as the wood must be mutilated to make the cup, so also must human nature be mutilated for one to become moral. The methods which would be used to do such a thing would bring calamity on the citizens.

Gao offers another analogy in 6A2 which is meant to criticize Mencius's view that human nature has an inborn tendency to seek goodness:

> Gaozi said, "Human nature is like whirling water. Give it an outlet in the east and it will flow east; give it an outlet in the west and it will flow west. Human nature does not show any preference for either good or bad just as water does not show any preference for either east or west."
>
> "It certainly is the case," said Mencius, "that water does not show any preference for either east or west, but does it show the same indifference to high and low? Human nature is good just as water seeks low ground. There is no man who lacks the tendency to seek the good; there is no water that does not flow downwards. Now by striking water and causing it to splash up, you may make it go over your forehead, and, by damming it up you may force it up a hill—but are such movements according to the nature of water? It is the force applied which causes water to act in this manner. When men are made to do what is not good, their nature is dealt with in this way."

Mencius's point is that in comparing the natural flow of water to morality, Gaozi has overlooked a strategic similarity between the two that actually proves the opposite of his claim. Just as water naturally flows downhill, so does human nature naturally move toward the good.

Xunzi: Dispelling Obsessions

> The thing that all men should fear is that they will become obsessed by
> a small corner of truth and fail to comprehend its overall principles. If
> they can correct this fault, they may return to correct standards, but if
> they continue to hesitate and be of two minds, then they will fall into
> delusion (*Xunzi*, "Dispelling Obsessions," Watson 1963: Chapter 21)

The Confucian master simply called Xunzi (Master Xun) was named
Xun Kuang (a.k.a. Xun Qing, *c.*310–220 BCE), and he seems to have
come from a different lineage of descent from Confucius than did
Mencius. Xunzi was interested in obtaining a clear enlightened
state of mind and arguably he can be seen as the greatest theorist of
epistemology in classical Chinese philosophy. The last great master
thinker in the Jixia Academy, Xunzi developed his epistemological
thinking as an intellectual. He emphasized humans' cognitive ability
to discern right and wrong through "disputation" (*bian*) and his views
on debate and argument are largely consistent with those of the Later
Mohist debaters known as the *bianshi* (Fraser 2012).

As for the sources of knowledge, Xunzi made no appeal to anything
transcendent as Mozi had done with his use of ghosts and spirits or
to an alternative state of awareness as in Lao-Zhuang thought. Instead,
he emphasized the importance of the senses in contributing to our
knowledge and in resolving disputes. Speaking of the use of general
terms, he writes,

> And how does one go about distinguishing between things that are the
> same and those that are different? One relies upon the senses. Things
> which are of the same species and form will be apprehended by the
> senses as being all the same thing. Therefore, after comparing such
> things with others of a similar nature, one may settle upon a common
> designation. In this way one arrives at a common name for all the
> things of one class, which everyone agrees to use when the occasion
> demands. (*Xunzi*, Watson 1963: Chapter 17)

In addition to the senses, Xunzi also recognized the (*xin*) as a source
of knowledge. Xunzi follows the pattern of all Chinese thought in
the classical period by associating the heart and mind (*xin*) together.
For him, the mind is never reducible to calculating reason devoid of

feeling. In fact, as a source of knowledge, rationality and feeling work simultaneously and complementarily in order to yield truth. Feeling and emotion are not enemies of rationality so long as they are not allowed to run amok or overwhelm what reason understands. Emotions must not prevent the heart-mind from considering all aspects of a knowledge claim. Likewise, discursive rationality will not be able to resolve epistemological quandaries if it excludes feeling and emotion. Xunzi's point is that the human heart-mind by which knowledge is gained is not to be thought of on the analogy of a computer or calculator. Just as the senses provide perceptual content, the heart-mind processes this information into concepts and yields understanding whenever it operates properly.

Xunzi held that to judge between competing views one has to keep one's heart-mind in a clear state (*da qingming*). This state is attained by making one's mind empty of preconditions and presuppositions and quietening emotion and passion. This is Xunzi's way of insisting that knowledge comes when we examine a problem by setting aside our assumptions or presuppositions. Some Western philosophers call this *bracketing* our presuppositions in order to allow experience/evidence to be described without prejudging it.[9] Xunzi has many accounts of persons who allow their emotions to cloud their reason and the following is only one of them:

> There was a man named Juan Shuliang who lived south of Xiashou. He was stupid and easily frightened. One night he was walking in the moonlight when, glancing down and seeing his shadow, he took it for a crouching ghost. Looking up, he caught sight of his own hair and took it for a devil standing over him. He whirled around and started running, and when he reached his home he fell unconscious and died. Is this not sad? Always when people see ghosts, it is at times when they are aroused and excited, and they make their judgments in moments when their faculties are confused and blinded. At such times they affirm that what exists does not exist, or that what does not exist exists, and then they consider the matter settled. A man, having contracted a chill from the dampness, proceeds to beat a drum and make an offering of a pig in hopes of effecting a cure. He wears out the drum and loses a pig in the process, that is certain, but no blessing of recovery follows as a result. (Ibid., Chapter 21)

According to Xunzi, in the process of knowing and arguing for one's knowledge, one must, negatively, discard all obscuring factors, presuppositions and overwrought emotions and, positively, be alert to other, easily neglected aspects of an issue in dispute. The function of the heart-mind in epistemology is not to perceive, that is the role of the senses. The heart-mind is the organ of understanding. "How does a man understand the Way? Through the heart-mind. And how can the mind understand it? Because it is empty, unified, and still." (Ibid., Chapter 21) Xunzi says,

> The heart-mind may be compared to a pan of water. If you place the pan on a level and do not jar it, then the heavy sediment will settle to the bottom and the clear water will collect on top, so that you can see your beard and eyebrows in it and examine the lines of your face. But if a faint wind passes over the top of the water, the heavy sediment will be stirred up from the bottom and the clear water will become mingled with it, so that you can no longer get a clear reflection of even a large object. The heart-mind is the same way. If you guide it with reason, nourish it with clarity, and do not allow external objects to unbalance it, then it will be capable of determining right and wrong and of resolving doubts. But if you allow petty external factors to pull it about, so that its proper form becomes altered and its inner balance is upset, then it will not be capable of making even gross distinctions.
>
> (Ibid.)

In Books 6 and 21 Xunzi offers lists of his opponents and diagnoses of their errors. In all these cases he charges that his opponents have placed too much emphasis on some part of the understanding process and thus created misunderstanding.

> Mozi was obsessed by utilitarian considerations and did not understand the beauties of form ... Huizi was obsessed by words and did not understand the truth that lies behind them. Zhuangzi was obsessed by thoughts of Heaven and did not understand the importance of man. He who thinks only of utilitarian concerns will take the Way to be wholly a matter of profit. He who thinks only of desires will take the Way to be wholly a matter of satisfaction. He who thinks only of law will take the Way to be wholly a matter of policy. He who thinks only of circumstance will take the Way to be

wholly a matter of expedience. He who thinks only of words will take the Way to be wholly a matter of logic. He who thinks only of Heaven will take the Way to be wholly a matter of harmonizing with natural forces. These various doctrines comprehend only one small corner of the Way, but the true Way must embody constant principles and be capable of embracing all changes. A single corner of it will not suffice. These men with their limited understanding saw one corner of the Way and, failing to understand that it was only a corner, they considered it sufficient and proceeded to expound it in engaging terms. Such men bring chaos to themselves and delusion to others. (Ibid., Chapter 21)

To prevent such confusions in understanding, Xunzi turned to the concept of *fa*, meaning "criterion" or "standard." He held that reasoning, whether analytically making distinctions or synthesizing diverse positions, operates by rules that approximate the way in which a geometer might judge a circle by using a compass. To know something is to be guided by these standards of reasoning to a conclusion. In Chapter 22 of *Xunzi*, he says the heart-mind (*xin*) draws distinctions among reasons, explanations, motions and desires; in much the same way, the eye draws distinctions among colors (Robins 2007).

Xunzi illustrates his views on standards by focusing on language. Language is one way of expressing our knowledge about reality by means of names (*ming* 名) and statements (*yan* 言). In Xunzi, "names" means nouns, singular and general terms. "Statements" means any utterance that conveys a thought, including commands and imperatives. Accordingly, language analysis is quite important in communicating knowledge. For example, calling someone a "son" places that person in a role that is subject to norms and expectations for how to live and not merely placing the person as a progeny of a particular set of parents. But when done correctly, both the knowledge about how to live and feel, as well as that of one's progeny is conveyed simultaneously. The crucial task of epistemology is not only to reveal how language is reporting facts and expressing someone's ideas but also a means to guide action or express passion and feeling. It is used to do all these things.

Xunzi relied on his structure of the epistemological process and understanding of language to dispel superstitious beliefs, correcting beliefs about the facts and calming emotional reactions to the world.

When stars fall or trees make strange sounds, all the people in the country are terrified and go about asking, "Why has this happened?" For no special reason, I reply. It is simply that, with the changes of heaven and earth and the mutations of the *yin* and *yang*, such things once in a while occur. You may wonder at them, but you must not fear them. The sun and moon are subject to eclipses, wind and rain do not always come at the proper season, and strange stars occasionally appear.

(Ibid., Chapter 17)

Xunzi's ultimate goal was not to use reason to turn everyone into religious unbelievers.[10] His point was that instead of fearing natural occurrences that happen according to the processes he considered "scientific" (*yin* and *yang*), it is human irresponsibility that should really be feared. When villagers fail to make provision for dikes to withstand floods, homes and persons are lost; when farmers fail to weed their crops, the harvest is slight. These are the real enemies of humankind according to Xunzi. To use the belief of Heaven's expression of pleasure or displeasure as an explanation for natural phenomena is to create fear about strange things. Such a belief is mistaken because weather, eclipses and the like belong to the parts of the world or they are examples of natural actions describable as the permutations of the *yin* and *yang*. Heaven and earth exist according to organizational patterns. This means crops must be planted in certain seasons and locations, suitable clothing must be worn according to the weather and villages must be built near adequate water supplies.

You pray for rain and it rains. Why? For no particular reason, I say. It is just as though you had not prayed for rain and it rained anyway. The sun and moon undergo an eclipse and you try to save them; a drought occurs and you pray for rain; you consult the arts of divination before making a decision on some important matter. But it is not as though you could hope to accomplish anything by such ceremonies. They are done merely for ornament. Hence the gentleman regards them as ornaments, but the common people regard them as supernatural. He who considers them ornaments is fortunate; he who considers them supernatural is unfortunate. (Ibid., Chapter 21)

Xunzi's most distinctive epistemological ideas are in Chapter 21 of the *Xunzi*. In this chapter he is not occupied primarily with how we know facts about the world, but how one can come to know the Way (*Dao*). While Xunzi says the heart-mind knows the Way by becoming empty, unified and still (i.e., by removing presuppositions and calming its passions), he takes a very different view than that of the Lao-Zhuang tradition. Instead of advocating ridding ourselves of all distinctions and abandoning discursive reasoning, Xunzi does not regard prior learning and obtained knowledge as something that prejudices our ability to know the truth. In Xunzi's understanding of emptiness, the inquirer should temporarily set aside prior learning, to turn toward the acquisition of something new: "not using what one has already stored up to harm what one is about to receive" (Robins 2007). He sees prior learning as essential to our storehouse of knowledge, and he recommends that we never cease learning and investigating. Such cumulative knowledge can save us from obsessions and superstitions and lead us to focus on activities that will create a more humane world.

Wang Chong (c.27–100 ce):
Critical Chinese Philosophy in the Classical Period

Wang Chong was a critic of the views on ontology, morality, religion and politics he received from earlier thinkers. His writings on these subjects were compiled into the work entitled *Critical Essays* (*Lunheng*). The work has 85 chapters. In these essays, Wang exhibits a thinker with a skeptical disposition, a critical intellect and a flair for originality in approaching philosophical problems. He held that a claim or belief must be supported by evidence.[11] Speaking of his own work in Chapter 61, he says, "And though the chapters of my *Critical Essays* may [only] be numbered in the tens, one phrase likewise covers them all, namely, 'hatred of fictions and falsehoods'" (Forke 1907). Of his method, he says, "I cite manifest instances in order to make the factual proof certain" (ibid., Chapter 48) and "In things there is nothing more clarifying than having an example, and in argument there is nothing more decisive than having evidence" (ibid., Chapter 67).

Wang is keenly aware of the tensions between empirical and rational pursuits of knowledge. He insists both must play a role in the advance of knowledge. One cannot depend only on sense experience because it can be deceptive. Intellectuality (*xinyi*) must be involved. In this sense, he takes a position on epistemology very much like that of Xunzi. He says bluntly that the Mohists did not use their intellectuality to verify things, but merely accepted what they heard as so-called eyewitness testimony and thus fell into deception (ibid.). Wang is skeptical of the use of experience alone in support of knowledge claims:

> Therefore, truth and falsehood do not depend upon the ear and eye, but require the exercise of intellect (*xinyi*). The Mohists, in making judgments, did not use their minds to verify things, but indiscriminately believed what they heard and saw. Therefore although their proofs were clear, they failed to reach reality. Judgments which thus fail to reach reality are difficult to impart to others, for although they may gain the sympathies of stupid [unlearned] people, they will not harmonize with the minds of the learned. (Ibid., Chapter 67)

On the other hand, Wang Chong certainly does not accept the Daoist solution to the problems surrounding rational argument either. Against the Daoists, he holds that history never affords any instances of men knowing what is true spontaneously without study or of persons being enlightened without inquiry and reasoning. For Wang, even the Daoist "perfected person" is not apt to bring about anything without study or to know anything in default of inquiry (ibid., Chapter 2).[12]

In his actual practice of testing differing positions and claims, Wang often uses the method known in Chinese as "arguing from a lodging place." This is similar to the strategy known in Western epistemology as "assuming an opponent's position for the sake of argument." Most often when he does this, Wang examines a belief that he believes is false (*xu* 虛) and practices what is called a *Reductio ad absurdum* technique. That is, he shows that an untenable or absurd result follows from accepting the belief. Here is an example of his approach:

> When the minister of Chu, Sun Shu Ao was a boy, he saw a two-headed snake, which he killed and buried. He then went home, and cried before his mother. She asked him, what was the matter? He replied, "I have heard say that he who sees a two-headed snake must die. Now, when I went out, I saw a two-headed snake. I am afraid that I must leave you and die, hence my tears." Upon his mother inquiring, where the snake was now, he answered, "For fear that others should see it later, I have killed it outright and buried it." The mother said, "I have heard that Heaven will recompense hidden virtue. You are

certainly not going to die, for Heaven must reward you." And, in fact, Sun Shu Ao did not die, but went on to become prime minister of Zhou. For interring one snake he received two favours. Does this make it clear that Heaven rewards good actions? No, this is idle talk. That he who sees a two-headed snake must die is a common superstition; and that Heaven gives happiness as a reward for hidden virtue is also a common prejudice. Sun Shu Ao, convinced of the superstition, buried the snake, and his mother, addicted to the prejudice, firmly relied on the Heavenly recompense. This would amount to nothing else than that life and death do not depend on fate, but on the death of a snake.

In the last lines of this passage, Wang puts himself in the place of one who believes this story, for the sake of argument. This enables him to show the absurdity of thinking that everything that Sun Shu Ao did in life up to and including becoming a prime minister had nothing to do with his talents and learning, but only with the death of a snake. Wang Chong is devoted to the development of a strategy for obtaining truth (*shi* 实) because of the failure of the common people to recognize the truth and their tendency to give themselves over to falsehoods. He wrote, "If the multitude in their works had not gone astray from truth and some discussions had not gone bad and become disordered, then Huan Tan[13] would not have written his works." (Ibid., Chapter 84)

According to Alexus McLeod's study of Wang's epistemology, truth (*shi*) is opposed to a certain kind of falsehood captured by the Chinese concept of *xu*, often translated as "falsity" as well as "emptiness" (2011: 39). In developing his epistemology, Wang clearly does not believe that all questions can be resolved because he insists that one cannot find the truth on the basis of partial evidence alone. Here his approach brings into light the distinction between belief and knowledge. Many more things can be believed than can be known. Believing something is not knowing it.

The sense of *xu* as "false" for Wang refers to a belief that is supported by "*merely apparent* qualities." Statements that have been shown false do not attract us, but *xu* falsehoods have attractive features—such as making us feel better about ourselves or life events, and thus they are difficult to give up believing. This way of understanding *xu* helps us to make sense of passages in which Wang talks as if such beliefs possess an allure that entices the undisciplined mind. Wang's implied point is that no one knowingly believes a falsehood. However, persons may believe (but not know) *xu*-type claims. They have an appeal or promise to them that is attractive. Wang writes that it is the nature of common people to enjoy strange stories and sayings, to delight in empty (*xu*) and absurd writings because truth (*shi*) is not easily or quickly substantiated, but flowery and empty speech astounds the hearers and excites their heart-minds. This is why even scholars with talent add things to and exaggerate the truth about affairs (McLeod 2011: 39)

Wang's epistemology is often characterized as the method of the four doubts, and it is so named because he expresses doubts about the *xu* beliefs associated with *hanwen* ("on heat and cold"), *qiangao* ("on reprimands"), *biandong* ("phenomenal changes") and *zhaozhi* ("results of moral behavior"). In his objections to *hanwen*, Wang undercuts beliefs such as that the ruler's joyful or angry *qi* could directly affect the weather, altering the temperature or producing storms. He holds that changes in weather are traceable to the "natural" causes of *yin* and *yang*. The conduct of human affairs has no influence on these processes in his view. In his doubt about *qiangao* beliefs, he questions the belief that Heaven interferes with the course of things through visitations, prodigies or portents, providing reprimands of bad conduct. His procedure is to reveal the assumption behind the belief. Such a belief assumes that Heaven must have a will or consciousness, otherwise how could it warn humankind or punish us? However, Wang argues that this assumption is an unshared one and that there is no way to prove or falsify it since anything that happens could be made to fit it. He doubts *biandong* beliefs because natural explanations can account for the occurrence of phenomena and events as well as they do. Finally, Wang has doubts about such *zhaozhi* beliefs as that the ruler's actions (and, by extension, those of all people) can influence Heaven to grant prosperity or longevity. Wang says that based on our observations we can recognize that humans are weak and inferior compared to Heaven, so it is impossible for the human being to move or change Heaven's operations since they are so much more superior than ours (Fung 2009: 293–5).

The question of fate/destiny (*ming*) was one that preoccupied many philosophers and we recall that Mozi was one of them. While Mozi argued that reality is not fated but that life's results are subject to Heaven's intention shown in the rewards and punishments meted out by ghosts and spirits based on our actions, Wang took a much different view. He argues that most, if not all, aspects of human existence are determined (*ming*) at birth. Not only are a person's gender, strength and physical being fixed, but also the individual's aptitude for learning, goodness, lifespan, likelihood of success and innate character are set as well (Nylan 2003: 745). Large sections of several of his essays are devoted to this topic (chs 1–7, 9–12, 42–3, and 53–5). In one of these, Wang writes:

> King Cheng's ability did not equal that of the Duke of Zhou. Duke Huan's intelligence fell short of that of Guan Chung. Nevertheless Cheng and Huan were endowed with the most glorious fate, whereas the Duke of Zhou and Guan Chung received inferior appointments. In ancient times, princes very seldom did not learn from their ministers. Possessing an extensive knowledge the latter would, as a rule, act as their fathers and instructors. In spite of their lack of sufficiency, the princes would take the place of sovereigns, and their ministers with all their accomplishments had to serve as their menials. That shows that rank depends upon destiny, and not on intelligence, and that wealth is good fortune, and has nothing to do with mental faculties.
>
> (Forke 1907: 146)

> In case a person predestinated (*ming*) for poverty, acquires wealth by his exertions and his energy, he dies, when he has made a fortune, and should another doomed to humility win honours by his talents and abilities, he will be dismissed, when he has achieved a position. They win wealth and honour by their energy and their genius, but are unable to keep it by fate and luck, just as a vessel holds but a certain quantity, and as a hand lifts but a certain weight. If a vessel holds just one pint, then one pint exactly fills it, but, as soon as there is more than one pint, it flows over. (Ibid., 147)

What is particularly interesting about Wang's arguments for the predestined (*ming*) character of persons is that they rely on the science of his day. That is, they make use of the *qi* theory of reality of early Chinese ontology. Here is a summary of how his argument goes in Chapter 4 of *Critical Essays:* The reason that so many things about a person or natural object are destined (*ming*) is because of the original endowment of *qi*, its quantity and quality, and the specific blend of *qi* which is constitutive of the object. For example, a person's *qi* actually determines what events and other persons he will encounter in life (external factors), as well as how he will react to them (internal factors) (Nylan 2003: 745).

Nevertheless, Wang rejected the idea that Heaven has any intention or that it establishes the destiny of all things according to some purpose. Instead, Wang thinks of Heaven's operations as spontaneous *wu-wei*.

> The Way of Heaven (*tiandao*) is one of effortless action (*wu-wei*). Therefore in spring it [Heaven] does not act to germinate, in summer to cause growth, in autumn to give maturity, and in winter to store up. But the *yang qi* comes forth of itself (in spring and summer), and things of themselves germinate and grow; the *yin qi* arises of itself (in autumn and winter), and things of themselves reach maturity and are stored up.
> (Forke 1907: Chapter 19, my change)

> Heaven uses the fluids of the five phases in producing all things, and man uses all these things in performing his many works. If one thing does not subdue the other, they cannot be employed together, and, without mutual struggle and annihilation, they cannot be made use of. If the metal does not hurt the wood, the wood cannot be used, and if the fire does not melt the metal, the metal cannot be made into a tool. Thus the injury done by one thing to the other turns out to be a benefit after all. If all the living creatures overpower, bite, and devour one another, it is the fluids of the five phases also that compel them to do so. (Ibid., 105)

Wang is extremely critical of the popular belief in ghosts and therefore of Mozi's position that Heaven gives out rewards and punishments through ghosts and spirits. His intention in rejecting this belief is actually twofold. First, he wants to counter the argument that ghosts and spirits make it possible for one's actions to correlate with one's success, benefit or longevity. For Wang, the natural endowment we have at birth is the destiny that makes these things happen. Secondly, he means to deny the existence of ghosts and spirits completely. They simply do not exist. Belief in ghosts is not merely a *xu* belief, he thinks it is demonstrably false. He offers this argument.

> Man is brought into existence by means of *qi*, and when he dies his *qi* is dissipated. It is the blood of the arteries that moves *qi* (in humans), and when a person dies the blood of his arteries rests (stops movement).

With this exhaustion (cessation of movement), *qi* is dissipated; with this, his physical frame decays; and with this decay, he becomes ashes and earth. How, then, can he become a ghost?

Since a dead man cannot become a ghost, he also cannot have consciousness. How may we prove this? From the fact that man, before his birth, has no consciousness. Before his birth, he forms part of the primal *qi* and upon his death he reverts to this *qi*. This *qi* is widespread and indeterminate, ... Before birth man is devoid of consciousness, and after death he reverts to this original condition of unconsciousness. ... Human death is like extinguishing a fire.

(Ibid., Chapter 62)

In pursuing this claim further, Wang offers several points. He rhetorically wonders why, if it is true that there are ghosts, there are not ghosts of other creatures (since all creatures are made from *qi* 氣). He also holds that if there were ghosts, they should surely outnumber living persons since there are many more people who have died than who are currently living.

If we focus specifically on Wang's method, we notice that he thinks knowledge is not limited to the information coming through our senses or our experience. Experience may be a source of knowledge, but our senses and the testimonies given by other persons based on what they saw or heard must be checked by the use of the intellect (i.e., reason and argument). Epistemologically, we must distinguish three philosophical categories: justified true belief (knowledge), demonstrated falsehoods and *xu* beliefs.

Knowledge as Justified Truth Belief in Plato

According to Plato (*c.*428?–348? BCE), in order to say we know something, we must have a "justified true belief." Like Wang Chong, Plato made a distinction between knowledge and belief. Belief is very much like opinion and is not necessarily grounded in any facts or supported by reasoned argument. A person could believe that the earth revolves around the moon, or that the tooth fairy does indeed leave quarters under a child's pillow in exchange for a tooth. The person could even believe that these are facts and act accordingly and even with great passion and enthusiasm. One might even die for a belief.

Yet without justifying such a belief through evidence and reason, it will remain only a belief and not something one knows. At the same time, if one knows that 2+2=4, it makes no sense to say he does not believe it. Within Plato's construction of these epistemological distinctions, knowledge implies belief. But it is not enough merely to believe something, even to believe it with all one's heart. To have knowledge, it is also a requirement that it be a true belief. One cannot *know* something that is untrue/false. We can know *that* something is false, but we do not know a falsehood. The final component of knowledge, according to Plato, is justification. Without justification, says Plato, all we have is simply an opinion even if it happens to be true, but we do not know it.

Even though his epistemology shows some parallels to that developed by Plato, Wang's parsing of the relationship between knowledge, truth, falsity and belief is somewhat different from Plato's and Mozi's. For Wang, there are justified true beliefs (knowledge), false beliefs and *xu* beliefs. Neither Plato nor Mozi offered a developed philosophical discussion of what Wang Chong called *xu* beliefs.

Tiantai Buddhism's Threefold Truth Epistemology

As we saw in Chapter I, in Tiantai Buddhist ontology, there is only one reality, not a two-fold structure of the phenomenal world of objects and a spiritual world. But the defining thesis of Tiantai is actually an epistemological one. It is the teaching of Threefold Truth (*san di*) put forward by the Tiantai philosopher, Zhiyi. Zhiyi held that the philosophy of Threefold Truth was not unique to Tiantai but was actually the teaching of all Buddhist schools. He also thought that twofold truth was readily obvious, but a third dimension of truth was often overlooked. Threefold truth may be described as follows: (1) We can make true statements about the world of existing things. These truths are about things that exist and their interactions in a network of interdependent causes. These are the truths of history, science, etc. about provisional existence (*jia di*). The truth of a statement here is verified by testing it over against the world of our experience. (2) It is also true to say that all things are empty (*kong di*) and have no permanence. There is no permanent essence to anything in our world of experience. Everything in reality is devoid of any self-nature. Of course, it is realization of this truth that liberates one from suffering because it breaks one's attachment to things and persons who are the objects of our desires. (3) But Zhiyi also argued that there is a third character of truth. It consists of the truth that the mundane or phenomenal world is real and at the same time it is impermanent and ultimately empty. This is truth as the Middle Way (*zhong di*).

> Now, if one knows that the mundane is not mundane [but empty], then the extreme [truth] of the mundane is put to rest, and if one realizes the non-mundane [the empty] is the mundane then the extreme [truth] of emptiness is put to rest. This is called "cessation as an end to both extremes." (Swanson 1989: 118)

My modifications added in the brackets in the quote above are designed to make clear that in Tiantai all threefold truths are identical and that only when one is taken as "more true" than another does one go astray epistemologically. As Paul Swanson translates from Zhiyi's *The Esoteric Meaning of the Lotus Sutra*, "emptiness is identical to [mundane] existence and the Middle Way" (ibid., 182). To put it differently, these are not three truths, but Threefold Truth.

The Threefold Truth epistemology of Tiantai means that objects of our experience may be studied and used. We may possess knowledge about how they interact in a nexus of interdependent causes, how to make various objects from other materials, how to use them for our benefit and the like. All the while, though, we are using and studying things that are empty in themselves; having this knowledge is liberating and enlightening because we can use it to break the attachments we have to things that are the sources of our suffering.

We may illustrate how the Threefold Truth epistemology works by applying it to an example taken from Buddhist tradition. There was an historical Buddha named Siddhartha. We may inquire as to his birthplace, disciples, travels, teachings and so forth. We may do literary and historical critical analysis of narratives told about him. The truth statements we make about all this are mundane truths about the Buddha. We may also make truth statements about his enlightened way of living, his freedom from attachment and overcoming of suffering. These are not symbolic truths, while the former are literal truths. These are not spiritual truths, while the former are material or empirical truths. They are statements about truth as emptiness. But we may move on to realize the truth that the mundane Buddha and all that can be said about him is also the empty Buddha, and the enlightened Buddha.

Zhiyi thought that persons had different epistemological capabilities that put them on divergent levels of truth. In *Esoteric Meaning* he says, "Teachings are basically as responses to capabilities. There are distinctions and differences in the texts because the capabilities [of inquirers] are not the same" (ibid., 165). Some people are only able to grasp truth in its mundane expression. For them, truth is the mundane and they are caught up in its pleasures, desires and attachments. They suffer because of this even though they may resist desires through moral action, prayer, devotion and the like. Others express truth only as emptiness. What others know as mundane, these persons know as illusory and impermanent. They detach from things and live apart from the mundane as much as possible. But for those who are capable of it, truth is seen for what it is, they live in the mundane, knowing it is real but also seeing its emptiness. Threefold Truth is perfectly integrated; three in one and one in three. And yet, there is one more thing to be said about Threefold Truth. In *The Great Calming and Contemplation* Zhiyi says:

> All three are empty because the path of speech and discursive thought is a dead end. All three are provisional because they are names only [in language only]. All three are the middle because they are identical with ultimate reality. (Donner and Stevenson 1993: 178)

The difference between the capabilities of persons explains epistemologically why some are able to grasp the threefold character of truth and others become fixated on either mundane truth or emptiness. In the *Lotus Sutra*, the Buddha expounds many parables. "The Burning House and the Three Carts" is one of the most famous of these, and it reveals the Buddha's explanation for teaching different people in varying ways and even for teaching what may be false on a mundane level. Ultimately, the point is that the Buddha makes use of the way of truth that is helpful for the specific person. This is called the use of "expedient means."

In the parable, a rich old man, upon seeing his house on fire, tried to save his children's lives. He warned them to get out of the house, but they were occupied in playing games. So, the old man said, "I have marvelous toy carts drawn by goats, deer and oxen waiting outside for you. You must come outside right now to get them." After the children reached safety outside, they discovered there were no toy carts as promised, but there were real carts filled with jewels (*Lotus Sutra*, Watson 2002: Chapter 5).

As Zhiyi uses this parable, he focuses on how Buddhism may have many teachings, some of which contradict another or may even be untrue as statements about mundane existence. But they are "expedient means" to enable people with different intelligence, education and capacity to gain the "jewel of enlightenment." In this case, it is not what a statement *says* that makes it a threefold truth, but what it *does*. This is what Jeeloo Liu rightly calls the pragmatic understanding of truth in Tiantai Buddhism (2006: 294).

But even given his philosophy of Threefold Truth, many interpreters still insist that Zhiyi holds that real truth is actually unspeakable and beyond human conceptualization. For example, Burton Watson observes of the stream of Mahayana Buddhism of which Tiantai is a sect, "Mahayana Buddhism has always insisted that its highest truth can never in the end be expressed in words, since words immediately create the kind of distinctions that violate the unity of Emptiness" (2002: xxviii). It seems correct to say that truth as Middle Way is something inexpressible since expressing it would involve making a statement that might be taken to be a mundane truth or truth about emptiness. For those who have attained enlightenment as Buddhas, truth is simply the Threefold Truth and it has no need of further expression.

Wang Yangming (1472–1529): Pure Knowledge

In order to understand the uniqueness and originality of Wang Yangming's epistemology, consider that in Western philosophy in the twentieth century, the British thinker Gilbert Ryle wrote deliberately about the distinction between "knowing that" and "knowing how" (1949: Chapter 2). "Knowing that" he took to refer to knowing whether a proposition was true or false. It was concerned with the facts of the world; the sum total of the true statements that could be made about the objects that furnish the world and their relationships to each other. "Knowing how" Ryle considered to be knowledge about the way to perform a task (how to make a table) or undertake an activity (how to swim, dance, etc.). Actually, this distinction is probably too neat. What knowledge is and the sources from which it comes are a good deal more complicated. Ludwig Wittgenstein showed that there are many uses for the word *know* and that the criteria for saying that one knows vary with the uses; as do the conditions for saying that some knowledge claim is *true*. *True*, like *know* has many uses in language and the grounds for saying something is true are set by the specific use one is making of the term (Wittgenstein 1953: pars 132, 149, 150, 151, 153 and 154; 1969: pars 5, 11, 18, 105, 162, 163, 167, 315, 323–6, 333, 336). This does not mean Wittgenstein was an epistemological relativist. The reason is that for each use, there is indeed a recognized set of conditions for making the judgment that a claim is true or false. Relativism might be taken to mean that "there is no truth; only various interpretations," or "what is true for me, may not be true for you" and the like.

On these terms, Wang Yangming's notion about what he called "pure knowledge" (*liangzhi*) is a particular use of *know* that includes both "knowing that" and "knowing how." In this way, Wang makes an interesting contribution to the conversation on epistemology. As we saw in our discussion of Wang's ontology, one component of *liangzhi* or "pure knowledge" is the direct and immediate apprehension of the Principles (*li*) of Heaven by which all things are ordered (space, time, cause and the like). But according to Wang Yangming's biography, while exiled in the Guizhou region, he experienced the direct enlightenment of "pure knowledge" and began teaching what he called "the unity of knowledge and action (*zhixing heyi*)," meaning that when one possesses this kind of knowledge there is no difference between knowing *what* one should do and spontaneously *willing to do it*. These are not two separate events, one epistemological and the other volitional.

Some interpreters associate "pure knowledge" with a kind of sixth sense, as something like the immediate perception of the "appropriateness/fittingness," "goodness" or "evil" of an action, but it is more than that.[14] Wang thinks that in pure knowledge one not only knows the good but also possesses a compelling love or attraction to it and is repulsed by evil and hates it.

[The Teacher said,] "Pure knowledge (*liangzhi*) is nothing but the sense of right and wrong, and the sense of right and wrong is nothing but to love [the right] and to hate [the wrong].

(*Instructions*, in Chan 1963a: Section 288, my change)

"Pure knowledge" is not the result of study. It does not come at the end of an argument as an inferred conclusion. It is direct and immediate. Wang's position is related to the characteristic Chinese conception of the "heart-mind" (*xin* 心) according to which the mind always involves feeling and is never merely a discursive instrument. The cognitive content that is before the mind is always simultaneously *felt* in a certain way without any separation between these according to Chinese thought. Only when we keep this in focus can we understand Wang Yangming's position that in "pure knowledge" there is a "unity of knowledge and action (*zhixing heyi*)."

Chan (Zen) Buddhism and Wang Yangming

Chan Buddhism developed in China between the sixth and eighth centuries. It is regarded as a uniquely Chinese form of Buddhism that later was transplanted into Japan where it became prominent as Zen. The Chinese word *chan* is used to translate the Sanskrit *dhyana*, which means "meditation." Although regarded as Chinese in origin and tenor, the founding legend of Chan is that the Buddha transmitted a private esoteric teaching, never written on any sutra, but passed only from one teacher (a.k.a. patriarch) to another. The 28th patriarch in this lineage of transmission is known as Bodhidharma (470–543), and he is said to have brought the teaching to China. In the history of Chan, there is a Northern and Southern School. The Northern followed Shenxiu (*c.*605–706) as its patriarch and the Southern followed Huineng (638–713). According to the *Platform Sutra of the Sixth Patriarch*, regarded as the canonical expression of Chan philosophy, the split between these schools arose over who should follow Hong-ren (601–74) who was the fifth patriarch of Chan, telling the story of Huineng's ascendancy to that role.

Chan does have an epistemology, but it is quite different from what we have encountered in our study of Mozi, Mencius, Xunzi, Wang Chong and others. In Chan, the objects of knowledge are not external things or even what Tiantai calls the provisional things of the mundane world. Chan's theory of knowledge is concerned with one's own mind and what is known by immediate, direct acquaintance. To know one's mind is to know the external world since the mind's conceptualization is identical with what we call the world. It also means that we can know other minds (other persons' minds) since everyone, at the most fundamental level, shares the same mind.

A clarification must be offered. When Chan philosophers claim that we know the world through our own minds, they do not identify *mind* with the thoughts presently in front of us. They mean one's *original mind*, before the mind was clouded over by experiences or distinctions. In our original minds, we have awareness of absolutely certain truth. D. T. Suzuki says this knowledge "is not derivative but primitive; not inferential, not rationalistic, not mediational, but direct, immediate; not analytical but synthetic; not cognitive, but symbolical; not intending but merely expressive; not abstract, but concrete; not processional, not purposive, but ultimate, final and irreducible; not eternally receding, but infinitely inclusive; etc." (1956: 34)

While it is generally agreed that Wang Yangming is influenced by Chan Buddhism, he also draws heavily from Daoist thought as we have seen in the Lao-Zhuang teachings. Wang practices meditative techniques associated with both Chan and Daoism. He is sometimes attacked for being overly Buddhist, but most, if not all, of the connections usually cited for Chan influence on Wang may also be accounted for by his early and ongoing interest in Daoism.[15]

In his exposition of the volitional force of "pure knowledge," Wang's position makes a novel contribution to epistemological thinking because he does not compartmentalize knowing and willing into separate activities as is characteristically the way of doing epistemology among Western thinkers. It seems obvious to a Westerner that knowing I should have my blood sugar checked is different from actually going to do it. I have to engage my will or choose to act on my knowledge. But there is an important component missing when we consider this same example from a Chinese point of view. From the Chinese view, when I know that I should have my blood sugar checked, accompanying this knowledge (bonded with it) is a feeling about it. This is an extension of the Chinese conception of the unity of heart and mind mentioned above. To greatly oversimplify the matter, we may say that this feeling may be one of attraction and desire, or repulsion and hate. It is these feelings that, if followed naturally, effortlessly, will lead me to act or omit to have my blood sugar checked. Wang says,

> The master of the body is the heart-mind (*xin*). What emanates from the heart-mind is the will. The original substance of the will is knowledge, and wherever the will is directed is an actualized act. For example, when the will is directed toward serving one's parents, then serving one's parents is actualized. When the will is directed toward serving one's ruler, then serving one's ruler is actualized. When the will is directed toward being humane to all people and feeling love toward things, then being humane to all people and feeling love toward things results and when the will is directed toward seeing, hearing, speaking, and acting, then each of these is actualized.
>
> (*Instructions*, Section 6, my translation)

In Western philosophy, when we speak of *willing* to do something, we often do so to mark acting in a way that did not come naturally, but rather in a manner that required effort, as though we had to overcome a desire born of a feeling toward something known. But Wang takes a different position.

> [The Teacher] said, "Knowledge is the original substance of the heart-mind. The heart-mind is naturally able to know. When it perceives the parents, it naturally knows that one should be filial. When it perceives the elder brother, it naturally knows that one should be respectful. And when it perceives a child fall into a well, it naturally knows that one should be commiserative. This is pure knowledge (*liangzhi*) of good and need not be sought outside. If what emanates from pure knowledge (*liangzhi*) is not obstructed by selfish ideas, the result will be like the saying "If a man gives full development to his feeling of commiseration, his humanity will be more than he can ever put into practice." However, the ordinary man is not free from the obstruction of selfish ideas. He therefore requires the effort of the extension of knowledge and the investigation of things in order to overcome selfish ideas and restore principle.
>
> (*Instructions*, in Chan 1963a: Section 8, my changes)

Even though Wang insists that moral efficacy accompanies moving on one's "pure knowledge," he does not believe that one is given the exact details of what to do in the particular circumstances and contexts of a life event or relationship.

> Pure knowledge (*liangzhi*) is to minute details and varying circumstances as compasses and measures are to areas and lengths. Details and circumstances cannot be predetermined, just as areas and lengths are infinite in number and cannot be entirely covered. If compasses and squares are truly set, there cannot be any deception regarding areas, and the possibility of correct areas in the world cannot be exhausted. If measures are well exhibited, there cannot be any deception regarding length, and the possibility of correct lengths in the world cannot be exhausted. If pure knowledge (*liangzhi*) is truly extended, there cannot be any deception regarding minute details and varying circumstances, and yet the possibility of minute details and varying circumstances in the world cannot be exhausted. (Ibid., Section 139, my change)

Moral discernment can come through reason and experience but when it does so, the natural interpenetration of knowledge and action is not present, as it is in pure knowledge.

> I asked, "It is by nature that the sage is born with knowledge and can practice it naturally and easily. What is the need of any effort?"
> The Teacher said, "Knowledge and action are effort. The difference lies in whether it is thorough or shallow and hard or easy. Pure knowledge (*liangzhi*) is by nature refined and clear. In the wish to be filial toward parents, for example, those [grasping the inborn] knowledge of filial piety can practice filial piety naturally and easily, merely follow the pure knowledge (*liangzhi*), and sincerely and earnestly practice filial piety to the utmost. Those who learn filial piety through study, and practice it for its advantage, must merely be alert at all times and be determined to follow the pure knowledge (*liangzhi*) and practice filial piety to the utmost that is all. As to those who learn filial piety through hard work and practice it with effort and difficulty, their obscuration and impediments are already quite great. Although they are determined to follow this pure knowledge (*liangzhi*) and practice filial piety, they cannot do so because they are hindered by selfish desires. They must apply a hundred efforts where others can

succeed by only one, and a thousand efforts where others can succeed by ten. Only then can they follow this pure knowledge and practice filial piety to the utmost.

(Ibid., Section 291, my changes)

As mentioned earlier, Wang makes reference to the famous case of seeing a child about to fall into a well cited by Mencius (2A6) to demonstrate that all humans have an inborn disposition to compassion. Wang says that when our heart-mind is operating by "pure knowledge" we will see and know that the child is about to plunge to its death and this will be accompanied by the natural feeling of compassion as something we are attracted to so overwhelmingly that we will jump to save the child.

I have never warned people against investigating the principles of things to the utmost nor urged them to live in deep seclusion, sit erect, and do nothing. My idea is that it is incorrect to interpret the investigation of the principles of things to the utmost as we come into contact with them to mean what I have described before as devoting oneself to external things and neglecting the internal. If an unenlightened student can really carefully examine the Principles of Heaven in the heart-mind in connection with things and events as they come, and extend his pure knowledge of the good, then though stupid he will surely become intelligent and though weak he will surely become strong. The great foundation will be established and the universal way [in human relations] will be in operation. And the nine standards of ruling a state will be united by one thread that runs through them completely. (*Instructions*, in Chan 1963a: Section 137, my changes)

According to Wang, the heart-mind in possession of "pure knowledge" is one with the Principle(s) (*li*) of heaven and earth. So long as it is not clouded or unobscured by selfish desires, its clear character will manifest itself in action. For Wang, the most interesting and important outcome of pure knowledge is its power to enable our moral discrimination in actual conduct. He does not argue that we can know scientific truths by means of such knowledge (e.g., whether there is evidence of water on Mars).

Zhang Dongsun (1886–1973):
Pluralistic Cultural Epistemology

In the early half of the twentieth century, Zhang Dongsun was one of the most important philosophers in China, especially owing to his efforts to establish, in dialogue with Western philosophy, a unique and new philosophical epistemology in the Chinese context. This approach has variously been labeled as Pluralistic Epistemology or Cultural Epistemology (Jiang 2002: 57). Zhang's epistemological theory was both pluralistic and deeply attentive to the role of culture in all aspects of knowing, so much so that Haridas Muzumdar (1956) characterized Zhang's work as the ground-breaking exposition of a "sociology of knowledge."

For Zhang, what counts as evidence, what we seek to know, what we think it is possible to know, what we notice through our senses, how we interpret our sense perceptions, what qualifies as a sufficient reason to say we know something all represent epistemological positions that are inevitably culturally defined and structured. Persons are not merely acculturated to observe festivals, organize themselves socially, or valorise certain heroes. They are also shaped by their cultures to operate epistemologically in different ways.

In his article "A Chinese Philosopher's Theory of Knowledge" Zhang sets out four guidelines for the study of epistemology:

1. A theory of knowledge and cultural history must be treated simultaneously.
2. Not only does concrete social thought have its background in cultural determinants, but also so do the logical forms and theoretical categories which structure epistemological philosophy.
3. The differences between Western and Eastern epistemologies can be explained from this point of view.
4. From this we may understand that Western philosophy is nothing but a particular form of epistemology characteristic of and for the use of Western culture, but that there are plural epistemologies deriving from the many diverse human cultures. (Muzumdar 1956: 12–13)

Zhang distinguished between perceptual and theoretical knowledge, but both types are socially and culturally constituted, even if perceptual knowledge also draws on the external world and its structure. He wrote:

It seems to me that human knowledge may be considered as having four elements, each penetrating into and mutually dependent upon the others. The first is the external "structure" [of the world available to our senses] which accounts for our immediate sensations. The external world being [known] merely [as] "structured," we can only know its "mathematical [structural] properties," to borrow a term from [Bertrand] Russell. As to its qualitative nature [the object in itself], we know nothing. But it must be pointed out that these mathematical properties are not static and rigid, but flexible and changeable. The second element is the "sensa," to use the terminology of neo-realism. Our sensation is a curious thing. Although externally aroused, it [i.e., the actual sensation] is different from the external world in nature. There may be said to be correspondence but not identity between the two. Sensation by its nature is something independent. The third element consists of "constructions." The ordinarily perceived tables, chairs, houses, friends and so forth, are "constructions." These constructions are often taken naively as independent self-existent things. But as a matter of fact, these things are constructed through the perceptions of the observer. The fourth element is what we have already discussed as "interpretation." These four elements are interdependent.

(Zhang 1939, my brackets)

Zhang thought that ultimately knowledge was constructed by the intricate workings of these four elements including content gathered through the senses, structural forms of pattern and order and concepts derived from our culture and sociality. We cannot have any direct knowledge of the external world as it is in itself (Jiang 2002: 63).

While much of what Zhang wrote about these four elements of epistemology is not as original as he thought, a great deal of it having been set out in British Empiricism and Kantian philosophy, there are some unique emphases worth noting. One of these is Zhang's lingering Buddhism from when he was a devotee of that tradition in his early life. Zhang, perhaps appreciating the problems Bertrand Russell and Ludwig Wittgenstein were both having with explaining the nature of an "object" in itself,[16] took the position that the objects of sensation do not have any ontological status themselves; there is no substance underlying the objects of our phenomenal experience.

This is not the same as to say that there is no external world. It is only to hold that the external world is not composed of fixed objects that cause experiences in us, but which we cannot know in themselves. Instead, our experience is of objects which are the products of mutually interdependent, transient relations. Zhang held that the term *matter*, like *mind* or *reality*, is an empty structural notion derived from the way some (i.e., specifically Western) cultural epistemologies work. Only some (e.g., Western) epistemologies even ask what is "real" or what is "matter."

The most obvious way in which all epistemology can be shown to be cultural is that knowledge is expressed in a particular language, or better put, *knowledge is linguistic thinking* or *knowing is through/in language.* Of course, language is a cultural product. Languages have grammar and structure and these embody a logic and rules for reasoning. For example, Zhang argued that the structure of Western languages leads philosophers to look for the essence (substance) underlying the attributes predicated of an object. So, he held that the investigation of the nature of substance itself became one of the central problems of Western philosophy but it did not arise in Chinese philosophy, because the language is differently constructed.

Zhang wrote:

> For example, when we say, "this is yellow and hard" yellowness and hardness are the so called "attributes" which are attributed to something, the something in this case being "this." The "something" in general is the substratum. With a substratum emerges the idea of "substance." This is the reason why in the history of Western philosophy no matter how different the arguments may be, pro and con, about the idea of substance, it is the idea of substance which itself constitutes the central problem. (Zhang 1939)

Zhang holds that Chinese language and culture did not set up categories as substance and attribute, so it did not even see as epistemological problems those which seem so obvious and evident to Western thinkers who do make such distinctions.

The differences between the cultural epistemologies of the West and China are even deeper. In Western thought, the law of contradiction or mutual exclusiveness is taken as a necessary truth of logic. Something must be either A or not-A. This kind of epistemological tool was not employed in Chinese philosophy because in Chinese language and culture relationality and inclusiveness were rooted in its correlative thinking. That is, something cannot be A at all, unless it is in relation to and participates in not-As. Zhang believes this explains in part why modern Chinese thinkers found the dialectical thinking of G. W. F. Hegel and Karl Marx more compatible with their epistemologies than other Western philosophies. Hegel and Marx both emphasized that new knowledge comes from a synthesis or correlation of previously regarded contradictions (e.g., the triadic structure: thesis, antithesis, synthesis).

Moreover, the concern over whether something exists or does not exist, while significant in Western epistemology, is also not a prominent preoccupation in Chinese philosophy. Zhang thinks this is because Western philosophers are always asking, "What is it?" The Chinese, on the other hand, confronted by the same situation, ask: "How should one react to it?" For Zhang, this means that Western thought is characterized by the "what-priority," Chinese by the "how-priority." The stress on how one must react to an experience has led Chinese philosophers to concern themselves with human affairs and how man must react to nature and his fellow human beings (Muzumdar 1956: 16).

Clearly, then, Zhang's pluralistic cultural epistemology has no room for the position that real or true knowledge transcends all cultures or for the idea that there is a universal set of criteria for knowledge or truth (such as the correspondence of a proposition or claim to external objects). Knowledge is always mediated through culture. Knowledge and truth are functions of the criteria set up within a specific cultural epistemology, and there is no way to approach "reality" that can be bleached free of the cultural constraints determining what one is looking for, what questions one asks, or what is taken as sufficient evidence for a belief.

CHAPTER III

哲学

Value Theory: Questions about the Nature and Application of Morality

Introduction

Ethics, or moral philosophy, is concerned primarily with the question of the best way to live and, secondarily, with whether this question can be answered philosophically. The main branches of ethics are meta-ethics, normative ethics and applied ethics. Meta-ethics concerns the nature of ethical thought, such as the use of moral concepts (i.e., brave, kind, spiteful, callous, etc.), whether there are absolute ethical truths and how such truths could be known. Normative ethics is more concerned with the questions of how one ought to act and what the right course of action is. This is where most ethical discussion is generated. Lastly, applied ethics goes beyond theory and steps into real-world ethical practice, such as questions of whether or when specific actions are morally permissible and how ethical recommendations relate to societal policies and laws.

This chapter concerns philosophical questions of morality and value. Some fundamental questions addressed by Chinese philosophers and explored in this chapter are these:

- How should we live?
- What is the ultimate purpose of our lives (to pursue happiness or pleasure, obey moral rules, please others or higher beings, follow our own interests)?
- What is the origin of our morality (do we invent it and agree to it, is it inborn or part of our nature, is it given by a higher being or intelligence)?

- What really makes something good or right to do (is it the consequences of the action, doing our duties or going by our passionate feelings)?
- Is morality universal or relative to its culture or the individual?
- What is most basic and important in morality: the actions we do or the sort of persons we are?

Confucius and the *Analects* on Self-cultivation and the Exemplary Person (c.500–300 BCE)

The first access that most people have into Chinese philosophy in general, and certainly into the thought of Confucius, is through the *Analects (Lunyu)*. This work is an anthology of selected sayings in which Confucius is often, although not exclusively, the main teacher. In this text, Confucius makes known his conception of the kind of project in which our human lives should be invested. The *Analects* gathers teachings and philosophical viewpoints of Confucius about what it means to be human, how to live a worthwhile and fulfilling life and even what it takes to lead and organize a state.[1]

Ren, Xiao and Li. What distinguishes the human being from other life forms for Confucius is the particular kind of being we are. Unlike other animals, the emergence of the human person is the coming of a being that requires others like itself, mutually interacting and creating each other, and doing so in such a way that we would say to become a person is a moral achievement, for being humane is inseparable from becoming a person. This characterization of Confucius's views on what it means to be a person is directly related to his often-delivered exhortation to his disciples that they should seek to be *ren* (仁). I do not take this concept as a moral virtue among others, not even as the highest one. I take Confucius to be referring to a way of being-in-the-world. The Chinese character is composed of two parts: "person (*ren* 人)" and what is usually taken simply as the number "2 (二)." Herbert Fingarette understands *ren* to refer to the value-laden process that exists when two *homo sapiens* are making each other into persons (Fingarette 1972: 227). While there are many analects in which it does seem that Confucius is talking about a trait of consummate human moral and interpersonal excellence when he speaks of *ren*, I take the term to be used to mark the achievement of becoming a person in itself.

The crucible in which this process of interaction with other persons begins is the family. In the family one learns how to treat others, and this carries over to life in the community and even the state (*Analects* 1.6, 11). Filiality (*xiao*) is more than an affirmation of the importance of family to the development of one's personhood and life fulfillment. It is a metaphor for relating to others beyond our birth family as though they were also relatives. In Confucius's thought, the institution of the family is the foundation of a well-ordered and civilized society. Indeed, he characteristically thinks of the relationship between ruler and subject on the model of a family. The ruler should care for all his subjects, as a father does for his children. In Confucian tradition, filiality found expression in what was called *the Five Relationships*: parent–child; spouse–spouse; older sibling to younger; ruler to subject; and friend to friend. Filiality in Confucian thought is a way of saying that it is in these paradigmatic relationships that we are "humanized." Being fully a person is being "humane," and that is being *ren*. Insofar as we do not actualize humaneness, we are to that extent still not yet fully persons because to be a person is more than to possess consciousness (even self-consciousness), intentions, desires and rationality. It requires cultivated reciprocity and the ability to evoke from others the sort of treatment given to persons. In these characterizations of Confucius's teachings, I have borrowed language used by Daniel Dennett (1976) but these distinctions and claims are embedded in the *Analects* teachings on *ren* and filiality.

In Book 4 of the *Analects*, the editor lays four aphoristic sayings together in sequence that suggest the earliest and most authentic of Confucius's views on filiality:

4.18 – The Master said, "In serving your parents you may gently dispute with them. But if it becomes clear you cannot change their opinions, you should resume an attitude of deference and not oppose them; even if discouraged, do not be resentful."

4.19 – The Master said, "While your parents are alive, you should not journey far afield; and if you travel, be sure to go to a specific known destination."

4.20 – The Master said, "A son who manages to carry on the household exactly as his father did for the three years' mourning period after his father's death, can be called a filial son."

4.21 – "You must always be aware of the age of your parents. On the one hand, it is a cause for rejoicing, on the other for anxiety."

In *Analects* 8.21, Confucius offers the appraisal of sage-king Yu that he had no faults and he provides as one illustration of this claim that Yu displayed filial devotion to the gods and spirits of his ancestors. In Book 11's collection of the record of Confucius's evaluations of his disciples and others, he praises Min Ziqian for his filialty (11.5).

In answer to inquiries, Confucius says that filial piety was best expressed by following the rites of propriety in relationships (*li* 澧) but he insists to Ziyou (2.7) and Zixia (2.8) that interactions between persons within our five relationships must always be funded by *proper feelings* of respect and affection, and not consist of merely performing one's duties. He tells Meng Wubo that a filial child never gives his/her parents anything to be anxious about (2.6) and when Ji Kangzi, head of the families who ruled the state of Lu, asks how to get his people to do their utmost for their neighbors and for the community, Confucius tells him to display filiality to his own elders and juniors (2.2).

The sayings collected in *Analects* 4.1–4.8 give us a pretty good picture of the *ren* person. This person is one who is able

1. to endure hardship and enjoy happy circumstances (4.2);
2. to identify without prejudice and with accuracy the individuals who are truly good and evil (4.3);
3. to be free from the desire to do wrong (4.4);
4. and to stand out from those who go astray (4.7).

Confucius refuses to say whether he knows anyone who has fully actualized *ren* personhood. Such a person is someone who has improved not this or that trait, but who has improved their very being itself, who is reaching beyond the current level of the human being to something higher. Accordingly, they do not become anxious whatever they might face in life (6.23, 9.29). In responses to Fan Chi's inquiries about *ren*, Confucius tells him that such a person has achieved success only after triumphing over challenge and difficulty (6.22). Moreover, *ren* persons establish others in establishing themselves. That is, they make those around them better (6.30).

In Book 5's collection of "Comments on Disciples and Personages," Confucius refuses to say that even the much-admired Zhonggong (Ran

Yong) is *ren* (5.5). He likewise says he is unsure whether his disciple Zilu (Zhong You) is *ren*, even if he possess the skill to be in charge of a city of a thousand households (5.8, 5.19). However, Confucius says that Yan Hui (Yan Yuan), his most-loved disciple, would go for months without departing from *ren* thoughts and feelings (6.11).

Book 12's "Collection of Teachings to the Disciples by Topics" begins with a series of analects on *ren*, first to Yan Hui (12.1), then to Zhonggong (12.22) and Sima Niu (12.3) in which Confucius offers the position that *ren* comes through self-cultivation and observing the rituals of propriety in interpersonal and social relations *li* (禮) (3.3). When speaking about what we may consider as morality, the term Confucius uses that is perhaps the closest in meaning is *li* and it is often translated as the ritual proprieties that guide conduct. *Li* refers to the way of comporting oneself that helps humans transcend animality, become human (i.e., develop humaneness, *ren*) and even transcend present ways of being human by raising themselves to ever higher expression captured by the concept of *junzi* (exemplary person, etc.).

Books 3 and 10 both contain numerous analects related to Confucius's teachings about the *li* that govern human relationships and assist us in transcending our animality. The *li* include the behaviors that indicate moral appropriateness and cultured decorum in the Five Relationships and beyond. They present behaviors displaying a person of moral character and refinement.

In speaking of exemplary persons (*junzi*), Confucius observes that they, "learn broadly of culture, discipline this learning through observing the *li* and moreover, in so doing, can remain on course without straying from it" (6.27). For Confucius, following the *li* is a way to develop humaneness (*ren*) (3.3). Observing the *li* is not merely about the superficial action (e.g., giving a gift of jade and silk or knowing when to play the bells and drums in a ceremony). It is about changing one's being internally (17.11).

Confucius realizes that *li* changes over time as human need requires and yet he does not approve of a relativistic view of *li*. He definitely values the *li* practiced during the Zhou dynasty and insists that some *li* simply should not be changed (2.23, 3.9, 3.21, 9.3). Confucius counsels rulers to prefer propriety (*li*) as a means to establish order rather than turning to law and punishment (2.3, 4.13). An exemplary person (*junzi*) disciplines his conduct by such proprieties (6.27, 15.18).

Yan Hui once reported, "The Master is good at drawing me forward a step at a time; he broadens me with culture and disciplines my behavior through *li*" (9.11). Indeed, we can best understand the importance of acting according to *li* in interpersonal relationships when we notice Confucius's response to Yan Hui's question about what is entailed in being truly *ren*. Confucius replies, "Do not look at anything that violates the observance of *li*; do not listen to anything that violates the observance of *li*; do not speak about anything that violates the observance of *li*; do not do anything that violates the observance of *li*" (12.1).

Being *ren* comes through self-cultivation and observing *li*, and it cannot be reduced to the dichotomy often found in Western moral theory that ethics is either concerned with action (doing) or character (being). Confucius recognizes the importance of both what persons *do* and the sort of person they *are*. A *ren* person will act in a certain way; and the construction of *ren* character cannot occur without doing the *li* acts derived from the lives of exemplary persons (*junzi*) in the past and present. However, Confucius does not provide the kind of extended philosophical discussion of character development which we find in Aristotle's notion of virtue in *Nicomachean Ethics* (Irwin 1985).[2]

Self-cultivation. Confucius responds to questions from a disciple named Zigong about the exemplary person by associating such spiritual and character development with the analogy of carving a fine piece of jade through a love of the proprieties (*li*) that govern our relationships (1.13, 9.13). There is no single word in the *Analects* for self-cultivation; but as a concept Confucius teaches, its imprint is present in the earliest stratum of his teachings. Self-cultivation is not simply learning from books; it includes character development, enhancement of talents (e.g., archery, music, building, management, etc.) and obtaining cultural refinement (*wen*) (5.15). Cultivating oneself into an exemplary person is never merely reduced to one's moral actions or values. Yet, Confucius advocates a plural value system in which morality is not the only form of life important for becoming *ren* even if no one responds who is morally deficient can be so regarded. Confucius allows too that in self-cultivation, everyone makes mistakes, but what is to be avoided is to repeat a mistake or fail to reform after making one (9.25).

In thinking of the dedication and commitment needed for cultivating oneself, Confucius calls on his disciples to give their utmost (*zhong*, 3.19). Self-cultivation does not occur automatically; it requires sustained and vigorous effort (5.15). Being willing to learn from others is crucial to self-cultivation. Confucius says, "When walking with two other people, I will always find a teacher among them. I focus on those who are good and seek to emulate them, and those who are bad remind me what needs to be changed in myself" (7.22). Confucius thinks of all persons as he does himself. They too are in need of refinement, learning and education. Persons must make something out of themselves.

Others can help us refine ourselves and move toward the goal of being exemplary persons. If others are of exceptional character, we should stand shoulder to shoulder with them (4.17), but if they are not, we should not imitate them, but look inwardly and examine ourselves (4.17) and we should not befriend anyone who is not as good as we are (9.25).

Confucius recognizes that the Way (*Dao*) he recommends to persons requires strength and effort (6.12), and he admits that he too is on the path to growth and transformation, that he has no natural propensity simply to change for the better (7.20). In fact, he worries that he will not grow morally, he will fail to understand appropriateness (*yi*) or he will be unable to reform his poor conduct.

An essential component of self-cultivation is a love of learning (*haoxue*). As Confucius puts it, "Study as though you can't catch up to it, as though you fear to lose it" (8.17). Speaking of his own quest for cultivation he says, "There are in a town of ten households, bound to be people who are better than I am in doing their utmost (*zhong*) and in making good on their word, but there will be no one who can compare with me in the love of learning (*haoxue*)" (5.28).

The commitment needed for one to walk the way of self-cultivation explains Confucius's disappointment in some of his disciples: "Zai Wo was sleeping during the daytime. Kongzi said, 'Rotten wood cannot be carved, and a wall of dung cannot be plastered.' As for Zai Wo, what would be the use of reprimanding him?" (5.10). Self-cultivation is a lifelong task that may be compared not only to carving ourselves into a fine piece of jade but also to building up a mountain: "if I stop even one basketful of earth short of completion, then I have failed completely" (9.19).

Exemplary Persons and Sages. The ideal toward which humans are moving for Confucius is expressed in the term *junzi*. Following

Roger Ames and Henry Rosemont (1998), "exemplary person" is the translation I use for *junzi*. The exemplary person in the *Analects* is a quite different moral ideal than those advocated in many Western moral philosophies. The Confucian exemplary person is not portrayed as "perfect." There is no abstract flawlessness held up as the goal for persons to achieve by Confucius. In fact, as noted above, mistakes are made by exemplary persons. Neither is the exemplary person the same ideal as we find in the Western notion of saint, for whom moral duty overrides all other values so that the saint does not rest or pursue other ends if there is yet remaining good to do for others.[3]

In their discussion of the approbationary remarks Confucius makes about persons, Ames and Rosemont hold that there are several categories of persons represented in the *Analects*. To make their case, they give particular attention to these three types of persons: apprentice (*shi*), exemplary person (*junzi*), and sage (*shengren*). The goal toward which the *shi* is striving is to become a *junzi*. What the *shi* does, the *junzi* is. In the *Analects*, the *junzi* is described, not instructed or taught, presumably because he does not need instruction.

> He has traveled a goodly distance along the way, and lives a goodly number of roles. A benefactor too many, he is still a beneficiary of others like himself. While he is still capable of anger in the presence of inappropriateness and concomitant injustice, he is in his person tranquil. He knows many rituals and much music, and performs all of his functions not only with skill, but also with grace, dignity, and beauty, and he takes delight in the performance. He is still filial toward his parents and elders, but now takes all under *tian* as his dwelling.
>
> (Ames and Rosemont 1998: 62)

The heart of the authentic teachings of Confucius in the *Analects* residing largely in the first strata of the text contains a number of analects concerned with the exemplary person. Six of Book 4's analects specifically describe this kind of individual. They never abandon *ren*, not even for one day (4.5). They always do what is appropriate (*yi*) (4.10, 16), cherish moral excellence (*de*) (4.11). They are not driven by their desires (4.10). Exemplary persons take the high road and not the low one (14.23), and they feel ashamed if their high-sounding words are not fully reflected in their deeds (14.27). Indeed, exemplary persons cherish their excellence of character and self-cultivation over land or thought of gain. Exemplary persons take as much trouble discovering what is right as lesser men take to learn what will pay (4.16). Confucius says,

> Wealth and rank are what people want, but if they are the consequence of deviating from the Way (*Dao*), I would have no part in them. Poverty and disgrace are what people deplore, but if they are the consequence of staying on the way, I would not avoid them. Wherein do the exemplary persons who would abandon their *ren* warrant that name? Exemplary persons do not take leave of *ren* even for the space of a meal. (4.5)

Book 15 of the *Analects* preserves a collection of aphorisms from Confucius on the exemplary person (15.19, 20, 21, 22, 23). The positions taken seem consistent with those we find in Book 4. Exemplary persons are the sort of individuals who are distressed by their own deficiencies, not by the failure of others to praise them (15.19). They cannot stand the thought of not distinguishing themselves in virtue and excellence (15.20). They make demands on themselves, whereas petty persons make demands on others (15.21). They are self-possessed, calm and not contentious (15.22). They promote others on merit, not on words (15.23).

In his instructions to his disciples, Confucius tells Zixia to seek to be a scholar–advisor (*ru*) for an exemplary person, not for a petty one (6.13). He approved of Shiyu's estimation of Qu Boyu, noting that Qu showed himself an exemplary person because when the way of Heaven was being followed in a state, he gave his service, but when it was not, he left government (15.7). And in an exchange with Ji Kangzi, Confucius makes clear why such a choice of association is possible. The ruler who is an exemplary person can affect the entire kingdom with appropriateness and moral excellence, like the wind that blows over the grass (12.19).

Confucius sets up no abstract upward limit for human development. Instead, he offers specific human examples of sages of the past: Yao, Wu, Wen and Shun. He looks back to them, but also forward to the novelty and creativity embodied in present and future persons. Persons such as Yao and Shun were actually theomorphized, just as some later follower did for Confucius in the last strata of the *Analects* text: "Confucius is the sun and moon which no one can climb beyond." (19.24) But these forms of valorization do not hold up these exemplars as perfect or flawless; neither do they mean that the most creative persons are those of the past. There is always the forward-looking vision in Confucian ethics.

Mohist Moral Philosophy (c.470–391 BCE)

While a study of Mozi's ethics and moral philosophy is of paramount importance to an understanding of Chinese philosophy, the dependence of his views on his ontological positions, especially as these are set out in books 8–37 and 46–9 of the work entitled *Mozi*, is sometimes underappreciated.[4]

An understanding of Mozi's views on reality begins with what he has to say about *tian*. In classical Chinese, the word *tian* has many uses. When in the compound "heaven and earth" (*tian di*), it is used for "reality" or "the totality of existing things." When occurring by itself, Heaven, it is most often used as "sky," or "nature," or as a nominative for some quasi-personal presence (i.e., more or less as a numinal person). This latter use predominates in Mozi's ontology and informs his moral philosophy.

In the *Mozi*, Heaven is often described as though it is an "agent" capable of acting with intentions (*yi*, *zhi*) and desires (*yu*) (e.g., Chapters 26–8). Heaven is praised as impartial, generous, wise, just and caring. It cares for humans and benefits the worthy by providing resources and blessings. Heaven has a *dao* that orders all things, including its relations with humanity. If we were to use a philosophical concept from the West, we could say that Heaven is "providential." By exercising its will as a decree or "mandate" (*ming*), it influences history, causing the rise and fall of rulers and states. Mozi insisted that Heaven—like gods, ghosts and ancestors—was a supreme power exhibiting the sort of behavior associated with that of a person and it was thought to be capable of rewarding and punishing behavior based on its own ultimate ethical standard (Graham 1989: 17, 49).

Holding such a position is one of the reasons Mozi is committed to a rejection of the philosophical position that the happenings in the course of reality's process are predestined or fated to take the form they do. Mozi's arguments gathered in the "Against Fate" chapters (35–7) of his text are an attack on the truthfulness of the claim that reality is fated (*ming*). As shown in Chapter II of our study, a principal argument used by Mozi against the position that reality is fated is a pragmatic one. Basically he says that if we accept the position that life is fated it would mean that one's position, health, wealth, success, longevity and the like are already determined and are not consequences of human effort or choices in life. If this were true, there would be no point in striving to be moral or working diligently to succeed in life. Mozi said:

> Nowadays, the world's officers and gentlemen, if they genuinely wish in their hearts to seek to promote the world's benefits and eliminate harms, then quite properly words like those which claim the existence of Fate (*ming*) cannot but be resolutely rejected.
>
> (*Mozi*, Johnston 2010: 37.10)

Mozi thinks a world in which the morally good suffer misfortune, the evil prosper, or rewards and punishments are dispensed for outcomes not in the control of persons to be unfair, full of harm and devoid of actions having any moral warrant. Such a world would not be purposive or meaningful, and humans could not rely on a connection between their actions and what they deserve. So, Mozi is driven to take his ontological position that the nature of reality and its processes cannot be determined in advance largely because of his views on moral philosophy.

All this is not to say that Mozi has no concept of what we might call "natural evil," that is, evils that are not connected to one's conduct or character. Chris Fraser makes use of a famous example from Mozi's life to show that even a worthy person may experience undesirable events:

> Master Mo Zi was sick. Die Bi approached and questioned him, saying: "Sir, you take ghosts and spirits to be all-seeing, to be able to bring about ill-fortune and good fortune, to reward those who do good and to punish those who do bad. Now you, sir, are a sage, so how is it that you are sick? Does it mean that there is in your words what is not good, or [is it because] ghosts and spirits do not see and know all?" Master Mo Zi replied: "Although I am caused to be sick, how does this mean that my words are all of a sudden not good or that ghosts and spirits are, all of a sudden, not all-seeing? There are many ways in which people can become sick. They can suffer from cold or heat. They can suffer from strain or fatigue. If there are a

hundred gates and only one is shut, then how, all of a sudden, can a robber not enter?" (*Mozi*, Johnston 2010: 48.20)

If we assume that Mozi was living the life of a sage and committed to goodness, the immediate question that arises is why, then, should Heaven (through the means of ghosts and spirits) send sickness his way, or allow him to become ill? Mozi takes the position that his illness does not disprove his position that ghosts and spirits enforce morality, rewarding the good and punishing the evil. He says that his sickness might be caused by some other factor that is intelligible (e.g., food, drink, imbalance of *yin* or *yang*, etc.), whether it is manageable or not, but he does not think that such situations are evidence for the claim that Heaven's operations are fated.

One could still inquire why ghosts and spirits do not intervene to prevent adversities, such as sickness or crimes against persons, protecting the good person from illness or wrongdoing. Chris Fraser holds that if we analyse Mozi's positions on the activity of Heaven, we will not find any example of his advocacy of *pre-emptive intervention*. According to Fraser, Mozi's position is the following:

> If we follow Heaven's way (*dao*), ghosts and spirits will help our endeavors to be a success. If we turn toward evil, Heaven will send calamities. However, in both cases we see that Heaven *reacts* to human action, but does not proactively or pre-emptively intervene to prevent distress caused by the operation of natural processes (i.e., *qi*, *yin/yang* and the five phases). In short, Heaven does not bring us benefits to *encourage* us to be good, but to *reward* us for being good. "Similarly, in the Mohist interpretation of history, Heaven does not intervene to prevent wicked tyrants from misgoverning their states and harming their people. Once they do so, however, it responds by punishing them and supporting challengers who depose them." (Fraser 2014: 16)

The disciples who collected the sayings of Master Mo into the *Mozi* summarize the teachings of their school as a set of ten doctrines and much of Mohist moral philosophy can be found in these ideas. The doctrines begin with the idea of "Elevating the Worthy" (*shang xian*). In this sense, the Mohists, like the Confucians, believe in a meritocracy. Leadership should depend on a person's competence and virtue without regard for the person's social status or family origin. So, living a virtuous life was a basic step to success and advancement. According to the doctrine of "Exalting Unity" (*shang tong*), the purpose of government is to achieve a stable social and economic order by spreading a unified conception of moral appropriateness (*yi*). Here we see that for the Mohists government's purpose is not to provide the greatest amount of liberty or freedom to its citizens. Nor should all the citizens be allowed to follow their own way of morality. The Mohists believe that the function of government is to create an ethos in which human beings can flourish and achieve their greatest potential. Mohists do not hesitate to recommend giving government the power to enforce a particular moral understanding of social life. With respect to the relationship of morality and law, the Mohists sought a society in which what was illegal was also immoral and what was legally permitted was also morally so.

Morality and Law	
Moral and Legal	Immoral and Illegal
Illegal but Moral	Legal but Immoral

Both morality and law seek to guide and even control human conduct. One way of thinking about the relationship between morality and law is by means of the table above. In Western civil libertarian societies, where the approach is to maximize one's free choice of how to live by minimizing the number of laws controlling conduct, actions falling in all four of the categories above can be found. Some Western models such as John Calvin's Geneva, various forms of Islamic caliphate rule and even proponents of the government's right to enforce a moral code such as Lord Patrick Delvin (1965), have been associated with the reduction of the relationship of law and morality to the top two categories only. Although we probably lack sufficient textual and historical material to know for sure, there is much in the *Mozi* text that suggests Mohists might also have supported such a limitation.

The Mohists use the concept of "Heaven's intention" (*tian zhi*) to underwrite their moral philosophy. They conceive of Heaven as a moral agent. Heaven's intentions represent an objective standard of what is morally right. Accordingly, they also argue that Heaven rewards those who obey its will and punishes those who defy it. Although we may find it odd in a philosophical text for the author to rely on religious belief, the Mohist doctrine of "Elucidating Ghosts" (*ming gui*) takes the position that social order can be maintained by encouraging belief in ghosts and spirits who reward the good and punish the evil.

Mozi holds that a coherent social order can rest only on a single, universal and objective morality. If a pluralism of moral values is allowed to exist in a culture, disorder and conflict will be the result. In itself, this is a crucial philosophical position, embracing moral universals and rejecting moral relativism. Mozi prizes order, stability and the transmission of a unified moral system over diverse expression of value choices among the populous. Mozi understands his preeminent philosophical task to be the defense of a true morality and the identification of the source from which this universal moral worldview originates.

While Confucians advocate a received traditional code of appropriate behavior (*li*) that was transmitted from one generation to another by exemplary persons, Mozi's view of the origin of morality is different. He even criticizes the Confucian position, accusing it of resting morality on an elitist consensus (i.e., the behavior of *junzi*). He thinks such a position is both unconvincing and flawed because it does not distinguish mere custom from true morality.

Mozi makes a sharp distinction between custom and morality. He holds that conformity to traditional customs (i.e., the Confucian *li* 禮) associated with exemplary persons does not ensure that their conduct is actually *morally* right. It proves only that this is the way the elite live. For Mozi, societies must be built upon actual, demonstrable moral truth that has always been true and will always be so. The fact that people *think* something is morally right to do does not make it so. Likewise, simply noticing the diversity in moral views does not mean that there is no universally true and correct morality. It could simply mean that some people are wrong (Fraser 2011: 142).

> Now the arguments of those who adhere to elaborate funerals and prolonged mourning say: "If elaborate funerals and prolonged mourning are really not the way of the sage kings, how do you

account for the fact that the *junzi* of the central kingdom practice them and do not stop them, implement them and do not abandon them?" Master Mozi said: "This is what is called '[considering] one's habits convenient and one's customs righteous (*yi*)'. Formerly, to the east of Yue, there was the country of the Kaimu. When a first son was born, they cut him up and ate him. They called this 'fitting for the younger brother'. When the paternal grandfather died, they carried the maternal grandmother away and abandoned her, saying: 'We cannot live with a ghost's wife'. If above, these things are taken to be government practice and, below, they are taken to be customs, and are carried out and not stopped, implemented and not discarded, then are they the way of true humaneness (*ren*) and appropriateness (*yi*)? This is what is called '[considering] one's habits convenient and one's customs as righteous (*yi*)'." (*Mozi*, Johnston 2010: 25.14)

Clearly the Mohists understand the problem known in philosophy as cultural relativity. They take the view that even if a practice is a matter of custom in a culture, it is not necessarily morally right. They look instead for objective moral standards which they called models, or *fa* (法).

Mozi makes use of the notion "*fa*" as a way of talking about the pattern, order and structure Heaven gives to reality. He holds that Heaven moves intentionally. As it does so, it follows models (*fa*) in a way analogous to how one who steers a ship makes use of a compass or a carpenter employs a square, plumb line or level (*Mozi*, Johnston 2010: 4.1 and 27.10). The instructions of Heaven given to worthy persons are examples of these models (*fa*) for living, but the behavior of exemplary persons in a culture is not sufficient, in itself, to be identified with universal true morality. It may be nothing more than custom. For Mozi, Confucius's failure to make this distinction is what led him astray. Indeed, Confucius's valorization of the Zhou dynasty's *li* was simply an elevation of one culture's customs over that of other communities. Mozi considers this to be a move lacking philosophical foundation and insists morality must rest on a true, objective and universal foundation from Heaven.

Not only does Mozi differ from Confucius on the foundation of morality in a metaethical sense, he also advocates an alternative normative ethics. He differs most sharply with the Confucians on the idea that caring for others should be scaled or graded based on who the other persons are and what is their relationship to us, recommending instead a concept he calls "inclusive concern" (*jian ai* 兼爱). We have seen that the Five Relationships play a strategic role in Confucianism and that we have different moral duties and are responsible for different actions based on what relationship we have with a person. In fact, the Confucian relational ethic is rooted in the cultivation of particular attachments. When thinking about what to do, I must first consider who is the other person involved and what is my relationship to him.[5]

The doctrine of "inclusive concern" (*jian ai*) is quite different from the Confucian reliance on the Five Relationships as conduct guides.[6] Mozi takes the position that in order to achieve social order all people must be concerned for each other, showing care for everyone. Practically speaking, this teaching means that in our relationship with others we should seek mutual benefit and express mutual respect. Mozi argues that the lack of "inclusive concern" is the source of all the harm and injury in the world, while attributing the exact opposite position to the Confucians.

> If this is so, then how can we not examine from what this harm arises? Does it not arise though inclusive concern? Master Mozi said: "It arises through *lack* of inclusive concern. Nowadays, feudal lords know only to be concerned for their own states and not to be concerned with the states of others, so they have no qualms about mobilizing their own state to attack another. Nowadays, heads of houses know only to be concerned with their own houses and not be concerned with the houses of others, so they have no qualms about promoting their own house and usurping another's. Nowadays, individual people know only to be concerned with their own person and not to be concerned with the persons of others, so they have no qualms about promoting their own persons and injuring the persons of others … When the people of the world do not all show concern for each other, then the strong inevitably dominate the weak, the many inevitably plunder the few, the rich inevitably despise the poor, the noble inevitably scorn the lowly, and the cunning inevitably deceive the foolish. Within the world, in all cases, the reason why calamity, usurpation, resentment and hatred arise is because inclusive concern does not exist.
>
> (*Mozi*, Johnston 2010: 15.2, my changes).

Mozi argues that the ultimate will of Heaven is inclusive concern toward others and that all *fa* (moral norms) that express inclusive concern are consistent with Heaven's will and objectively and universally true. Moreover, the actions that represent inclusive concern will bring about desirable consequences for the greatest number of persons. In the language of Western moral philosophy this is called *utilitarianism*. In the long run, the consequences for the greatest number of people would be best if we were fair and just. Fairness and justice represent inclusive concern that is also the will of Heaven (Ivanhoe 2000: 15). But we cannot simply say that Mozi is either a utilitarian or that he believes universal morality comes exclusively from Heaven. In Western philosophy, these might be more easily separable lines of justification for moral norms, but in Mozi's thought they are intertwined and mutually supporting.

With respect to the moral guidelines for rulership, for example, Mozi holds that providing food, clothing, shelter, preventing war and not over-taxing the people will, in the long run, be in everyone's interest and thus these must be Heaven's norms (*fa*). Such actions are examples of inclusive concern, the will of Heaven. On the other hand, actions which benefit only a few or benefit a few at the cost of the many were condemned by Mozi as examples of moral wrongs. The "Moderation in Funerals" (*Jie Zang*) sections of the *Mozi* are devoted to showing that the filial obligation on the part of children to have elaborate funerals for their parents is a misplaced custom that contradicts true morality. Elaborate funerals are unprofitable for the persons involved and for the village too. Likewise, those sections in the *Mozi* that criticize aggressive war making stress that armaments and war represent wastes of human capital and lives; only defensive wars can be justified morally.

When Mozi teaches inclusive concern, he does not mean that in order to be morally appropriate we should have a feeling of emotional love or attachment to all persons; neither does he mean that morality requires self-sacrifice. He is not advocating that all persons love each other in such a way as to make everyone into a friend or even that one should love another in the same way that one loves himself. He is not calling on persons to deny their own interests or to sacrifice themselves for others. "By comparison, inclusive concern and exchange of mutual benefit are quite different from these things" (*Mozi*, Johnston 2010: 15.4).

What Mozi is calling inclusive concern is more like what Western moral philosophers today call "reciprocal altruism." That is, we help others because we want to be able to expect their help in return. The moral order (*fa*) of Heaven operates in such a way that our own interests include those of others. Mozi thinks that this process will work as follows.

> Now if I am to seek to promote the world's benefit and eliminate the world's harm, I shall choose "inclusive" as being right. As a result, [people] will use their acute hearing and keen sight to help each other see and hear; they will use their strong and powerful limbs to help each other in action; and they will use principles to encourage mutual instruction. As a result, those who are old, without wives and children, will have the means of support and nourishment through their old age, and those who are young and weak, or who are alone without a father or mother, will have the means of help and support while they grow into adulthood. (Ibid., 16.4)

> If, for a moment, we take as a basis what the former kings wrote, in the worlds of the *Da Ya* it is said: "No words are without response, no virtue is without reward. If you present me with a peach, I repay you with a plum." This, then is to say that those who are concerned for others must themselves receive concern, and those who hate others must themselves be hated. (Ibid., 16.13, my change)

We may wonder whether Confucius realizes the importance of extending the particularized concerns of the Five Relationships into the community at large. The answer is, of course he did. But he seems to believe that the spread of moral concern will arise in a different manner than Mozi's reciprocal altruism. He thinks it will result from formed habits of action. In practicing concern toward those within our Five Relationships, we will habitualize our hearts to carry over our actions to others. In being a filial son toward my father, I come to act filially toward other fathers as well. Once the root takes hold, the Way grows from it (*Analects* 1.2, 1.6). Mencius later defends the Confucian position by calling this the extension (*tui*) of the moral virtues we have learned from close relationships to people more generally as a kind of operative moral principle (1A: 7).[7]

Lao-Zhuang Views of Morality (c.350–139 BCE)

The *Daodejing* takes the position that when we try to make something happen in the world by our own reasoning, plans and contrivances, we inevitably make a mess of it. If we take our hands off of the course of our lives and move with the *Dao*, it will untangle all life's knots, blunt its sharp edges and soften its harsh glare (*DDJ*, 56a). For the philosophical masters in the Lao-Zhuang tradition, only when people abandon oneness with the *Dao* do they begin to make distinctions in morality, politics, aesthetics and religion. When humans speak of beauty and ugliness, courage and cowardice, good and evil, these are discriminations of our own making, they do not belong to the *Dao* itself. The *Daodejing* makes this point in the passage below by specifically mentioning several of the distinctions made in Confucian moral and social philosophy: humaneness (*ren*); appropriateness (*yi*); filial piety (*xiao*); and kindness (*ci*).

> When the great *Dao* is abandoned, humaneness (*ren*) and appropriate-
> ness (*yi*) appear.
> When wisdom and erudition arise, great hypocrisy arises.
> When the six relationships [between persons] are out of harmony, then
> you have filiality (*xiao*) and kindness (*ci*).
> When the state is in chaos, "loyal ministers" appear on the scene.
>
> (*DDJ*, 18)

Distinction making in morality is regarded as a kind of disease in Lao-Zhuang tradition. This "disease" is likewise condemned in the *Zhuangzi* (e.g., Watson 1968: 45–6, 68–9, 72 and 74). In Lao-Zhuang, it is not so much the lack of inclusive concern that is the source of all the world's moral evils as it is in Mohism, but rather the fighting and struggling over these human-made distinctions that causes strife and injury (*DDJ*, 18, 38). The solution, then, is not to begin this process at all, or to empty oneself of it by forgetting such distinctions and returning to unity with the *Dao*. Being empty is a way of talking about getting rid of the distinctions that tie us in knots and erupt in the desires that are the source of our all-human suffering, violence and immorality. Thieves arise from stealing. Stealing arises from the distinction that this thing is mine not yours. Once this distinction is made, greed emerges and drives a person to steal and become a thief.

If we empty ourselves of such distinctions in the very beginning, the whole degenerate process dissolves and we are free to be one with the *Dao* and live out of a sense of its presence and power. The resulting conduct is what Lao-Zhuang masters called by the moral concept, *de* 德 (ibid., chs 10, 21, 23, 28, 38, 41, 49, 51, 54, 55, 59, 60, 63, 65, 68, 79).

Just as we have seen with respect to the term *tian*, *de* also has multiple uses. In Chinese, it is used as "excellence," "virtue," "power" or "charismatic force." It is not a good idea to reduce the meaning of *de* to any one of these translations exclusively. So, in what follows, the term is left untranslated and this gives the interpreter a chance to place it in context and see the actual work it is doing in a passage.

> To act with no expectation of reward;
> To lead without lording over others;
> Such is mysterious *de* (*xuande*). (Ibid., 10b, 51b)

> Cultivate the *Dao* in your person, and the *de* you develop will be genuine.
> Cultivate the *Dao* in your family, and the family's *de* will be more than enough.
> Cultivate the *Dao* in your village, and the village's *de* will long endure.
> Cultivate the *Dao* in your state, and the state's *de* will be abundant.
> Cultivate the *Dao* throughout the world, and the world's *de* will be pervasive. (Ibid., 54b).

In the Lao-Zhuang project, emptying oneself of moral distinctions does not leave behind an amoral and certainly not an immoral agent. Although the person has set aside or emptied himself of human moral designations and does not view life and relationships through the lens they represent, he is now empowered by a presence *(Dao)* that results in the expression of great *de*.

De is not shown through effort, striving or training. It is exhibited with the sort of effortlessness for which Daoists use the concept *wu-wei* (無為, ibid., chs 2, 3, 10, 43, 47, 57, 63, 64). "The [persons who possess the] highest *de* do not strive for *de* and so they have it" (ibid., 38). These characters 無為 (*wu-wei*) were rendered into English by the previous generation of translators as "nonaction." Consequently, many interpreters understood *wu-wei* to mean that the *Daodejing* was recommending quiescence and inactivity as the way to practice the *Dao*. But the *Daodejing* says clearly that persons should be active.

Act, but as *wu-wei*.
Be active, but do not let your conduct be intentional and deliberative.

(Ibid., 63)

Wu-wei is a concept used for a type of conduct. We typically think that morality is concerned only with our actions. But upon reflection we notice it can also focus on our omissions (things we should have done but did not do). Both action and omission are types of conduct. *Wu-wei* is another kind of discriminator for conduct. It differs from action in being nondeliberative and nonintentional. It differs from omission in the doing of something. It is felt as natural and spontaneous conduct coming directly from the storehouse of *Dao* and its limitless *de* inside the person.

This emphasis on acting effortlessly, naturally and spontaneously may seem somewhat problematic for a person steeped in Western moral traditions. Characteristically, Western philosophers insist that in order to act morally we must think about what we are choosing to do and weigh out the consequences. But in Lao-Zhuang, moving naturally along with the *Dao* results in the highest moral efficacy (*de*). *Wu-wei* conduct is the way out of the tangles we have created for ourselves by the institutions, rules and distinctions that clutter our minds and generate tension in our life together. The morality of *wu-wei* conduct lies in the fact that it accords in the situation with an efficacy that can only be attributed to the *Dao* and not to the result of human wisdom, planning or contrivance. This is the meaning of the claim that the person who is moved by the *Dao* exhibits profound and mysterious *de*.

The *Daodejing* does not say that this efficacy ignores or has no connection with the standard virtues we use as distinctions in moral language. This is not the point of the text's thoroughgoing criticism of such discriminations. The text takes the view that following the demands and rules set up by convention as though they were ends in themselves will lead only to frustration and misery, whereas *wu-wei* conduct rooted in an experience with *Dao* will result in "gaining the world," and things will be in harmony. Everything becomes well ordered (ibid.: 3). Should barons and kings be able to express it (*de*), the myriad creatures will transform themselves (ibid., 37).

What seems clear philosophically is that the Lao-Zhuang teachers advocate a position on the origin of moral knowledge and the impetus of ethical behavior that is ultimately unassailable by reason. Any criticism we might make of the Lao-Zhuang position can be deflected simply by saying that the critic has no experience of being one with the *Dao* or of having received its power (*de*).

This Daoist response is related to the association of emptying oneself of moral distinctions with the feminine in Lao-Zhuang. The *Daodejing* makes an explicit analogical connection between emptiness and the female:

> Know the male but preserve the female
> And be a ravine for all the world.
> If you are ravine for all the world, constant *de* will never leave you.
>
> (Ibid., 28)

In Lao-Zhuang, femininity represents receptivity, probably because in sexual relations, the female receives. To the would-be follower of the *Dao*, the *Daodejing* asks:

> Opening and closing Heaven's gate,
> Can you play the part of the female?

When the text speaks of opening and closing Heaven's gate, it is referring to the entry into a state of alternate awareness, devoid of the commonplace distinctions we make habitually. If a person succeeds in playing the part of the female, he will receive an awareness of the *Dao* and the person will be enabled to enact boundless *de*.

> Hold on to the great image and the whole world will flock to you.
> Coming to you they will suffer no harm, be peaceful, secure and
>   prosperous. (Ibid., 35)

In the *Zhuangzi*, the essay in Chapters 8–10 devoted to an exposition of *Dao* and *de* reflects well the themes found in the *Daodejing*. The essay represents a clear break in the text often using the first person and employing illustrations of its points internally. One of the most important literary evidences used by the writer is the specific compound *daode*. The most crucial difference between the *daode* essay and the *Daodejing* is that the essay makes no mention of the concept *wu-wei*. Instead, the stress is on returning to naturalness and embracing one's "inborn nature" (*xingming*).[8] The writer of the *daode* essay says, "My definition of expertness has nothing to do with humaneness (*ren*) and appropriateness; it means being expert in regard to your *de* that is all. My definition of expertness has nothing to do with humaneness or appropriateness; it means following the true form of your inborn nature, that is all." (*Zhuangzi* 8; Watson 1968: 103)

There is an argument throughout the *daode* essay that human society has been on a steady decline from the distant past when persons ceased following the *Dao* and expressing its *de*. The author argues that holding elite Confucian values, such as humaneness and appropriateness, and the making of other moral distinctions, is actually the source of confusion, unlawfulness and disorder. The writer of the essay claims that it was not until the *Dao* and its *de* were cast aside that the Confucian emphasis on humaneness and appropriateness entered, and the distinctions made by men created disorder and disharmony (ibid., 101, 105, 106). This claim is parallel to that made in *Daodejing* 18.

The author also argues that the use of rules and rituals of conduct (*li*) as in Confucianism is not the proper means by which one can become moral and enjoy a fulfilling life, but naturalness and spontaneity born of unity with the *Dao* resident in one's inner nature are the true means for such an achievement.

> If we must use cords and knots, glue and lacquer to make something firm, this means violating its natural virtue. So the crouchings and bendings of *li* [i.e., proprieties] and music, the smiles and beaming looks of humaneness and appropriateness, which are intended to comfort the hearts of the world, in fact destroy their naturalness.
>
> (Ibid., 100)

In *Zhuangzi* Chapter 9, the author makes the point that the domestication of horses destroys their nature, and "as far as inborn nature is concerned, the clay and the wood surely have no wish to be subjected to compass, curve and plumb line" (ibid., 104–5). The author says Confucians huff and puff after humaneness and stand on their tiptoes to reach appropriateness, but if the *Dao* had not been cast aside, no one would have ever even called for these values. Everyone would have lived by "inborn nature" and expressed true *de* (ibid., 105).

Elsewhere in the *Zhuangzi* we see an interest in trying to describe what it is like for one to act in *wu-wei*. These passages may certainly be connected in sentiment and philosophical function to the remarks we have noted about *wu-wei* in the *Daodejing*. The "perfected person's" (*zhenren*) *de* comes from oneness with the *Dao*, so that he flows in life spontaneously and effortlessly, without thought. *Wu-wei* conduct exhibits the efficacy of action and possesses the emotional feel that can only be associated with examples; it cannot be explained in language. Moving in *wu-wei* is like the ferryman in the gulf of Shangshen who handles his boat with commensurate skill (ibid., 200), the amazing hunchback cicada catching man (ibid., 19, 199), Bohun Wuren's skill in archery (ibid., 230–1), Qing who makes bell stands that seem to be the work of the spirits (ibid., 205–6) and Chui the artist who can draw free-hand as true as a compass or T-square (ibid., 206). All of these stories are examples of persons who seem to be able to perform in highly skilled and efficacious ways without deliberation and who report feelings of naturalness, effortless and spontaneity as they act. These examples are presented as analogues for what it is to *wu-wei* and express moral excellence (*de*).

Mencius (c.372–289 BCE): Morality as Cultivated Human Nature

The *Mengzi* records Mencius's position that human persons are distinct from other sentient creatures in having four propensities (*siduan*) that dispose them to view reality and human persons through what can be called a moral lens. Another way of saying this is that humans "moral" (as a verb) naturally in the same ways that a kernel of corn yields corn and not tomatoes. According to Mencius, humans do not have to learn to feel compassion toward other sentient beings or be disposed to act morally. Of course, Mencius realizes all humans must learn specific human or cultural moralities, but he argues that they are enabled and inclined to do so because of incipient drives in their natural endowment. A crucial passage that sets out this understanding follows:

> My reason for saying that no man is devoid of a heart-mind (*xin*) sensitive to the suffering of others is this. Suppose a man were, suddenly,

to see a young child on the verge of falling into a well. He would certainly be moved with compassionate apprehension, not because he wanted to get in the good graces of the parents, nor because he wished to win the praise of his fellow villagers or friends, nor even because he disliked the cry of the child. From this it can be seen that whomever's heart-mind is devoid of compassion is not human, whomever's heart-mind is devoid of shame is not human, whomever's heart-mind is devoid of courtesy and modesty is not human, and whomever's heart-mind is devoid of moral discretion is not human. The heart-mind's compassion is the seed of humaneness; the heart-mind's shame, of dutifulness; the heart-mind's courtesy and modesty, of observance of propriety; the heart-mind's moral discretion, of wisdom. Humans have these four seeds (*duan*) just as they have four limbs. For a person possessing these four seeds to deny his own potentialities is for him to cripple himself; ... If a man is able to develop all of these four seeds, it will be like a fire starting up or a spring bubbling up. When these are fully developed, he can tend the whole realm within the Four Seas, but if he fails to cultivate them, he will not be able even to serve his parents. (*Mencius* 6A10, my translation)

In this passage, Mencius is making the difference between his position and that of Mozi very clear. He holds that all humans have inborn moral endowments, just as assuredly as we are born with four limbs. His point about the child on the verge of the well is that these endowments will naturally incline us toward compassionate action. The cultivation of these seeds enables a person to increase in humaneness just as a fire continually builds or a spring that has begun to vent will flow ever more strongly (6A6). Mencius believes a person can, by virtue of cultivating his inborn moral endowments, find a special kind of energy that he calls "flood-like energy" (*haoran zhi qi*) that brings joy over his decisions and power to perform virtue. That is, a person becomes a lover of the good and the right as a result of moral self-cultivation.

Mencius takes the interesting position that for the cultivated person doing what is right pleases the heart-mind in the same way that succulent meat pleases the palate (6A7). He likens the morally accomplished individual to a connoisseur of fine food or music. The significance of this way of arguing by analogy for moral philosophy is that Mencius is indicating his position that the moral cultivation of such a person will so refine his judgment that he can rule the entire realm humanely like Yao or Shun, the sage-kings of the past, and he will love doing so. Self-centered actions such as greed, dishonesty or corruption fall away because they no longer hold any attraction. What one desires will be directed toward the good. On the other hand, if we try to interact with our world without the benefit of having cultivated our incipient moral endowments, we will wander around lost and puzzled or even become evil and wicked. Mencius says:

> For a man to give full realization to his heart-mind is for him to understand his own nature, and a man who knows his own nature will know Heaven. By retaining his heart and nurturing his nature, he is serving Heaven. (7A1, Lau 2003: 182)

> There are cases where one person is twice, five times or countless times better than another person, but this is only because there are people who fail to make the best of their native endowment.
>
> (7A6, ibid., 163)

In Western philosophy since the early modern period (*c.*eighteenth century), philosophers have taken the view that the human mind at birth is a blank slate and that experience furnishes it with ideas and concepts as the senses provide it with information. John Locke (1632–1704) is one philosopher associated with this position. Under this theory, moral dispositions and beliefs derive from one's acculturation and socialization. When extended to moral philosophy, this position leads to the view that morality is a human invention. However, recently, philosophy and evolutionary science have moved in tandem toward a coherent assault on the blank slate theory and more toward an appreciation of certain natural and hereditable endowments that may be similar to what Mencius pointed to in the 300s BCE. For example, a fruitful area of comparison between Mencius's position about natural moral endowment and the position of Steven Pinker that there is a language instinct is worth pursuing (Pinker 1994). Moreover, a substantial amount of research in moral ethology done by Frans De Waal and others invites us to connect Mencius's position with the findings of evolutionary ethics and the hereditary transmission of a number of important moral dispositions and behaviors (e.g., cooperation, reciprocity, compassion and others).[9]

Nevertheless, when reading Mencius, we cannot forget what we have learned about early Chinese ontology. In Mencius, there is no object that is a self or soul, such as we find in Western philosophy. The fact that Mencius chooses the process metaphors of agriculture to describe the way in which the nature of the heart-mind thinks morally (i.e., moral seeds that grow and develop an individual into a full-blown moral person) reveals that he was being consistent with the ontology of the early Chinese worldview in which he was steeped. The Chinese word for *nature* (*xing* 性) is related to a word that means "to be born" or "to live/grow" (*sheng*). So to speak of the nature of a thing can refer to the defining characteristics of a thing as these will develop over the course of time, if given a normal, healthy environment. Mencius is using the term "human nature" in this sense. Accordingly, the Chinese view of human nature with which Mencius is working may be summarized in this way: humans are in the process of "selfing," but as they do so, they make use of preloaded propensities that lie behind the complex and dynamic conduct that comes to define them as selves.

Of course, we actually have no problem accepting this idea of developmentalism with respect to the body. We realize that it is endowed with incipient messaging by which it grows, changes and takes shape through a process that is inborn. Mencius's point is that we "person" as well as "body." But here we are speaking of verbs, not exclusively of nouns. To the extent these concepts function as nouns (the body, the self), they are naming an ongoing process not a fixed, immutable object.

About these views, Dennis Arjo writes, "Mencius presents a sophisticated and plausible moral psychology that unites our basic psychological endowment with our moral nature. Since he argues that all humans have these hearts, Mencius is able to equate their development into moral virtues with proper human development" (Arjo 2011: 457). In fact, Mencius identifies four cardinal Confucian moral virtues, associating each with one of the incipient seeds with which humans are naturally endowed. These virtues represent the blossoming of the seeds:

- humaneness eventuates from the seed of compassion,
- dutifulness comes from an inner sense of shame,
- proper observance of the proprieties (*li*) that guide relationships is rooted in the seed of courtesy and modesty, and

- the virtue of wisdom derives from the seed of practical moral discretion.

However, even inborn moral endowments cannot develop into virtues without cultivation. Mencius laments that he had heard some people say they were unable to actualize one or more of the virtues. He holds that such persons are "destroying themselves" (4A10). In one case, Mencius and King Xuan of Qi engage in a dialogue about the king's having spared an oxen being led to slaughter for use in a ritual. The king says, "I cannot bear its frightened appearance." Mencius tells the king that this feeling is the kind he should act upon in order to be a great monarch. The king replies that he did not understand the usefulness of his feelings until Mencius explained it to him. Mencius had, in effect, helped the king reflect on and appreciate the function of his innate moral sensibilities (Van Norden 2011: 93). As the dialogue progresses, Mencius tries to help the king understand that while the king feels it is right to show compassion to the ox, he is not showing the same compassion to his people who are suffering from high taxes and wars (1A7).

One way of accessing Mencius's ideas on morality is to notice how they are embedded in his responses to Mozi, who is a principal target of several philosophical assaults in the *Mengzi*. For example, Mozi advocates "inclusive concern" calling for persons to treat all others alike morally without any partiality. Mozi thinks impartial concern is a realistic moral norm because it has nothing to do with emotional attachment for others. It consists of treating everyone without favoritism in order to produce the best consequences for all concerned. In his response, Mencius is not so much bothered by the universality of Mozi's ethical system, as by Mozi's aligning morality with the beneficial consequences or profit of an action and his association of such utility with the establishment of the norms (*fa*) of inclusive concern.

Mencius argues that judging what is moral to do based on the concept of benefit means losing sight of the nature of morality itself. He holds that doing what is the morally right thing may not benefit us or be profitable to the greatest number, but it might be acting according to our natural, inborn moral endowments. Mencius observes:

> Life is something I desire; appropriateness is also something I desire.
> If I cannot have both, I will forsake life and select appropriateness.

... It is not the case that only the worthy person has this heart-mind (*xin*). All humans have it. The worthy person simply never loses it. A basket of food and a bowl of soup, if one gets them then one will live; if one does not get them then one will die. But if they are given with contempt, then even a homeless person will not accept them. If they are trampled upon, then even a beggar will not take them.

(*Mencius* 6A10, Van Norden 2011: 89)

The moral self in Mencius's philosophy is described by means of an agricultural analogy, as we have seen. There is much about a seed that grows naturally but its health and development can be enhanced by cultivation and care. Likewise, humans grow morally in a similar fashion and just as growth of a crop is gradual, development of a person into a humane (*ren*) being is likewise so.[10]

It is very important that we understand Mencius's position. His position cannot be falsified by the simple fact of human wrongdoing. He does not mean that humans are innately programmed to be moral; nor that they will automatically grow into morally good beings. Here the comparison between Mencius's position and the irresistibility of a kernel producing corn breaks down. He means that human nature is predisposed or inclined by means of inborn tendencies to act morally, but not that morality is unavoidable.

Mencius insists not only on the gradual nature of self-cultivation and the effort required to achieve it but also on the importance of a certain kind of environment as necessary to produce the morally mature person. Circumstance can affect us, just as our natural endowments may do so. Evil and violent times can retard the youth, just as drought can harm the crops (6A7; 6A9). The great and luxuriant trees of Ox Mountain are beautiful, but if constantly lopped by axes, we cannot be surprised if the mountain appears bald and ugly. The same is true of a person who repeatedly cuts down the sprouts of his moral intuitions and follows a way of immorality (6A8). Such a one will appear evil. The environment in which one lives, the persons whom one befriends or the net result of habitual activity may destroy the evidences of the natural endowment of Heaven.

Still, Mencius says that water naturally flows downhill, if dikes and dams do not restrict it. By analogy, human beings tend toward the good, just as water flows downhill (6A2). So, against Mozi, Mencius argues that moral self-development is not rooted in our assessment of the consequences of behavior, but in human nature itself and the sensibilities that, if heeded, lead us to the virtues.

Xunzi (310–220 BCE):
On the Carving and Polishing of the Human Being

By the time Xunzi matured into a position as the leader of the Jixia Academy in the third century BCE, the situation in China was grave indeed, much worse than in Mencius's day. The chaos, violence and political corruption of Xunzi's time influenced his thinking and interpretation of Confucius's teachings. In short, the context made him feel that it was obvious that Mencius was wrong about the moral structure of human nature. Unlike Mencius, Xunzi believes that human nature is disposed to self-interest and that, left alone without moral guidance and the restrictions of law, self-interest will degenerate into selfishness and breed disorder and chaos. Goodness will not grow from within like corn stalks from kernels, because human inclinations are not the four propensities Mencius identified, but desires for beautiful sights and sounds, comfort and power. Unless controlled, these and other desires become violence, wilful violation of others, and destruction. Xunzi says,

> People's nature is bad. Their goodness is a matter of deliberate effort. Now people's nature is such that they are born with a fondness for profit. If they follow along with this, then struggle and contention will arise, and yielding and deference will perish therein. They are born with feelings of hate and dislike. If they follow along with these, then cruelty and villainy will arise, and loyalty and trustworthiness will perish therein. They are born with desires of the eyes and ears, a fondness for beautiful sights and sounds. If they follow along with these, then lasciviousness and chaos will arise, and proprieties of conduct (*li* 禮) and the standards of appropriateness, proper form and good order, will perish therein. Thus, if people follow along with their inborn nature and dispositions, they are sure to come to struggle and contention, turn to disrupting social divisions and disorder, and end up in violence.
>
> (*Xunzi*; Hutton 2001: 284, my changes)

Given his position on human nature, we can understand why Xunzi holds that persons must be transformed by the influence of teachers and models and follow especially the guidance of morality and ritual proprieties of human conduct (*li*) handed down to each generation. Individuals require substantial external control to become fully moral and humane (*ren*). In the development of his moral philosophy, Xunzi makes use of craft analogies: woodworking, jade carving, home construction and not the agricultural metaphors used by Mencius. He thinks of human nature as crooked wood that requires the steaming and straightening of a frame in order to be good. He also compares human nature to blunt metal that requires honing and grinding in order to become sharp, as well as to raw jade that requires cutting and polishing in order to become something of worth.

> A warped piece of wood must wait until it has been laid against the straightening board, steamed, and forced into shape before it can become straight; a piece of blunt metal must wait until it has been whetted on a grindstone before it can become sharp. Similarly, since man's nature is evil, it must wait for the instructions of a teacher before it can become upright, and for the guidance of the proprieties of conduct (*li*) before it can become orderly. If men have no teachers to instruct them, they will be inclined towards evil and not upright; and if they have no proprieties of conduct to guide them, they will be perverse and violent and lack order. In ancient times the sage kings realized that man's nature is evil, and that therefore he inclines toward evil and violence and is not upright or orderly. Accordingly they created proprieties of conduct and laid down certain regulations in order to reform man's emotional nature and make it upright.
>
> (Ibid., 277–8, my changes)

A fundamental question in moral philosophy which goes beyond that of human nature concerns just what is the origin of morality as a form of life itself. In the context of classical Chinese philosophy this was understood as the problem of the origin of the proprieties of conduct (*li*) governing human interactions. Xunzi addresses this problem directly:

> From what did *li* arise? I say: Humans are born having desires. When they have desires but do not get the objects of their desires, then they

cannot but seek some means of satisfaction. If there is no measure or limit to their seeking, then they cannot help but struggle with each other. If they struggle with each other then there will be chaos, and if there is chaos then they will be impoverished. The former kings hated such chaos, and so they established rules and the standards of appropriateness in order to allot things to people, to nurture their desires, and to satisfy their seeking. They caused desires never to exhaust material goods, and material goods never to be depleted by desires, so that the two support each other and prosper. This is how the proprieties of conduct (*li*) arose. (Ibid., 265, my changes)

If all matters pertaining to temperament, will, and understanding proceed according to proprieties of conduct, they will be ordered and successful; if not they will be perverse and violent or slovenly and rude. If matters pertaining to food and drink, dress, domicile, and living habits proceed according to *li*, they will be harmonious and well regulated; if not they will end in missteps, excesses, and sickness. If matters pertaining to deportment, attitude, manner of movement, and walk proceed according to ritual, they will be refined; if not they will be arrogant and uncouth, common and countrified. Therefore a man without *li* cannot live; an undertaking without the proprieties of conduct cannot come to completion; a state without *li* cannot attain peace.

(*Hsun Tzu*; Watson 1963: 424–5, my changes)

Xunzi believes that if Mencius were correct and human nature were such as to move persons toward the good like water flowing downhill, there would be no necessity for the emergence of morality or the proprieties of conduct.

If human nature is bad, then one simply must side with the sage kings and honor the proprieties of conduct (*li*) and appropriateness (*yi* 義). Thus, the press frame originated because of crooked wood. The ink-line arose because of things that are not straight. Lords and superiors were established and *li* and *yi* were made clear because of the fact that human nature is bad. Looking at it in this way, it is clear that people's nature is bad, and that their goodness is a matter of deliberate effort.

(Ibid., 253, my changes)

There seems to be a crucial difference between Xunzi and Mencius to be noted here. For Mencius, the seeds of morality are inborn. While we have to cultivate them, nevertheless the universe does imprint and embed them in human nature. But for Xunzi, the proprieties of conduct are created by humans, and we might have different ones from those we now live by. The moral distinctions might also change over time.

Nevertheless, much of what Mencius says does not contradict Xunzi's view of the proprieties (*li*); but if pushed far enough philosophically, it seems he would be forced to maintain that there is a limit to the extent to which morality can change and it is established by the inherent moral "seeds" in all persons. But all this depends on what view we take of Mencius's position on the question from where the seeds of human nature come. Are they endowments of Heaven as some have interpreted him to believe or perhaps they become part of human nature only after a long history of action and decision in the development of the human species much as a contemporary evolutionary ethicist might claim, in which case his position may be compatible with that of Xunzi.

Xunzi certainly does not believe that Heaven gives us a nature that is disposed to goodness and compassion, or even impartial care (Mozi's *jian ai*). In Chapter 17 of the *Xunzi*, he makes the point that Heaven does not care about human behavior at all or how the course of things affects humans. Heaven cannot be appeased or persuaded to bring humans good fortune. If there is good fortune for humans, they make it happen through responsible government and well-ordered society. Neither does Heaven make people poor or bring calamities. Heaven has no will and no mind, and thus does not act to bring judgment or reward, quite to the contrary of what Mozi had said.

> If you strengthen agriculture and textile production and moderate expenditures, then Heaven cannot make you poor. If your means of nurture are prepared and your actions are timely, then Heaven cannot make you ill. If you cultivate the Way and do not deviate from it, then Heaven cannot ruin you. … If agriculture and textile production are neglected and expenditures are extravagant, then Heaven cannot make you wealthy. If your means of nurture are sparse and your actions are infrequent, then Heaven cannot make you sound in body.
>
> (*Xunzi*, Hutton 2014)

Xunzi's ultimate goal is that we should cease fearing a Heaven that cannot act because it lacks a mind and will. He warns that it is human irresponsibility that should really be feared. The enemies of humankind are villagers who fail to make provision for dikes to withstand floods and homes and persons are lost, or farmers who fail to weed their crops and the harvest is slight, or a corrupt government takes more than is appropriate. No one is to blame but humans. Xunzi has no doubt that the proprieties of conduct (e.g., moral discriminations of right and wrong, etc.) were established by the sage-kings to prevent such calamities. He is a humanist and he believes that human beings invented morality, they did not discover it within or have it disclosed to them by Heaven (Goldin 2005: 126). If the sage-kings had not invented these proprieties, there would have been no civilization and no order.

Accordingly, Xunzi's view is that the sage-kings were moral experts of a sort. In fact, we should adopt the moral practice and advice that they offer even when, perhaps especially when, we cannot appreciate for ourselves the considerations supporting it (Tiwald 2012: 275). Several fundamental moral issues arise for anyone taking such a view. One of the most significant is the moral difference that exists when one does something based on following another's authority and when one does it for oneself or on one's own knowledge. In terms of its implications for one's character, should we make the same appraisal of one who acts rightly because he follows the example or instruction of an authority, as we do of one who acts rightly as a result of his own judgment or desire?

Justin Tiwald argues that Xunzi distinguishes the moral expert as model (*you fa*) from the expert as teacher (*you shi*). Xunzi thinks we need a moral teacher because the teacher knows which particular acts are appropriate instantiations of the proprieties (*li*). But one displays moral expertise when one acts according to *li* without the aid of a teacher (ibid., 278; *Xunzi* 2, 4.10, 8.11, 23.1). The moral expert has cultivated himself to the point of acting autonomously in each new situation, whereas the novice is still blind to the full sense of why a particular action is a full expression of the right thing to do. In his chapter "Cultivating the Self," Xunzi puts the matter in the following way:

> *Li* is that by which you correct your person. The teacher is that by which to correct your practice of the proprieties of conduct. If you

are without ritual, then how will you correct your person? If you are without a teacher, how will you know that your practice of *li* is correct? ... If you do not concur with your teacher and the proper model but instead like to use your own judgement, then this is like relying on a blind person to distinguish colors, or like relying on a deaf person to distinguish sounds. You will accomplish nothing but chaos and recklessness ... The *Odes* says, "While not knowing, not understanding, he follows the principles of the Lord on High [*bu shi bu zhi, shun di zhi ze* 不識 不知順帝之則]." This expresses my meaning.

(*Xunzi* 2.11, Tiwald 2012: 280)

For Xunzi, moral experts consistently do the correct thing on the basis of their own aptitude and volition (*Xunzi* 8.11, Knoblock 1990: 81). Moral experts are exceedingly rare, nevertheless almost all humans spend their entire lifetimes dependent on experts and teachers. In Xunzi, such experts are the sages (*shengren*), moral teachers (*shi*) and selected rulers. The sages are recognized as experts through the sheer force of the life they lead. They have, in word and deed, established morality and the proprieties of conduct (*li*) are derived from their examples. Teachers are those who serve society after thorough study and intensive education. They are relatively few in number because no society can afford to provide all citizens with such extensive training. Some rulers are moral experts based on their education and training. This is the basis for Xunzi's claim that the citizenry should typically regard their leaders as moral experts and obey them even if it is not clear why or how the direction of the ruler is the correct one. In Xunzi's view, no ruler who betrays his people or does not provide for their needs and for social harmony is displaying moral expertise.

Buddhist Moralities in the Chinese Context

The Way of Precepts

In Chinese Buddhism, the moral life is understood in a way similar to the notion of Threefold Truth in its epistemology. There are multiple levels. On the one, Buddhist morality looks in many ways like a conventional moral system. At this level are the ordinary lay followers of the Buddhist way. Various Buddhist schools share the basic code of ethics called the Five Precepts used for the guidance of life when a seeker is at this level. These precepts prohibit harming sentient beings, stealing, sexual misconduct, lying and intoxication. The specific Buddhist philosophical justification of these precepts is that following them guides one away from the desires that cause suffering. Many people spend their entire lives at this level. However, following precepts may also function as part of a training regime leading to higher enlightenment. In fact, many Buddhist sects add to these basic rules three (making eight precepts) or five (i.e., making ten precepts) as part of a progressive training regime. The Ten Precepts (*dasa sila*) are taken as appropriate for monks and nuns, as following them typically best fits the monastic life. Here is a commonly used list of the Ten Precepts:

1. Refrain from killing sentient creatures.
2. Refrain from stealing.
3. Refrain from sexual misconduct.
4. Refrain from incorrect speech (lying but also manipulating and using hurtful words).
5. Refrain from consuming intoxicants.
6. Refrain from taking food at inappropriate times (after noon).
7. Refrain from singing, dancing, playing music or attending entertainment programs (performances).
8. Refrain from wearing perfume, cosmetics and decorative accessories.
9. Refrain from use of luxurious instruments (sitting on high chairs, sleeping on soft beds, etc.).
10. Refrain from accepting money.

The goal of training by means of precepts is to enable one to extinguish one's attachments and desires (i.e., reach nirvana).

The best-known companion concept to Buddhist morality at the level of precepts is the concept of *karma*. *Karma* may be regarded in its most basic sense as the product of one's past actions. These products may be behavioral consequences, mental conditions or physical states that result from one's acts. The psychological habits and states caused by one's actions are as much karmic results as are the physical ones. The physical ones may be the length and condition of one's life and the social karmic results may be the effects on one's friendships, wealth, family life and the like.

At the level of ordinary knowledge, folk beliefs coming into Buddhism evolved the idea that one's *karma* is the source of constant rebirth, and that at death one pays for the *karmic* debt of the weight of one's immoral deeds in a set of 18 hells that are judicial courts. Then, after paying one's debt, a person enters the wheel of rebirth that casts one back into the mundane world in the form of being most appropriate to what remains after one's *karmic* debt is paid. If one's *karma* is pure then one becomes a celestial being, freed from the wheel of rebirth and the phenomenal world of the mundane forever.

Individuals living by moral precepts may stand out among others as good and ethical. They may receive awards and recognitions. We may seek them out in our relationships. In its highest forms, this is the Buddhism of compassion for the world that seeks to remove evil and suffering by living a pure life and contributing to the welfare of others. But while such persons are still thinking of life and existence under moral precepts, they remain "in training" and to that extent somewhat still in bondage to volition, and names and forms of discrimination that persons use. They are still subject to mental anguish, physical attunement and even to the self.

Among the many Buddhist philosophical and even religious schools, there is a great deal of controversy and mutual criticism. Much of it centers on the function of morality in the ultimate aim of Buddhism. Some sects in the Theravada School of Buddhism hold that many, perhaps most, human beings are not able to reach enlightenment and, thus, should follow the way of precept and morality and pass through life with as little suffering and harm to themselves and others as possible.

However, in other sects of Buddhism, there is a higher morality than that of following precepts. Of course, even those who attain the higher level of moral life may be able to do so only as a result of the training they undertook by first following moral precepts. Yet, a crucial difference occurs when the training eventuates in enlightenment. In nirvana's extinguishment of desire and vanishing of suffering, all moral precepts are dispensed with as well. One who has climbed to the heights no longer needs the ladder. Once a person is emptied of the desires moral precepts are meant to control and erase, then there is no longer any need for morality, nor any function for it. An enlightened one transcends ethics and precepts and is set free from morality totally. Obviously, any unenlightened person who discards morality will plunge into evil and suffering. However, the enlightened one freed from attachment and desire lives above and apart from all moral expectation and moves through existence as one who has transcended morality. Such a person neither causes suffering nor experiences any. Those who are able to achieve enlightenment are often called Arhats or Luohans in Chinese. In many forms of Chinese Mahayana Buddhism, 18 Luohans are revered as followers of Buddha who have reached enlightenment but continue to dwell among us. In popular Buddhist piety, persons seek aid, support and guidance from one or more of the Luohans who are regarded as possessed of supernatural powers.

Confucianism and Buddhism on Moral Precepts

1. Celibacy was already an established custom among Indian ascetics when the Buddha enjoined its practice on his monks and nuns. In China, however, not only did celibacy play no role in its indigenous moral practices (*li*) but it also transgressed the familialism at the heart of Confucian teachings. The continuation of the family line was a duty in Confucianism. The emphasis placed on producing progeny was stated by Mencius: "There are three things which are unfilial, and to have no posterity is the greatest of them." A celibate son, renouncing his sacred duty to the family line for a life as a Buddhist monk, thus, seemed to threaten the very cohesiveness of Chinese society.

2. The monastic life itself became institutionalized in India, where it existed as an autonomous social body outside of secular authority. In China, on the other hand, the existence of a class of non-productive monks offended the sensibilities of the Confucian work ethic. It was also decried on purely pragmatic grounds by generations of government officials who saw in it a loss of vital sources of tax revenue and manpower.

3. Breaking attachments to persons and things, extinguishing desires so that one will find the serene peace of nirvana in one's inner life is a central teaching in Buddhism. Texts such as the *Dhammapada* make this clear: 91, 92, 94, 134, 185–7, 200, 210–12, 221, 284–5, 335–59. In Buddhism there is a strong sense of self-denial and a

feeling that having desires, possessions and position are morally debilitating; but such a view is alien to Confucianism.

4. In Buddhism, harmony comes through withdrawal and removing oneself from things to which one is attached, and which, in turn, can cause suffering and distress. The result is a kind of placidness that emerges as one has extinguished desire and attachment. If one is not attached to family, friends, career, nation and such, one will not be affected by what happens to them. In contrast, the Confucian understanding of harmony is much different. For Confucians, harmony must play out in relationships, as one is immersed in the messiness of family and village life. Harmony is found in the Five Relationships. But in Buddhism, harmony comes in isolation and turning inward. This isolation may be physical, as in becoming a monk and moving to a monastery, or spiritual, as one remains in the world but not of it. Persons are encouraged to make themselves like an island in Buddhism. In Confucianism, harmony is a social achievement, requiring many persons to cooperate.

5. In Buddhism, there is an important stress on self-cultivation, and this is also an emphasis in Confucianism. However, the manner of self-cultivation is very different. In Buddhism cultivation is resistance to corruption and attachment, keeping oneself pure in mind and body. This wisdom comes through meditation, not study, art, music or intellectual conversation as in Confucianism. But more strikingly, of course, is that the result of self-cultivation in Buddhism is the awareness that there is no self to be enlightened or to escape suffering. Confucianism does not follow this path.

6. In contrast to the Confucian ideal of an exemplary person (*junzi*), the Buddhist holds up the ideal of the *Brahmana*. This is one who has by restraint and contemplation freed himself from passions and blame. This person is nonviolent. He is in complete control of his body. He meditates alone and finds the path himself. He keeps aloof from others and does not frequent houses of friends. All these characterizations of the spiritual ideal of Buddhism run in different directions from the exemplary person who is quite involved in family, state and interpersonal relations.[11]

The *Hua-yan* Bodhisattva

For many Buddhist schools, the highest moral attainment is Buddhahood, in which one personifies in body and spirit the cosmic Buddha in life. Everyone has an inherent Buddha nature and the expression of this in all actions is the goal. In contrast, *Hua-yan* (Flower Garland) Buddhism valorizes the form of existence known as Bodhisattva as the supreme accomplishment. To be a Bodhisattva is to dwell in the margins between experienced enlightenment and the moral and karmic views of those around one. Bodhisattvas can enter into the Buddha realm at any time, but they take a vow to continue serving and working with the ordinary beings of the world as instruments of compassion and guides to enable them to achieve enlightenment.

What is it that a Bodhisattva does that makes such a person a distinctive moral being? The Bodhisattva is free from desire and suffering. The Bodhisattva has experienced nirvana, but out of compassion helps others escape from the world of woe and misery, teaching them to cultivate the way of enlightenment by continuing to engage with them in the world conceived of under the condition of moral precepts. The Bodhisattva has already abandoned desires and the discriminations of the mundane world that are the cause of suffering. Such a one dwells in this world with a mind that transcends the causes of suffering and even has no attachment to the self. Those still caught in this world are attached to the self and to the discriminations of existence, and they suffer because of the desires such attachment creates. When a Bodhisattva lives among such people, the difference is obvious and the other sentient beings see that the Bodhisattva does not suffer. This draws them to their Bodhisattva savior who is perfuming existence (see Chapter I) by simply living in enlightenment among those still trapped in attachment, desire and suffering.

The Way of Morality in Chan Buddhism

Recall that *chan* in Chan Buddhism comes from the Sanskrit *dhyana* that means "meditation." Though meditation practice is not the only practice employed in Chan, its central role in epistemology and ethics is important to understand. The function of meditation in Chan is different than reaching intellectual conviction through study of texts and arriving at conclusions based on disputation and argument. One way of gaining clarity on how meditation functions in morality and ethics is to contrast the approach of Chan with the Western manner of doing ethics.

In some streams of Western morality, the task is to determine the duties or moral rules that should guide contact and then to follow them. Indeed, the prominent Western philosopher Immanuel Kant wrote more than one work dedicated to the identification of these duties and their application.[12] Moral norms function in ways similar to how a pilgrim traveling in a country would use a map. The way of Chan is much different. In Chan, the task is not to use reason or even a calculus of consequences of actions in order to arrive at duties and rules, but rather a person readies himself to act morally by putting himself in an altered state of consciousness through meditation. This state is empty of content, such as rules and duties. Indeed, one who practices Chan meditation (sitting meditation) as a source of ethics does not say that he "knows" what to do or "knows" what is right. He has set aside the need to speak of the ethical life as connected to the possession of some kind of moral knowledge. Neither does one who is in this state have a need to draw bearings from culture, community or any sacred book. In fact, one empties himself of all of these, does not check oneself against them, sets them aside and gives no deliberation or place to them. Then, one's original Buddha nature comes into awareness. One does not learn moral truths in this state, but it is, nevertheless, from this state that appropriate action arises.

Western morality counsels a person not to act in a situation of moral import until he has weighed out the options rationally and calculated the possible outcomes and consequences for the widest range of persons involved. Only then can one know what to do. In this sense, reasoning plays a role not merely in setting out the rules and guidelines that illuminate action but also in helping one assess the actual conduct to undertake. Chan Buddhism has a contrasting approach. In Chan, the person seeks a shift away from the rational and calculating mind. Meditation is a sort of alternate consciousness that enables one to act spontaneously without calculation or deliberation.

A further contrast between Chan and Western morality can be drawn. An important task in Western morality is the strengthening of the will so it can resist the pull of desires to act contrary to what is right. Doing what is right in Western philosophy is portrayed as a struggle of the will, a test of strength of character to stand up against temptation or to choose the good and right over self-interest. In Chan one result of meditation is acting without effort and any feeling of conflict and resistance from the will.

Zhu Xi (1130–1200): Fashioning the Human Being

Whereas Western philosophers often engage in a discussion of the ultimate meaning or goal of human life, frequently associating it with happiness, Zhu Xi identifies the fundamental purpose of human life as equilibrium or harmony (*zhonghe*). He takes his inspiration for this view from the classical Confucian text called the *Zhongyong*.

> Before the feelings of pleasure, anger, sorrow, and joy are aroused it is called equilibrium (*zhong* 中). When these feelings are aroused but each and all attain due measure and degree, it is called harmony (*he* 和) … When equilibrium and harmony are realized to the highest degree, heaven and earth will attain their proper order and all things will flourish. (Chan 1963: 98)

Moral activity is the means by which this harmony occurs.

For Zhu Xi, the purpose of philosophy in general and morality specifically is self-mastery, not merely self-realization. Such mastery occurs in the midst of life and its many-layered relationships with others and not in solitary meditation. Zhu is not advocating a return to the original state of the mind as still equilibrium because that condition is one of inactivity. He holds that being human implies engaging the world and others.[13] Indeed, when one engages the world, what follows is the arousal of feelings, thoughts, plans, aspirations and what Zhu called "the seven emotions." The task of moral reflection, then, is to enable persons to find harmony in interaction with other persons with whom we have daily relations.[14] The way to harmony is following the Principles (*li* 理) that are the webbing of reality (see Chapter I's discussion of Zhu's ontology). The instrument by which harmony is produced and Principles and feelings are interrelated is the heart-mind (*xin*).

Therefore, self-cultivation for Zhu Xi ultimately means learning how to make equilibrium (*zhong*) manifest in our outer actions (Metzger 1977: 94). Cultivating oneself is the art of bringing one's moral activity into authentic reflection of the goodness inherent in the human heart-mind in the form of Principles (Adler 2008: 59). In his "Letter to the Gentlemen of Hunan," Zhu Xi writes:

> So long as in one's daily life the effort at seriousness and cultivation is fully extended and there are no selfish human desires to disturb it, then before the feelings are aroused it will be as clear as a mirror and as calm as still water, and after the feelings are aroused it will attain due measure and degree without exception. This is the essential task in everyday life. (Chan 1963: 601)

Self-cultivation brings the still and active phases of life into an interpenetrating harmony (Adler 2008: 65). Stillness is never an end in itself, an error Zhu believed Buddhism to have made. Rather, its purpose is to nourish activity (ibid., 77). The kind of harmony Zhu Xi recommends is not so much "knowing yourself" as Socrates would have it, nor is it identical with Aristotle's highest good as *eudaimonia* (i.e., human flourishing), but the position that harmony is an expression of both the Socratic and Aristotelean projects.

However, we may wonder whether harmony is a sufficiently robust and satisfying ultimate value for human life. Would not happiness or virtue be more worthy? Is there something that intuitively seems somewhat deficient if, upon reflection or life's end, I can only say, "I lived a life in harmony with my own self and others?" Moreover, if harmony is the supreme good, does such an end really call us to the highest levels of achievement as humans? Consider and contrast Zhu Xi's notion with that of Friedrich Nietzsche's "will to power." For Nietzsche, the most fulfilling life is one that transcends itself, that leaves behind the mediocre precisely because such a person is *not* constantly adjusting his attitudes, goals, desires and actions to harmonize with those of others. For Zhu, embracing such a philosophy would be the height of selfish desire. Even the advocacy of such a philosophy of life would be taken as a demonstration of how cloudy one's heart-mind has become and how ultimate Principles have been hidden behind the veil of desire. He says:

Now if you cannot see Principles (*li*) clearly, it is not that you do not know what they are but rather that they are obstructed by things. Now the ordinary means [of dealing with this problem] is to rectify the many evil distractions in the mind. Only then can [Principles be seen] … The big problem is that persons frequently are unwilling to give up their old understanding. If intelligent, they will see what is not right and change it. (Gardner 1990: 123)

When the person is born, he understands Principles (*li*) without expending any effort. People nowadays are mired in confusion; only when the sages have spoken to them repeatedly [through their texts] are they willing to take leave of it. But if they are already stupefied and do not even know to pursue Principles, in the end they will become mere beasts. (Ibid., 104)

Zhu Xi says the foremost problem facing human beings is the obscuring and polluting nature of material desires. This is not to say that he believes desire is, in itself, the root of immorality and suffering, as we might find in Buddhism. Zhu holds that desires for food, drink, reproduction and so forth are shared by all human beings and cannot be eliminated. But it is the lack of regulation and control of desires that is the source of the problems of immorality and suffering. Accordingly, Zhu often describes the ideal state of the heart-mind as *gong* (i.e., impartiality, public and universal), and the problematic elements that get in the way as *siyu* (i.e., selfish, private and individual) (Shun 2005: 1). Individual and selfish desires, if not regulated, create a separation between a person and others. One will become morally dull or dead to others. To illustrate what he means, Zhu Xi makes use of an analogy drawn from two other Neo-Confucian thinkers, Cheng Hao (1032–85) and Cheng Yi (1033–1107).

In medical books, a paralyzed arm or leg is said to be unfeeling. This expression is perfect for describing the situation. The humane (*ren*) person regards all things in the universe as one body; there is nothing which is not a part of him. If he regards all things as parts of himself, where will his feelings not extend? But if he does not see them as parts of himself, why would he feel any concern for them? It is like the case of a paralyzed arm or leg: the life-force (qi 氣) does not circulate through them so they are not regarded as part of one's self. (Angle 2009: 78)

When persons do not regulate their desires, they cease to feel and apprehend Principles (*li*). However, one who is able to practice reverent and still equilibrium feels himself to be one body with other beings, not regarding their needs and interests as external to one's own.

Zhu Xi borrows a Buddhist image to speak of regulating our selfish desires, comparing this activity to polishing a mirror. The brightness of the mirror is *gong* and *siyi* is the dust that may becloud it (Gardner 1990: 145, 146). To put this another way, a person whose moral activity is pure in form will be a sage (*shengren*) (*Conversations* 4.17). The actions of his body are like clear water that allows the Principles of the Supreme Ultimate to show through for all to see. Whereas, someone whose actions arise from selfish desire (*siyu*) is like muddy water obscuring the Principles as though hiding a pearl beneath the waters.

Nonetheless, the Principles are not obliterated, even in an evil person. A person may concentrate his efforts on cultivating and transforming himself, on clearing the water or polishing the mirror as it were. This is done by self-cultivation. Such study is not merely for moral development. The more one learns, the more the Principles of things reveal themselves as a result. Zhu Xi likens this process to finding the heart-mind we lost because of our selfish desires. As if to dramatize the point he is making, Zhu makes reference to the folk belief prevalent in his day that crows demonstrate filial piety when they disgorge their food to feed their offspring or parents. Zhu thinks that to describe this behavior in moral language is to make a grave mistake, but his reasoning may be surprising.

Zhu Xi holds that animals such as crows can express Principles in one direction only. He is not saying that crows have intelligence to express Principles but are nonetheless unable to practice filial piety. He means, instead, that animals, because of the way the *qi* of their five phases is shaped, *must* express Principles as they do. Crows do not decide to feed their offspring, nor do they forego their own nourishment in order to provide food for their hatchlings. Zhu's point is that they cannot help but act in this matter. In this sense, his point is very close to what we mean when we say that animals act in a certain way "by instinct" (Fung 1953: 2:553, n. 1). The crucial difference between humans and other life forms is that persons can choose whether to act on their desires. Humans are not automatons being driven "in one direction" by the Principles. This explains why only humans are interested in self-cultivation and why only humans can be sages. It also provides Zhu with a philosophical explanation for the rise of evil and its presence only in the world of human beings, not in nature.

Wang Yangming (1472–1529): Moral Willing as Moral Knowing

While Wang Yangming is surely quite critical of Zhu Xi's thought, nevertheless he is influenced by the Neo-Confucian thinkers who went before him. For example, he adopts the moral vision of Neo-Confucianism that the goal of the fully human person is to think of his activity and relationships as forming one body with all things without differentiation (Cua 2003: 762). Wang's version of this teaching is expressed in this way in *Instructions for Practical Living:*

> The great person regards heaven, earth, and the myriad things as one body (*yiti*). He regards the world as one family and the country as one person. Those who make a cleavage between objects and distinguish between the self and others are small men (i.e., "petty persons," *xiao ren*). That the great man can regard heaven, earth and the myriad things as one body is not because he deliberately wants to do so, but because it is natural to the humane nature of his mind that he do so. Forming one body with heaven, earth and the myriad things is not only true of the great man, for even the mind of the small man is no different. Only he himself makes it small. Therefore, when he [the great person] sees the child about to fall into a well, he cannot help a feeling of alarm and commiseration (*Mencius* 2A.6). This shows that his humaneness forms one body with the child. Again, when he observes the pitiful cries and frightened appearance of the birds and animals about to be slaughtered, he cannot help feeling an "inability to bear" their suffering. This shows that his humanity forms one body with birds and animals. (Chan 1963a: I.195)

For the great person who moves by what Wang calls "pure knowledge" (*liangzhi*) (see Chapter II), there is a direct awareness of being one with the child about to fall into the well and acting on that awareness. Here I intentionally use the word *awareness* in order to avoid any dichotomy between "feeling" and "thought" that turns up in Western thought, since these are combined in the Chinese notion of "heart-mind" (*xin*). This awareness gives the agent a unifying perspective for experiencing and dealing with all persons, things, events and affairs. Such a person expresses humaneness (*ren*) in all relationships, a habit that is capable of indefinite expansion and ultimately embraces the whole universe. This is why Antonio Cua characterizes Wang's moral vision of humaneness as seeing "the universe as a moral community" (Cua 2003: 762).

When he asked about the difference between the meaning of humaneness (*ren*) as he understood it and Mozi's doctrine of inclusive concern, Wang Yangming replies that this can only be found out through personal realization (Chan 1963a: sec. 196).

> For instance, in the matter of serving one's parents, one cannot seek for the Principles (*li*) of filial piety in the parent. In serving one's ruler, one cannot seek for the Principles of loyalty in the ruler. In the intercourse with friends and in governing the people, one cannot seek for the Principles of faithfulness and humaneness (*ren*) in friends and the people. They [i.e., all these Principles] are all in the mind. It is the mind that manifests Principles. When the mind is free from the obscuration of selfish desires, it is the embodiment of Heavenly Principles (*tianli*) which requires not an iota added from the outside. (Ibid., sec. 3)

In this passage, Heavenly Principle (*tianli*) as a norm or standard is discovered by introspection, turning back into oneself. Knowing what is good or evil, right or wrong, belongs to a certain sort of clarity of the mind. Wang writes, "The thousand sages are all passing shadows; pure knowledge (*liangzhi*) alone is my teacher" (Ivanhoe 2000: 68). Wang, maybe because he is following Zhu Xi's teachings on this particular point, is concerned that selfish desires can disturb our oneness with the nature of reality and the quiet harmony it brings. The basic ontology behind this teaching has already been introduced: our minds and the world share the same Heavenly patterns (*tianli*). The only thing that prevents us from realizing this fact is that the clarity of our minds is clouded by selfish desires.

Wang likewise follows Zhu Xi's use of the medical analogy of numbness (*buren*) to describe the general lack of feeling for the welfare of people, creatures and things caused by selfish desires obscuring "pure knowledge." This expression fits well into Wang's overall picture, within which we and the world are "one body." In the language of Wang's day, the term *buren* not only meant to be "unfeeling" toward suffering or distress; it was a medical term describing paralysis in some part of the body, referring to our inability to act (Ivanhoe 2011: 282).

For Wang, pure knowledge *(liangzhi)*, if unobstructed by self-centered desires, spontaneously responds to any moral situation in a seamless process of perceiving, understanding, judging, willing and action (Ivanhoe 2002: 99–100). Cua holds that Wang Yangming's philosophical views on *liangzhi* with respect to morality may be divided into these categories: moral consciousness, moral discrimination, deliberation and changing circumstances and extension and achievement (Cua 2003: 770–3).

Moral Consciousness. According to Wang, *liangzhi* is a form of consciousness that is best understood by means of an analogy about vision. It is a type of knowing that can be compared to seeing clearly, without any fuzziness or distortion. In this sense, *liangzhi* is neither an object upon which the rational mind deliberates nor a product of the senses. It is a direct, unmediated apprehension that is an intrinsic capacity *(benti)* of the human consciousness (Chan 1963a: sec. 274). What it makes manifest are "Heaven's Principles *(tianli)*," that Wang also identifies with the Dao of reality (ibid., secs 165, 169, 265, 284). What is apprehended through *liangzhi* can be known by all persons without any relative subjectivity entering into it (ibid., sec. 189). In fact, *liangzhi* only appears when selfish desires are set aside (ibid., sec. 4).

> The human heart-mind *(xin)* is naturally able to know. When it perceives the parents, it naturally knows that one should be filial. When it perceives the elder brother, it naturally knows that one should be respectful. And when it perceives a child about to fall into a well, it naturally knows that it should intervene *(Mencius* 2A.6). This is *liangzhi* and need not be sought outside [of the mind]. (Ibid., sec. 8)

As a direct moral awareness before our consciousness, Wang speaks of "the vision of *ren* (仁)" and in this, "pure knowledge" *(liangzhi)* is not a precept or set of precepts, but more like seeing an aspect or dimension of something that another person misses, because his heart-mind is clouded by selfish desires.

Moral Discrimination. How one is to distinguish right from wrong, good from evil, is one of the most basic problems faced by moral philosophy. A common way of dealing with the problem of discrimination is to identify some set of moral rules that should guide action, as in deontological ethics. Another way is to perform a kind of calculation of the outcomes of a possible action and choose the act that minimizes harm to the greatest number of people, or maximizes benefit for most persons, as in utilitarian ethics. Aristotle held that the person of virtuous character would, by virtue of a long habitual history of choosing good, select the best action habitually and without need for deliberation.

Where does Wang Yangming's philosophy of the power of *liangzhi* to discriminate actions fit among these other models? Wang believes that our puzzles over what to do morally are rooted in the way in which our selfish desires obscure and cloud the native functioning of *liangzhi* (ibid., sec. 162). Absent the obstruction caused by our selfish desires, we are never confused about how to act.

Deliberation and Changing Circumstance. "Pure knowledge" (*liangzhi*) displays the agility required by the constantly changing processes and events of life. In contrast to a moral theory that might take fixed and universal principles and try to conform and adapt them to new situations and dilemmas, *liangzhi* grasps Heaven's Principles and moves with reality seamlessly, without the intervention of rational analysis and deliberation. Even so, Wang does not deny the value and power of deliberation and reasoning, and he thinks that our normal use of it leaves little doubt about what we should do (morally speaking); nevertheless he gives two cases of moral perplexity that he believes illustrate the deficiency of reasoned deliberation in guiding us morally. One is Shun's puzzle about whether to marry without telling his parents and the second is King Wu's dilemma over launching a military expedition before burying his father. Wang says that Shun's choice to marry and King Wu's pursuit of the campaign both represent the exercise of *liangzhi* because only it can fully grasp the minute details of varying circumstances. In this case, the way through the conflict of established standards for guiding behavior could not be known rationally but it could be "seen" through *liangzhi* as an "instant realization" (ibid., sec. 139).

As philosophers we may feel some hesitancy to accept Wang's analysis. How can we distinguish Shun's and Wu's choice through *liangzhi* from simply "doing what they wanted to do" or what "their consciences told them to do"? Wang anticipates this criticism, or something very close to it. He insists that while *liangzhi* is inherent in all persons, it is the distinguishing characteristic of the mind of the sage. As one prepared by study and deep reflection, the sage's grasp and awareness of *liangzhi* is beyond the ordinary. So, one who does not practice as a sage cannot hope to be able to experience the internal powers of *liangzhi*.

Extension and Achievement. "Pure knowledge" (*liangzhi*) is also the power by which we can expand the creativity of heaven and earth by making novel decisions and interactions that emerge into being at the living edges of the move from the present to the future. Moreover, the vision enabled through *liangzhi* makes the universe into a moral community not just of human persons but also of natural things. Once selfish desires are eliminated, the *liangzhi* vision of the sage is clear and moral failure falls away. The sage's will becomes pure and sincere (ibid., sec. 101).

Like Zhu Xi, Wang saw himself as the defender and champion of the true lineage of Confucianism coming through Confucius to Mencius. However, Wang does not employ the same kinds of metaphors we see in Mencius, those that interpret the development of the human being on the model of agriculture. It will be remembered that for Mencius, all humans are born with four innate moral endowments. With proper cultivation, these seeds will grow into a healthy and morally upright human. In contrast, Wang's metaphors were drawn from Zhu Xi's work. He "spoke of the moral mind as like the sun shining behind clouds and as a clear, bright mirror hidden beneath dust" (Ivanhoe 2000: 60).

This shift in metaphor amounts to a very different kind of approach to self-cultivation. Instead of thinking primarily of development, as the agricultural metaphors of Mencius, and even the rigorous learning process of Zhu Xi suggest, Wang is bringing forward a "discovery" model of moral self-awareness. He does not hesitate to talk about sudden and complete moral enlightenment, as though the clouds of desire and confusion blow away and the sun suddenly comes bursting through.

For Wang, the experience of moral enlightenment brings not only new knowledge about what is right and good but also transforms our desire and affections, so that we freely act in a moral way. This is a crucial point. Wang is not saying that we have only a cognitive gain in moral knowledge, and then we must use our will to redirect our desires and passions to act upon that knowledge. He is saying that the knowledge we gain is will-transforming. P. J. Ivanhoe calls our attention to the distinction in Chinese between "real knowledge" (*zhenzhi*) and "ordinary knowledge" (*changzhi*) (ibid., 62). Ordinary knowledge is just that. It is the sort of commonplace knowing that everyone has. Real knowledge is what Wang is pointing to: knowledge that brings together the cognitive and volitional dimensions of our experience.

In the sense of morality, possessing "real knowledge" is knowing what one should do and at the same time being motivated to do it. It is self-activating knowledge. In *Instructions for Practical Living*, Wang makes it clear that possessing *liangzhi* is an experience in which knowledge and action are not separated (Chan 1963a: sec. 5). He holds that "real knowledge" forms a bond between knowledge and action similar to being attracted to a beautiful color or being repulsed by a bad odor.

In *Instructions for Practical Living*, Wang expands on his philosophical idea of the unity of knowledge and action (will). The novelty of this approach lies in its bringing together epistemology and morality. Wang's experience of enlightenment discloses to him that moral choice is not the result of a separate analytical process or discrete volitional one. If one depends upon reason to make a calculus of the consequences of one's actions, or to divine the rules and exceptions applying to a situation, before one engages his will, he will very likely be led wrongly. Xu Ai (1487–1518), Wang's first disciple and also his brother-in-law, recorded this conversation with Wang:

> I did not understand the teacher's (i.e., Wang's) doctrine of the unity of knowledge and action … Therefore I took the matter to the teacher … I said, "For example, there are people who know that parents should be served with filial piety and elder brothers with respect but cannot put these things into practice. This shows that knowledge and action are clearly two different things." The teacher said, "The knowledge and action you refer to are already separated by selfish desires and are no longer knowledge and action in their original substance. There have never been people who know but do not act. Those who are supposed to know but do not act simply do not yet know. When sages and worthies taught people about knowledge and action, it was precisely because they wanted them to restore the original substance, and not simply to do this or that

and be satisfied ..."The teacher said, "... I have said that knowledge is the direction for action and action the effort of knowledge, and that knowledge is the beginning of action and action the completion of knowledge. If this is understood, then when only knowledge is mentioned, action is included, and when only action is mentioned, knowledge is included. The reason why the ancients talked about knowledge and action separately is that there are people in the world who are confused and act on impulse without any sense of deliberation or self-examination, and who thus only behave blindly and erroneously. Therefore it is necessary to talk about knowledge to them before their action becomes correct. There are also those who are intellectually undisciplined and think in a vacuum. They are not at all willing to make the effort of concrete practice. They only pursue shadows and echoes, as it were. It is therefore necessary to talk about action to them before their knowledge becomes true. The ancient teachers could not help talking this way in order to restore balance and avoid any defect. If we understand this motive, then a single word [either knowledge or action] will do. (Mou 2009: 407)

Wang's position is that being able to will what is right to do is an immediate realization of knowledge of the right. No one who truly has knowledge will fail to practice it.[15]

Dai Zhen (1724–77):
The Proper Place of Desire in Morality

Not all subsequent Chinese philosophers share the negative attitude of Zhu Xi and Wang Yangming toward desires. Dai Zhen explores the concept of desire and human nature carefully.[16] Both Zhu and Wang are very suspicious of human desires, comparing them to muddy water that obscures our vision of a pearl beneath it, or clouds that conceal the sun. For both of these thinkers, desires cloud our clear awareness of Heaven's Principles and inhibit our true moral knowledge and right activity. We will not be able to realize coherence with the Principles of Heaven (*tianli*, 天理) until we successfully suppress the impulses of our desires.

Taking a rather starkly contrasting view, Dai Zhen thinks we cannot be fully virtuous *until our moral behavior and desires go hand-in-hand.* In order to be virtuous, one must not only do the good, but also desire to do the good and feel satisfaction in doing the good. Dai holds that there is something philosophically at stake about our development as moral beings in the view we take toward desire. Justin Tiwald puts this well:

> If we see our work in moral self-cultivation as primarily subtractive or eliminative—as a matter of overcoming bad feelings and desires so as to let the refined parts of nature act of their own accord—then, Dai, maintains, it makes no sense to think of moral education as contributing to the growth and maturation of the moral understanding. What we learn in the process of study might be understood as having instrumental value, helping to free us from the grip of our bad dispositions and realize the dormant moral sensibilities in ourselves, but once that is accomplished the content of our knowledge would seem to play no constitutive part in moral comprehension.
>
> (Tiwald 2009)

Dai holds that there is another difficulty for moral philosophy arising from the devaluing and elimination of desires. Zhu Xi's and Wang Yangming's attack on desires actually leave us blind to what really matters to others (what *they* desire) and to the possible detrimental effects of our actions (what they do not *want* done to them). Moreover, we will not even be capable of recognizing what contributes to our own well-being if we extinguish all of our own desires. Zhu and Wang think it is enough to stress that desires are not bad in themselves, so long as we regulate them. This may be a sufficient response to Dai and it can be that he has overlooked it. But Dai's point may also be somewhat different. He is not saying that we should ignore the regulation of desires, but that we should actively consider the desires of others and even our own when ascertaining what we should do morally. In this sense, his point does not seem to be addressed by Zhu or Wang. In fact, he seems to be on target in his criticism of their views. They both suggest that moral knowledge is rooted in moving to a place of stillness in our minds where Heaven's Principles are clear and evident and that this can only be done by leaving desires behind entirely. For Dai, however, suggesting that the perfectibility of a moral agent lies in the elimination of all desire is misguided and wrong. Instead, the exemplary person may most surely be known by one exhibited feature. An exemplary person is one who *desires* virtue.

According to Dai, since desires differ among persons and may be the source of conflict and disharmony, this is the point at which the "cognitive mind" may be a guide. In his *Evidential Study of the Meaning and Terms of the Mencius*, Dai Zhen says:

> When I do something to others, I should examine myself and think quietly: would I accept it should someone do the same thing to me? When I demand something from others, I should examine myself thinking quietly: were this demanded of me, could I do it? When I gauge the response of others by my own, Principles will become clear. The Principles of Heaven refers to the Principles that are differentiated on the basis of what is natural. The Principles that are differentiated on the basis of what is natural means this: gauging the feelings of others by one's own so that there is fairness in every [action].
>
> (Chin and Freeman 1990: 70)

The "cognitive mind's" application of the method of reciprocity (*shu*) that Dai sets out in the quote above represents the superiority of human moral actions to those we notice in birds and beasts. Reciprocity has a long and venerable tradition in Chinese philosophy. It is found both in Confucius and Mozi, but Dai makes use of the concept as a tool of moral judgment and not simply as a virtue in itself (i.e., "Do unto others what you want them to do to you"; or "Do not do to others what you do not want done to you"). The actual function of Dai's guideline is to describe the method of the "cognitive mind's" operation in moral judgment in such a way as to say that the logic is to take oneself and extend it to others. What an application of this tool yields is what Dai calls "invariant norms" (*buyi zhi ze*) that are not merely subjective but principles that can attain a kind of universal agreement across all times and places (Tiwald 2009).

One major difficulty arises here. If the act of moral judgment, of which only humans are capable, is guided by taking myself (i.e., my desires) and extending it to others, it is at least possible that I may seriously misjudge the well-being of others who might benefit a great deal more from some action than I would. I might well treat others in deeply deficient ways simply because I lack the desires that they have.

Dai may see this problem. He writes, "If one genuinely returns to oneself and reflects on the true feelings of the weak, the feudal, the dull, the timid, the diseased, the elderly, the young, the orphaned, or the solitary, can those [true feelings] of these others really be any different from one's own?" (Tiwald 2009). In this sense, then, Dai may be suggesting that when the "cognitive mind" works properly in making a moral judgment, it does not strictly consider only *how I would want to be treated*, but rather it considers *what needs the weakest and most disadvantaged have* and acts on that principle.

For Dai Zhen, there is no need for persons to renegotiate or decide anew in each generation, based on the operations of their "cognitive minds," what moral principles should guide action. We have the examples and teachings of the sage-kings and philosophers of the past. These can serve as instructions for all people. "The system of proprieties (*li* 澧) is the order and arrangement of heaven and earth." (Chin and Freeman 1990: 156) Nevertheless, Dai Zhen is not recommending a simple return to the authority and tradition of past teaching. His point is that what we learn from the classics is not merely the principles of action of the past but also how to apply our "cognitive minds," helping it to see the morally salient features of our actions and relationships. The classics provide nourishment to our minds.

Mou Zongsan (1909–95): Moral Metaphysics

Mou Zongsan coined the term "moral metaphysics" and understands this activity to be primarily occupied with the most basic existential inquiries of humans, such as "What should I do?" and "What makes my life meaningful?" (Cheng 2009a: 430). He argues that in doing moral metaphysics one must notice a two-directional movement between the human and Heaven. One movement is upward, from the human toward Heaven and is represented in the *Analects* and the *Mencius*. The other is in a downward direction, from Heaven toward the human, represented by the *Zhongyong* and the "Ten Wings" (i.e., the *Commentaries on the Book of Changes*) (ibid., 431–2).

In his study of Zhu Xi and other Neo-Confucians, Mou used the philosophical framework of the German philosopher Immanuel Kant (1724–1804), but offered a reading of the Neo-Confucians as a corrective to points where he believed Kant had gotten it wrong (Tan 2009: 559). He understands Kant's view to be that morality is not derived from empirical experience (i.e., it was *a priori*). In the *Groundwork on the Metaphysics of Morals* (1785) and *The Critique of Practical Reason* (1788) Kant develops a method for identifying the pure moral duties humans have by subjecting any candidate duty to its rational derivation from what he calls the Categorical Imperative: "act always on the maxim which you can will to be universal law."[17]

For Mou, the Neo-Confucian philosophy of the *equilibrium* (*zhong* 中) in the heart-mind of every person, where the Principles of Heaven are known immediately, is to be preferred to Kant's approach. He extends his theory by the claim that sagehood in Confucian practice represents the realization in practice of the "oughts" or "duties" of the moral law that Kant identifies with the maxims of morality. Mou realizes that his position requires one to commit to a metaphysics (ontology) in a way that Kant's does not. This is one of the reasons he inverts Kant's way of speaking about "the metaphysics of morals," by which the German philosopher means to identify what were the presuppositions for morality as we have it. Mou uses the concept of "moral metaphysics" to focus on the transcendent sources of morality. He calls this the "teaching of complete virtue" (*cheng de zhi jiao*). He thinks that the Neo-Confucians, such as Zhu Xi, Wang Yangming and Dai Zhen, have ontological (transcendent) levels to their moral theories that Kant lacks, thereby making theirs more complete analyses of ethics philosophically.

Kant holds that in order for us to have morality, we have to presuppose as the foundation to all moral duty that the human being has autonomy (i.e., is free). However, he does not think that a scientific or empirical description of human behavior will locate freedom. Instead, empirical description will be directed by the concept that all events have a cause and would, therefore, always seek to provide a comprehensive causal explanation for human action and never appeal to freedom. The presupposition that humans are free, one of the basic postulates to moral life, must be, then, about a dimension of reality that is not describable by science. Kant calls this the noumenal realm, whereas science deals with the phenomenal world. Mou finds this approach unsatisfactory both ontologically and morally. He holds that Neo-Confucian thinkers have the correct philosophical exposition of this problem.

In Neo-Confucianism, for example, moral knowledge of Principles (*li*) is a direct, immediate awareness of the heart-mind, and actual moral practice is the creativity of the sages within the cosmic process (ibid.). Creative free action, according to Mou, is a manifest reality in the lives of the sages, not merely a postulate of practical (moral) reason as Kant holds (Mou 1968: 10–13, 43–5). Mou argues that the sages connect the finite (what Kant calls the phenomenal world) with the infinite (i.e., Principles or what Kant calls the noumenal world) revealing that freedom is a fact of reality, shown in moral action, and not merely a postulate of practical reason or way we think of ourselves as existing in the world. Mou understands this position to be a type of completion of Kant's work.

In Kant, the highest good is the exact coincidence of virtue and happiness; that happiness occurs in exact proportion to our virtuous living. But Kant says the confluence of optimal virtue and happiness does not and cannot occur in this world because the natural and physical laws of empirical reality operate without regard for virtue or morality. They just do what they do without considering the moral action of an individual. We cannot expect any necessary connection to exist between happiness and even the most careful observation of our moral duties (Kant 1993: 123). Accordingly, morality requires that we postulate both an immortal soul (i.e., that our lives extend beyond the years given us here and now) and a supreme power able to bring virtue and happiness together (i.e., God). Together with the postulate of freedom mentioned above, these two presuppositions make up what Kant calls the transcendental foundations of morality (i.e., practical reason) to work in Kant's thought (ibid., 129–32).

Mou objects to this analysis in Kant because he thinks personalizing the process that brings virtue and happiness together only pushes the problem to another level. Kant will have to explain why such a being as God (who belongs to the noumenal and not the phenomenal world!) should be interested in bringing about the coincidence of virtue and happiness. Mou does not see how postulating God provides assurance that virtue and happiness will coincide. How do we know philosophically that a being of supreme power wishes to bring virtue and happiness together?

In contrast to Kant's approach, Mou turns again to the sage as an example of one who unites Heaven's Principles through free action and thereby realizes the unity of virtue and happiness (Mou 1985: 323). He argues that the sages as concrete examples proved that Heavenly Principles can be manifested in human practice and need not require postulation of an afterlife (Mou 1971: 257). The sages live lives uniting happiness and virtue. Mou holds that an appeal to concrete lives is preferable to the bifurcated reality of Kant's phenomenal and noumenal distinction. The sage attains Heaven's Principles through autonomy (his virtue) and he brings benefit and happiness through creative action. In this way, Mou holds that the sage completes Kant's philosophy by uniting the kingdom of nature (phenomenal world) and the kingdom of ends (noumenal world) (Mou 1985: 323).

CHAPTER IV

哲学

Political Philosophy: Questions about the Nature and Purpose of Government

Introduction

Political philosophy is the normative study of government, relationships between individuals and communities, rights and justice. In this chapter we will explore some fundamental questions related to the creation of society and government as these are handled by Chinese philosophers. Some questions we will explore are the following:

- What is the natural state of humans, prior to government and law (are they free, equal, independent or social; are they inevitably in conflict or do they live in innocent bliss)?
- From where does government arise (a contract between persons, the recognized superiority of some persons to lead, or the decree of a higher power)?
- What are human laws and from where do they come (do we arrive at them by participatory exchange of views, do they derive from the nature of reality, are they codifications of the lives of exemplary persons, or are they decrees of government or rulers or a divine being)?
- What is the best form of government?
- Are there checks and balances on government/rulers?
- Is revolt against the ruler or government ever justified?
- What is the proper balance between governmental authority and individual liberty of expression and thought?

- What is the role and responsibility of government to implement justice and how should it do it (in distributing goods, for example, are there rules of entitlement, fairness, equality of opportunity)?[1]

Confucius (551–479 BCE) on Rulership and the Function of Government

In the *Analects*, the ideal ruler is called a sage-king. This is no accident because Confucius's understanding of government may be characterized as a meritocracy. Speaking to aspiring young political rulers, Confucius says, "Do not worry over not having an official position; worry about what it takes to have one. Do not worry that no one acknowledges you; seek to do what will earn you acknowledgment" (*Analects* 1.1, Ames and Rosemont 1998: 92). Such a view is quite different than rule by the vote of the people (democracy) or by the elite (aristocracy) or even by a hereditary lineage through a single king (monarchy). Confucius's notion of political leadership is expressed simply as "only the worthy should rule." His strong belief in meritocracy is directly related to his position that the ultimate purpose of government is correcting the life circumstances and situations of the people in order to establish what is proper (ibid., 12.17). This broad sweep brings within the scope of government the power and responsibility to help in natural disaster, enable the free and responsible flow of trade, protect the people from internal and external enemies and advance the self-cultivation of the citizens. According to Confucius, in order to care so profoundly for the people and to orient the political functions of government to their self-improvement, the ruler must be morally upright himself. If he is, all the people will follow. The character of the ruler is like the wind and that of the citizens is like grass. The people will bend in the direction the wind blows (ibid., 12.19).

This is quite a different point of view than one that relies on law and punishment to create order in a society. Of course, Confucius does not doubt that order might be created by strict laws and severe punishments. But in his view, order is not the ultimate purpose of government. The cultivation of a humane and harmonious society is. Under a government of strict law and severe punishment, the people might try to avoid being caught by obeying the law. But there is no guarantee they are growing in moral cultivation so they can be self-governing.

Lead the people with administrative injunctions and keep them orderly with penal law, and they will seek to avoid punishments but will be without a sense of shame. Lead them with virtuous excellence (*de* 德) and keep them orderly by observing propriety (*li* 禮) and they will develop a sense of shame and will become self-ordering. (Ibid., 2.3)[2]

Political philosophy is often taken to possess a dual emphasis. On one hand is the philosophical rationale for an ideal social order and on the other hand is the sense that the real world requires compromises and applications that may be principled but are certainly less than the ideal. For example, Confucius does not address the question whether moral character actually guarantees political effectiveness. The reason he does not talk about this problem may well be that he makes no distinction between political efficacy, getting things done and doing so rightly. Confucius does not believe any given ruler has a "divine right" to be king. Right to rule, he holds, must be earned by the evident force of the ruler's self-cultivation and his implementation of the corrections of real or potential harms to the people, thereby winning their respect and loyalty. "If proper in their own conduct, what difficulty would they have in governing? But if not able to be proper in their own conduct, how can they demand such conduct from others?" (ibid., 13.13).

The sage ruler is no mere ideal in Confucius's teaching. He believes there were actual historical instantiations of such rulers and named specifically Yao and Shun. We may wonder why, then, Confucius is known to be the person "who keeps working toward a goal the realization of which he knows to be hopeless" (ibid., 14.38). The reason for such hopelessness is not thought by Confucius to be a flaw in his philosophy of rulership but more that his ideal requires that sages be in power, but these people are rare in the real world (*Analects* 7.26).

The objective of political policies and laws in Confucian political theory is to create a harmonious society by cultivating the people.[3] The ruler and government should provide citizens an environment in which they can cultivate themselves and live exemplary lives. Accordingly, politics means rectifying (*zheng zhe, zheng ye*, ibid., 12.17) situations and practices that prevent cultivation. Moral and social ritual (*li*) is an indispensable instrument in this task (Tan 2001: 468–91). An objection that presents itself immediately is that such a goal may make too little provision for individual rights and personal autonomy.

What is often overlooked in this comparison is the character of the citizens. In a Confucian theory of government, the ruler's example, complete with his care for his people, is the wind blowing across the grass (*Analects* 12.19). This means the people are shaped by the ruler's example to value the relationships and mutuality that he expresses. Therefore, the drive for free expression takes place in this context, not in one in which an individual is at liberty to choose to do whatever he wishes so long as it does not harm or injure another.

While the authenticity of the following passage as traceable to Confucius is arguable, nevertheless this text from the "Li Yun" chapter of the *Book of Rites* (*Liji*) purports to give a picture of how Confucius's image of a proper society was understood in the Warring States Period (prior to 221 BCE).

> Zhongni (i.e., Confucius) was one of the guests at the Ji sacrifice; when it was over, he went out and paced back and forth on the terrace over the Gate of Proclamations, looking sad and lamenting. What made him lament was the state of Lu. Yan Yan was by his side and asked him, "Master, why are you sighing?" Confucius replied, "I have never seen the practice of the Great Dao and the eminent men of the Three Dynasties, but I aspire to follow them. When the Great Dao was followed, a common spirit ruled the world. Men of talent, virtue, and ability valued mutual trust and cultivated harmony. They did not love only their own parents, nor treat only their own sons as sons. Provision was secured for the aged till their death, employment for the able-bodied, and the means of raising up the young. People showed kindness and compassion to widows, orphans, childless men, and those who were disabled by disease, so that they were all sufficiently provided for. Men had work and women had homes. Possessions were not wastefully discarded, nor were they greedily hoarded. People enjoyed laboring for others. In this way selfish schemings were discouraged and did not arise. Robbers, thieves, and rebellious traitors were unknown, and doors remained open and unlocked. This was the period called Grand Unity." (*Book of Rites*, "Li Yun"; Legge 1885: Section 1)

This portrayal of the Confucian political ideal makes no appeal to technology or abundance of material resources. Neither does it assume there will be an absence of natural disasters. It emphasizes the excellence of the ruler that infects the people with a spirit of harmony, thereby creating a flourishing society. This is why the Grand Unity of the "Li Yun" chapter of the *Book of Rites* is contrasted with the society of the Small Tranquility in the same chapter.

> Now that the Grand Dao has fallen into disuse and obscurity, hereditary families rule the kingdoms. People love only their own parents as parents, and cherish only their own sons as sons. People accumulate things and use their strength only to their own advantage. Noblemen believe in their right to hereditary power. They seek only to build strong city walls, trenches and moats for security. The proprieties of conduct (*li* 澧) and what is right are used to enforce the relationship between ruler and minister; to ensure affection between father and son, harmony between brothers, and the sentiment of concord between husband and wife; to establish institutions and measurements; to organize farms and villages; to honor the brave and the wise; with a view to their advantage. Schemes and plots multiply, and armed conflicts arise. And so it was that Emperor Yu, King Tang, King Wen, King Wu, King Cheng, and the Duke of Zhou obtained their distinction. Each of these six great men attended to the rules of propriety to manifest their appropriateness and demonstrate their sincerity, identify error, exemplify humaneness (*ren*), and promote courtesy, thus promoting virtue. Rulers who did not follow this way were driven out by those who had power and condemned. Such was the Small Tranquility. (Ibid., Section 2)

Although the Small Tranquility state is not completely bankrupt, it is an incomplete realization of the ideal.[4]

Mencius's (c.372–289 BCE) Political Philosophy

It is a pity that Mencius's political philosophy is often neglected in a study of Chinese thought. One reason this is so is that Mencius conceives of politics and rulership as a branch of morality. D. C. Lau observes that for Mencius "the relationship between the ruler and the subject was looked upon as a special case of the moral relationship that holds between individuals" (*Mengzi*, Lau 2003: xxxviii).

Mencius does not speculate about the beginning of government. Instead, he is interested in describing a philosophical ideology of humane government *(renzheng* 仁政*)* for those rulers who will listen to him. Mencius is a *shi* 士, or scholar who traveled from state to state, seeking to be a ruler's political advisor. He receives compensation and housing from rulers for his service. These traveling advisors often had a significant influence on the ruler, and some of them even became powerful high-ranking officials themselves.

For Mencius, humane governance means "governance that tolerates no suffering of others" *(bu ren ren zhi zheng)* (ibid., 4A1; also see 1A7). Mencius holds that a ruler who practices humane governance should do at least the following things:

- reduce punishment and taxation (1A5),
- rejoice with his people (1B1), make sure the masses are neither cold nor hungry (1A7),
- take no pleasure in executions (1A6),
- allow no one to starve to death (1A4), and
- take care of the four types of people who are the most destitute (widows, widowers, old people without children, and young children without fathers) (1B5). (Xiao 2006: 266)

In the year 319 BCE, Mencius was in the city of Liang, capital city of the state of Wei. King Hui of Liang invited the wisest scholars from all of China to offer their advice on how to govern. Mencius was given a royal audience. The king asked him to provide guidance for how to make his state wealthy.

> If your Majesty says, "how can I profit my state?" The chief counselors will say, "how can I profit my plan?" And the nobles and commoners will say, "how can I profit myself?" Superiors and subordinates will seize profit from each other and the state will be endangered. When the ruler in a state that can field 10,000 chariots is assassinated, it will invariably be by clan that can field 1000 chariots. When the ruler in a state that can field 1000 chariots is assassinated, it will invariably be by a clan that can field 100 chariots. 8000 out of 10,000 or 800 out of 1000 is certainly not a small amount. But if one merely puts appropriateness last and profit first, no one will be satisfied without stealing more. Never have the humane left their parents behind. Never have

the righteous put the ruler last. Let your Majesty speak only of humaneness (*ren*) and appropriateness (*yi*).

(*Mengzi* 1A1, Lau 2003, my changes)

The strategy Mencius employs in giving political counsel to king Hui is to argue that obsession with profit is itself unprofitable (Van Norden 2011: 85). Mencius takes a position similar to that of Confucius: "to act with an eye to personal profit will incur a lot of resentment" (*Analects* 4.12, Ames and Rosemont 1998). However, "A humane man is the most powerful" (*ren zhe wu di*) (*Mengzi* 1A5; also see 7B3 and 7B4, Lau 2003). One who has the Way will have many to support him; one who does not have the Way will have few to support him (ibid., 2B1).

Xiao Yang argues that Mencius thinks a ruler pursuing humane government is able to do so because of his inner nature and not because it is merely expedient. Mencius is no utilitarian in his political theory, recommending a political action based on its favorable consequences. He holds, "Humans all have hearts that cannot bear the suffering of others. The Former Kings have such hearts, and that is why they have government that cannot bear the suffering of others" (ibid., 2A6). Here we see an argument for humane (*ren*) governance. Practicing humane governance is not based on one's belief that it will necessarily profit one's country in the long run; rather it is a natural expression of the meritorious ruler's heart-mind that is intrinsically compassionate and must manifest such moral disposition in his actions (Xiao 2006: 267). Mencius even claims,

> That which an exemplary person (*junzi*) follows as his nature, namely humaneness (*ren*), justice, propriety (*li*), and wisdom, is rooted in his heart-mind (*xin*), and expresses itself in his face, giving it a glowing appearance. It also shows in his back and extends to his limbs, rendering their message intelligible without words. (*Mengzi* 7A21; also see 4A15)

Mencius travels from state to state seeking to find a ruler who will practice "humane government." He thinks a state ruled in such a manner by a virtuous person will be one free of crime because the people have their needs met. Whereas in a state driven by profit, the people's needs are neglected and lawlessness results.

Mencius holds that the obligation of humane government is to ensure that the basic needs of the people are met. In contemporary political discourse, we call this "social justice." In contrast, Mencius is not intent on teaching that the role of government is to maximize civil liberty. Freedom of expression, speech and thought were not principal themes in Mencius's thought. In fact, he advocates an educational system in the ideal state that instructs people about how to conform to acceptable patterns in their relationships, as parent, child, ruler, minister, spouse and friend (ibid. 3A4). Mencius provides specific advice about how the state should help secure the livelihood of the people, including recommendations about everything from tax rates to farm management to the pay scales for government employees (ibid. 3A3). In giving advice to King Xuan, Mencius makes clear his views:

> Now if you should practice humaneness in the government of your state, then all those in the Empire who seek office will wish to find a place at your court, all tillers of land to till the land in outlying parts of your realm, all merchants to enjoy the refuge of your market-place, all travelers to go by way of your roads, and all those who hate their own rulers to lay their complaints before you. This being so, who can stop you from being a true King? (Ibid., 1A7)

Mencius is not making the utilitarian argument that the king should rule humanely in order to enjoy the benefits of his kingdom. He is saying that a ruler whose heart-mind leads him in this way will be recognized for his virtue and his kingdom will prosper.

The analogy Mencius uses for rulership is that of parent–child. A ruler should be to his subjects as a father is to his children. No father wants to see his children starving or freezing. All fathers want to see their children have opportunities for success and a fulfilling life. A humane ruler, according to Mencius, should have the same heart-mind. If the ruler can extend his love for his own children to cover the people over whom he is sovereign, the people will love him just as they love their own parents. As JeeLoo Liu observes, "Clearly, what Mencius thought is the opposite of Machiavelli's teaching, it is far better to be loved than feared if the ruler cannot be both" (Liu 2006: 83).

Mencius is not the only thinker to occupy the role of an advisor. There were many others. One of these may have had a direct influence on Mencius's political philosophy. Shang Yang lived in the middle period of the Warring States. He was born around 390 BCE and died in 338 BCE. Xiao Yang stresses that we have no record of Mencius and Shang encountering each other and there is no direct mention of Shang Yang in the *Mengzi* (Xiao 2006: 262). However, their positions on political philosophy are opposing and given the specifics of Mencius's points, it is hard to believe that he was unfamiliar with Shang's views. After all, Shang was the primary theorist behind the empire building of his time, including the rise of the state of Qin to the most powerful among the warring states. With respect to the ability of a humane ruler to survive, Shang preferred a strong military over the practice of social justice.

> A country of a thousand chariots is able to preserve itself by defending itself, and a country of ten thousand chariots is able to round itself off by attacking others; even [a bad ruler like] Jie would not be able to twist words to subdue his enemies. If a country is incapable of attacking other countries, or defending itself, then [even a humane ruler like] Yao would have to surrender to stronger countries. Based on this observation, we know that whether a country is taken seriously and respected by other countries depends entirely on its force. Therefore, force is the basis on which a country gains both prestige and respect.
>
> (*Shang Jun Shu*, 182/325 quoted in Xiao 2006: 263)

For Mencius, though, the question of government is not a strategic one about power, but a moral one, directed toward care for the people.

According to the *Mengzi* text, Mencius touches upon the removal of the ruler on several occasions. He says ministers should not hesitate to depose a ruler who repeatedly refuses to listen to admonitions against his serious mistakes (Lau 2003: 5B9). Speaking of historical instances in which rulers were removed, Mencius says a sovereign who mutilates humaneness (*ren*) or cripples rightness (*yi*) is an outcast, even if he is an emperor (ibid., 1B8). Mencius offers the first fully coherent defence of the replacement of government in Chinese philosophy. If the king is not humane, if he abuses the people instead of taking care of their welfare, he can be legitimately removed. For Mencius, anytime the ruler abuses his power in this manner, he ceases to be a genuine (*zhen*) ruler.

> Mencius said, "It was by humaneness (*ren*) that the three dynasties[5] gained the throne, and by not being humane that they lost it. It is by the same means that the decaying and flourishing, the preservation and

perishing, of states are determined. If the sovereign be not humane, he cannot preserve the throne from passing from him. If the Head of a State be not humane, he cannot preserve his rule." (Ibid., 4A3)

Mencius said, "Jie and Zhou's losing the throne, arose from their losing the people, and to lose the people means to lose their hearts. There is a way to get the kingdom: get the people, and the kingdom is got. There is a way to get the people: get their hearts, and the people are got. There is a way to get their hearts: it is simply to collect for them what they like, and not to lay on them what they dislike. The people turn to a humane ruler as water flows downwards, and as wild beasts fly to the wilderness ... If among the present rulers of the kingdom, there were one who loved humaneness, all the other princes would aid him, by driving the people to him." (Ibid., 4A9, my changes)

However, although Mencius held that the validity of rulership rests on the people's judgment, he does not think that the task of replacing the ruler should be placed in the hands of the people. In this case he is not a defender of popular revolution. Instead, the ruler should be removed by his own ministers in the ruling class, whom Mencius calls "Heaven's Delegated Officials" (*tianli* 天吏) (ibid., 2A5, 2B8).[6] The reason Mencius takes this position is the people lack the political expertise and certainly the military wherewithal to succeed in removing a ruler. A populist uprising will bring the whole nation into chaos. But his justification for deposing of an unjust ruler shows more clearly than any other feature of his thought that he has moved away from the older explanation that the rise and fall of dynasties and centers of power is a result of the Mandate of Heaven (*tianming*) or Heaven's authorization of the ruler and his kingdom. Mencius's position does not employ this grammar. Instead, he takes the view that the right of a king to rule, or the legitimacy of the government bureaucracy as a whole, rests with the people. This is not to say that the people should choose their own rulers as in a democracy, but in Mencius's ranking, "people are most valuable, land and grain are next valuable, and the ruler is least valuable."

Mencius lives in a time when the various neighboring dukes were constantly attacking one another and they were all committed to increasing their own power and prestige. He believes that if the king is intent only on acquiring wealth or territory, his people will surely suffer. At the same time, Mencius recognizes that not all warfare can be avoided. Sometimes war is necessary. We might call Mencius's view his theory of a "just war." For Mencius, a just war should have these characteristics:

- War should be a regrettable last resort since Mencius believed it would inevitably bring great suffering and waste upon the people. However, Mencius does not limit the war powers of a ruler merely to defensive ones, as Mozi does (*Mozi* 19.3). He holds war should not be entered into lightly and neither should it pre-empt other means of restoring justice and the well-being of the people, whether internally or externally (Van Norden 2011: 86). One of his sayings has become a Chinese proverb: to try to rule by means of brute force is as ineffectual as "climbing a tree in search of a fish" (*Mengzi* 1A7; Lau 2003).

- A war must have a just purpose or end in mind. It should not be pursued for expanding territory, gaining wealth or increasing power. A just war restores the well-being of the people. Internally, war (or revolutionary action by the ministers) may be used to remove an unjust ruler when there is no other effective means.

- Going to war with another kingdom or country can only be justified if it is corrective and not merely punitive. The analogy Mencius uses is that war between states is what punishment is to a criminal within the state. Shang Yang uses this exact analogy, but he stresses the punitive force of the action, not its corrective one (ibid., 7B4).[7] In contrast, Mencius argues that war with another country can be undertaken only if it brings benefit to the people of the other country. This is an interesting shift in focus. Mencius is directing our philosophical attention beyond the consequences for the king or his people. Mencius holds that the point is if the people of the enemy country have been exploited, abused or starved, they will welcome deliverance. In fact, they will not put up resistance. Mencius believes they will actually bring food and drink to reward the incoming troops. For him, winning a war is equivalent to winning the hearts of the people. In all just wars, one state must occupy the high moral ground and be rectifying the conditions of abuse being implemented by the other state. (Ibid., 1B11)

Lao Zhuang and Yellow Emperor Daoists on Rulership and Government

In introducing the Lao-Zhuang tradition, we have often noted the overlap between the teachings of the *Daodejing* and those sections of *Zhuangzi* most reliably traced to the historical Zhuang Zhou and his disciples. This remains true with respect to the political philosophy characteristic of this tradition as well.

The *Daodejing* took form in the turbulent period known as the Warring States (*c.*475–221 BCE). During all this disruption, rulers ignored the common people and their needs.

> The court is resplendent;
> Yet the fields are overgrown.
> The granaries are empty;
> Yet some wear elegant clothes;
> Fine swords hang at their sides;
> They are filled with food and drink;
> And possess wealth in exceeding abundance.
> This is known as taking pride in robbery.
> Far is this from the Way! (*DDJ*, 53)

In the *Daodejing*, individuals are cautioned not to seek favor or position in the government. "To gain favor is to be in the position of a subordinate. When you get it be worried; when you lose it be worried" (ibid., 13). But this philosophical text does say that if one is in a position of rulership, he should embody the *Dao* and thereby work for the good of all (ibid., 16). However,

> The greatest of rulers is but a shadowy presence;
> Next is the ruler who is loved and praised;
> Next the ruler who is feared;
> Next is the one who is reviled, those lacking in trust are not trusted.
> The greatest rulers are careful and stand by their word. (Ibid., 17)

In this connection, the text is famous for its aphorism that ruling a state is like cooking a small fish (ibid., 60), the point being that the least amount of tampering is best, as though the ruler should allow the *Dao* to take its course unaided and without manipulation by government policies. Rulers should not make a display of themselves and not build up armament or wage war. While a cultivated person (e.g., a Confucian), as a well-educated and trained ruler, may sometimes use weapons and wage war, the one who has the *Dao* does not rely on such strategies and knows that fine weapons are inauspicious instruments (ibid., 31). Even a victory is not a thing of beauty because it is erected on the destruction of human beings. "One who delights in the slaughter of human beings will not realize his ambitions in the world."

> Follow what is correct and right in ordering your state.
> Follow what is strange and perverse in ploying your troops.
> Follow *wu-wei* and gain the world.
> How do I know that things are this way?
> Because of this.

> Sages say,
> I do nothing (*wu-wei*) and the people transform themselves.
> I choose stillness and the people regulate and correct themselves.
> I *wu-wei* and the people prosper on their own.
> I am without desires and the people simplify their own lives. (Ibid., 57)

Actually, to rule a state properly according to the *Daodejing* is quite opposite to anything recommended in other political traditions of China in the classical period.

> In ancient times, those good at practicing the Way did not use it to
>   enlighten the people, but rather to keep them in the dark.
> The people are hard to govern because they know too much.
> And so to rule a state with knowledge is to be a detriment to the state.
> Not to rule a state through knowledge is to be a blessing to the state.
>   (Ibid., 65)

Of course, the *Daodejing* is not saying literally that a ruler is not to use his knowledge, and the text does not mean that there should be some conspiracy to keep the people uneducated and ignorant. It means that what is called "knowledge" by the Confucians and the Mohists is filled with discriminations and values of human making and definition. Trying to rule by these will tie the state into knots and create the circumstances for criminality and violence among the people. Once the ruler is empty of these and governs without using such "knowledge," the state and the people will settle down and order themselves. Government's role is to enable the people to order themselves, not to impose it from outside.

No philosophical inquiry makes it more obvious that the *Zhuangzi* is a composite text of teachings that sometimes differs in focus than does the subject of rulership and government. In the logia associated with the historical Zhuang Zhou (Chapters 1–7) and his disciples (Chapters 17–28), rulership is not held in high esteem and involvement at court is to be avoided. The positions taken in these sections parallel closely those of the *Daodejing*. Whereas, in those passages in *Zhuangzi* connected with what is called Yellow Emperor Daoism, political activity is not rejected if the ruler undertakes it in *wu-wei*.

The logia in Chapters 1–7 of *Zhuangzi* show that Daoist philosophical masters have no use for positions as officials or rulers. Instead, they recommend that the world be left to the processes of the *Dao* that orders things itself, without man's help (*Zhuangzi* 1, Watson 1968: 32–3). Indeed, trying to force the world into a pattern is something the perfected person (*zhenren*) must avoid. Political machinations run counter to what is natural. Of rulers who rely on political strategies, laws and structures, Jie Yu said:

> This is a bogus virtue! To try to govern the world like this is like trying to walk the ocean, to drill through a river, or to make a mosquito shoulder a mountain! When the sage governs, does he govern what is on the outside? He makes sure of himself first, and then he acts. He makes absolutely certain that things can do what they are supposed to do, that is all. (Ibid., 7; 93)

The teachers who were sources of this material create a story according to which even the great sage ruler Yao, when he visits the four masters of Gushe Mountain, realizes that there is no need for government and that the affairs of human politics can be forgotten by the one who follows the *Dao* (ibid., 2; 34).

Zhuangzi's disciples also reject rulership. To explain why Zhuangzi was never a ruler, the disciples provide us with an account of the master fishing on the Pu River when two ministers from the King of Chu come to ask him to rule over all the territories of Chu (ibid., 17; 187–8). Zhuangzi refuses, saying he would rather be like a turtle content to have his tail in the mud than be the long-dead sacred tortoise in the palace of the king. This distaste for official position and government rulership is very clear throughout Chapters 17–28. For example, Zhuangzi tells his old debater *(bianshi)* friend Huizi that he has no desire to rule (ibid., 17; 188). Chapter 28 contains several logia all dealing with rulership. Some of these are designed to show that when they were approached with the offer of rulership, famous Daoist masters refused it, went into hiding, or even committed suicide rather than rule (ibid., 28; 310, 312, 313–14 and 321–2). Consider this example of the disciples' attitude toward rulership:

> The men of Yue three times in succession assassinated their ruler. Prince Sou, fearful for his life, fled to the Cinnabar Caves and the state of Yue was left without a ruler. The men of Yue, searching for Prince Sou and failing to find him, trailed him to the Cinnabar Cave, but he refused to come forth. They smoked him out with mugwort and placed him in the royal carriage. As Prince Sou took hold of the strap and pulled himself up into the carriage, he turned his face to heaven and cried, "To be a ruler! A ruler! Could I alone not have been spared this?" It was not that he hated to become their ruler; he hated the perils that go with being a ruler. Prince Sou, we may say, was the kind who would not allow the state to bring injury to his life. This, in fact, was precisely why the people of Yue wanted to obtain him for their ruler. (Ibid., 28; 311)

In sharp contrast to these sentiments about political involvement and the place of government, we see the Yellow Emperor logia on rulership largely in Chapters 11–16 of the *Zhuangzi*. In making its point about rulership, this section takes as its hero the Yellow Emperor and says that in his early period of rule he used humaneness and appropriateness "to meddle with the minds of men." What followed was a history of consternation and confusion, all the way down to the Confucians and Mohists who are mentioned by name (ibid., 11; 117). We also find in *Zhuangzi* the story about the Yellow Emperor visiting Master Guang Cheng on top of the Mountain of Emptiness and Identity (*Kongtong*) (ibid., 11; 118–20). When the Yellow Emperor learns the essence of the Perfect Dao, he "withdrew, gave up his throne, built a solitary hut, spread a mat of white rushes, and lived for three months in retirement" (ibid.). When the Yellow Emperor returns to rule thereafter, he follows *wu-wei* (effortless action) and becomes an immortal. The point of these teachings is that the Yellow Emperor creates disaster when he rules as a Confucian or Mohist would, meddling with persons' minds, but when he rules in *wu-wei*, he is glorified and the world is well ordered.

> Emptiness, stillness, limpidity, silence, *wu-wei* are the root of the ten thousand things. To understand them and face south is to become a ruler such as Yao was; to understand them and face north is to become a minister such as Shun was. To hold them in high station is the *de* of emperors and kings, of the Son of Heaven; to hold them in lowly station is the way of the dark sage, the uncrowned king [i.e., Confucius]. Retire with them to a life of idle wandering and you will command first place among the recluses of the rivers and seas, the hills and forests. Come forward with them to succor the age and your success will be great, your name renowned, and the world will be united. In stillness you will be a sage, in action a king. Resting in *wu-wei*, you will be honored; of unwrought simplicity, your beauty will be such that no one in the world may vie with you. (Ibid., 13; 142–8)

In this passage, the much-honored Confucian sage-kings Yao and Shun are not blamed for the confusion and disorder of the world, but their success and greatness is attributed to the fact that they practiced *wu-wei*, emptiness and stillness. Any true ruler should follow their example. To forsake them is to follow the way of the dark sage, known as the uncrowned king (Confucius).

Legalism and the *Hanfeizi* (c.280–233 BCE)

The term "Legalist School" (*fa jia*) first appeared in Sima Qian's *Records of the Historian* in about 90 BCE. If we take the term to refer loosely to Chinese philosophers of the classical period whose common conviction was that law rather than morality was the most reliable ordering mechanism for society, we are on firm ground. A number of philosophers associated with this school were active in government and as imperial consultants from the mid-300s to *c.*200 BCE. For example, Shang Yang (d. 338 BCE) was a chancellor of the Qin state and Shen Buhai (d. 337 BCE) held a similar positon in the Han state. Master Han Fei (Hanfeizi, 280–233 BCE) served as an advisor in the Han state, just prior to its annexation by the Qin when China's first empire was created in 221 BCE (Wong 2003).

Han Fei has no well-developed theory of the state of nature, but what he has is an adequate view for explaining the origin of government as an institution: strong enforcement and control of behavior is needed to bring order to the state and develop the society.

> If people had to wait for arrow shafts that are naturally straight, then for a hundred generations there would be no arrows. If they had to wait for that is naturally round, then for a thousand generations there would be no chariot wheels. If in a hundred generations there is not a single arrow shaft that is naturally straight, nor a single piece of wood that is naturally round, how is it that every generation is able to ride around in chariots and shoot down birds with arrows? It is because they used the way of straightening and bending (i.e., rule of law).
>
> (*Han Fei Tzu*; Watson 1964: 357)

Although it is generally agreed that Han Fei was influenced by Xunzi's views on human nature, he does not think that human nature is evil. He simply holds that all humans act in their own self-interest.

> The carriage maker … hopes that men will grow rich and eminent; the carpenter fashioning coffins hopes that men will die prematurely. It is not that the carriage maker is kindhearted and the carpenter a knave. It is only that if men do not become rich and eminent, the carriage will never sell, and if men do not die, there will be no market for coffins. The carpenter has no feeling of hatred towards others; he merely stands to profit by their death. (Ibid., 86)

As Han Fei interprets it, the human actions that seem to mark individuals as humane and caring or as evil and miserly are actually very much dependent on the *conditions* in which one lives and not primarily on human nature. He is not a complete economic determinist, of course, but he feels resources and scarcity play a role in the extent to which one will follow the laws and moral norms of society.

> In olden times, men did not need to till, for the seeds of grass and the fruits of trees were sufficient to feed them; nor did women have to weave, for the skins of birds and beasts were sufficient to clothe them.

Thus, without working hard, they had an abundance of supply. As the people were few, their possessions were more than sufficient. Therefore the people never quarrelled. As a result, neither large rewards were bestowed nor were heavy punishments employed, but the people governed themselves. Nowadays, however, people do not regard five children as many. Each child may in his or her turn beget five offspring, so that before the death of the grandfather there may be twenty-five grand-children. As a result, people have become numerous and supplies scanty; toil has become hard and provisions meager. Therefore people quarrel so much that, though rewards are doubled and punishments repeated, disorder is inevitable. (*Hanfeizi*, Chapter 49; Liao 1939)

In taking this position, we see that far from maintaining that humans have a nature that is good or evil and from their nature arises their moral conduct, Han Fei insists that human moral action is a by-product of the socio-economic environment in which they find themselves.

Based on this analysis, Han Fei argues that creating a state in which the resources are sufficient is one way to encourage moral goodness and social order. Likewise, if a ruler wants his people to work diligently, he must motivate them by an appeal to their self-interests. The ruler should set up policies and administrate the state so that whenever an individual is maximizing his own self-interest the action will also enlarge the public interest of the state.

We can see, then, that for Han Fei rulership is not the expression of the virtue and character of a ruler of merit as Confucius or Mencius might have had it. Neither is it an expression of a virtuous ruler who follows the Way of Heaven as Mozi insists. In fact, for Han Fei, even a ruler who is morally deficient in his own personal life may nevertheless be a good ruler. The test is whether he can use political instrumentation to manage the self-interests of the various power centers and the common people. Instead of having as its end the creation of a community in which people are humanized and encouraged to cultivate themselves morally, Han Fei thinks of politics as a form of social control, a set of tactics that must be balanced and re-balanced based on the people's preferences and distastes, for these are the guides to what they perceive to be in their self-interest.[8]

Han Fei largely separates politics from morality, taking an approach to rulership that Confucius would not condone. To put it succinctly, Confucianism insists on rule by the virtuous (i.e., a meritocracy) and the ultimate goal of the state as a harmony between morality and politics. Hanfei thinks of both the ruler and politics as *amoral*. In fact, he thinks persons of virtue and morality may actually be detrimental to the state. In the chapter "Eight Fallacies," he makes this claim:

> The presence of kind-hearted men implies [i.e., leads to] the existence of culprits [i.e., defilement] among the magistrates; the presence of humane men, the losses of public funds; the presence of superior men, the difficulty in employing the people; the presence of virtuous men, the violation of laws and statutes; the appearance of chivalrous men, vacancies of official posts; the appearance of lofty men, the people's neglect of their proper duties; the emergence of unyielding heroes, the inefficacy of orders; and the appearance of popular idols, the isolation of the sovereign from the subjects. (Ibid., Chapter 47)

How can the presence of kind hearted persons lead to defilement among the magistrates or the ministers of the government? Han Fei says it works like this: if a person administers his office by kindness and not by justice and application of the law, he may be subject to emotions and thereby manipulation. A humane (i.e., *ren*) man, caring for the people's needs, might allow his compassion for the poor and needy to go too far and exhaust public funds or he may be led to levy heavy taxes to pay for free riders benefiting from the state's generosity. Han Fei gives this example of what the Confucian humane men involved with government in his day say,

> "Give the poor and the destitute land and thereby provide men of no property with enough." However, if there are men who were originally the same as others but have independently become able to be perfectly self-supporting, even without prosperous years or other income, it must be due to their diligence or to their frugality. Again, if there are men who were originally the same as others but have independently become poor and destitute without suffering from any misfortune of famine and drought or illness and malignancy or calamity and lawsuit, it must be due to their extravagance or to their laziness. Extravagant and lazy persons are poor; diligent and frugal persons are rich. Now, if the superior levies money from the rich in order to distribute alms among the poor, it means that he robs the diligent and frugal and rewards the extravagant and lazy. (Ibid., Chapter 50)

So, we can see the very direct way in which Han Fei thinks that the kinds of persons and conduct valued by Confucians, whether it be humaneness (*ren*) or becoming an exemplary person (*junzi*), can work to counter-purposes of the state, the well-being of the people and a just order. When his views are extended like this, we may ask whether he has crossed the line from the position that politics is *amoral* to the position that politics is *anti-moral*, and that, indeed, it should be so, although he may not go quite so far.

Han Fei sets out five political tactics necessary to a viable government:

- the use of the power of position;
- the employment of administrative methods;
- the making of laws;
- taking hold of the two handles of government—reward and punishment; and
- the effortless action (*wu-wei*) of the ruler.[9]

The "power of position" (*shi* 勢) is a term used in Chinese military texts to refer to the strategic advantage that one army has over another by occupying the high ground. Han Fei recommends that rulers employ their political power and authority to bring order to the society. Bryan Van Norden quotes this passage from the *Hanfeizi:*

> IfYao and Shun had relinquished the power of their positions as rulers and abandon the law, and instead went from door to door persuading and debating with people, without any power to encourage them with veneration and rewards will chorus them with punishments and penalties, they would not have been able to bring order to even a few households. (Van Norden 2011: 191)

The employment of administrative methods (*shu* 術) included the appointment of someone to government office based on their merit. Han Fei sees favoritism as a severe problem in the government of the Han dynasty. The responsibility of the ruler, then, is to achieve his policies and tasks by appointing capable ministers. Likewise, ministers should not perform the duties of another. They should not exceed their appointed assignments or overstep the boundaries of their office. In the "Using Persons" (*Yong Ren*) chapter of his work, Han Fei proposes that the people be made to exert their strength for public causes and thereby avoid the usurpation of the ruler's authority by self-seeking ministers (*Hanfeizi*, Chapter 27; Liao 1939).

The creation of laws is another tactic necessary to the ideal state in Han Fei's view. For him, the determination of law is the right of the ruler.

> Government through law exists when the ruler's edicts and decrees are promulgated among the various departments and bureaus, when the certitude of punishments and penalties is understood in the hearts of the people, when rewards are given to those who respect the law, and when penalties are imposed on those who violate the rulers' decrees.
>
> (*Han Fei Tzu*; Watson 1964: 336)

Han Fei holds that other allegiances, whether custom, tradition or moral values, cannot be allowed to compete with law. The dutiful son of the father (the Confucian filial son) must not be allowed to break the law in order to be filial (Chapter 49). The state, the law, the ruler, must come first.

> Men of today who do not know the right way to political order, all say, "Win the hearts of the people." If they should think of winning the hearts of the people and thereby attaining political order, then even Yi Yin and Kuan Chung would find no use for their statesmanship and the superior would listen to the people only. The intelligence of the people, however, cannot be depended upon just like the mind of the baby ... if his [the baby's] boil is not cut open, his trouble will turn from bad to worse ... Yet he keeps crying and yelling incessantly as he does not know that suffering the small pain will gain him a great benefit.
>
> Now, the superior urges the tillage of rice fields and the cultivation of grassy lands in order to increase the production of the people, but they think the superior is cruel. To perfect penalties and increase punishments is to suppress wickedness, but they think the superior is severe. Again, he levies taxes in cash and in grain to fill up the storehouses and treasures in order thereby to relieve famine and drought and provide for corps and battalions, but they think the superior is greedy. Finally, he traces out every culprit within the boundary, discriminates among men without personal favoritism ...

and unites the forces for fierce struggle, in order thereby to take his enemies captive, but they think the superior is violent. These four measures are methods to attain order and maintain peace, but the people do not know that they ought to rejoice in them.

(Chapter 50, Liao 1939)

In short, the ruler does not take his directions from the common people and Han Fei seems not to think them sufficiently intelligent or prudent to take seriously in the matters of rulership and law making.

It is just such a view that leads Han Fei to refer to the tactics of rewards and punishments as the "two handles" of government. "When handing out rewards, it is best to make them substantial and dependable, so that people will prize them; when assigning penalties, it is best to make them heavy and inescapable, so that people will fear them" (*Han Fei Tzu*; Watson 1964: 343). His position is that rulers must structure government in such a way that it is in the best interest of the citizens and the ministers alike to act for the common good and not merely for their private desires. "When a sage governs the state, he does not wait for people to be good in deference to him. Instead, he creates a situation in which people find it impossible to do wrong" (ibid., 357).

> For this reason, the intelligent ruler, in bestowing rewards, is as benign as the seasonable rain that the masses profit by his graces; in inflicting punishments, he is so terrific like the loud thunder that even divines and sages cannot atone for their crimes. Thus the intelligent ruler neglects no reward and remits no punishment. For, if reward is neglected, ministers of merit will relax their duties; if punishment is remitted, villainous ministers will become liable to misconduct. Therefore, men of real merit, however distant and humble, must be rewarded; those of real demerit, however near and dear, must be censured.
>
> (*Hanfeizi*, Chapter 5; Liao 1939)

Even if all the other tactics of governing are followed, chaos can still be the result if one has an ineffectual ruler. Han Fei thinks of penal law as the expression of the ruler's power and control over society. However, he is not recommending arbitrary laws established at the whim of the ruler, or designed only to aggrandize the ruler's power and luxury.

If the lord of men institutes difficult requirements and convicts anybody whosoever falls short of the mark, then secret resentment will appear. If the minister disuses his merit and has to attend to a difficult work, then hidden resentment will grow. If toil and pain are not removed and worry and grief are not appeased; if the ruler, when glad, praises small men and rewards both the worthy and the unworthy, and, when angry, blames superior men and thereby makes Po-i and Robber Chê equally disgraced, then there will be ministers rebelling against the sovereign. (Ibid., Chapter 27)

While Hanfeizi raises a number of cautions against the values and strategies of the Confucians, in Chapter V, "the Dao of the Ruler," he makes use of a vocabulary taken from the *Daodejing*, but he gives it a quite unique meaning. For example, Han Fei instructs the ruler to be "empty" and "still." But these are not disciplines designed to put him in touch with the *Dao* and enable him to move in *wu-wei* as they are understood to do in the Yellow Emperor tradition of the *Zhuangzi*.

Be empty and reposed and have nothing to do [i.e., *wu-wei*], then from the dark see defects in the light. See but never be seen. Hear but never be heard. Know but never be known. If you hear any word uttered, do not change it nor move it but compare it with the deed and see if word and deed coincide with each other. Place every official with a censor. Do not let them speak to each other. Then everything will be exerted to the utmost. Cover tracks and conceal sources. Then the ministers cannot trace origins. Leave your wisdom [i.e., do not state your views] and cease your ability [i.e., do not recommend policies or acts yourself]. Then your subordinates cannot guess at your limitations.

Han Fei is intentionally using Daoist concepts, but interpreting them in his own way. The ruler should be "empty" means the ruler should not reveal his opinions or policy desires. He should "be still" by not handing down a policy or taking any action himself (i.e., let others do it). By not taking action,

He [the ruler] makes it so that the worthy refine their natural talents, while he makes use of those talents and employs them. Thus, he is never lacking in ability. He makes it so that when there are achievements he gets the credit for their worthiness, and when there are errors the ministers take the blame. Thus, he is never lacking in reputation ... The ministers perform the work, and the ruler enjoys the final achievement. (Van Norden 2011: 196)

Political Views of the *Masters of Huainan (Huainanzi)* (139 BCE)

As a synthetic work completed by a collection of editors at the Huainan academy, the *Masters of Huainan* does not reject the Confucian virtue of humaneness (*ren*) as we saw done in the *Daodejing* and in the *Zhuangzi*. However, it seeks to correct the followers of Confucius for teaching humaneness (*ren*) in the wrong manner. We might expect this from a work compiled during the ascendancy of Confucian influence, but it also strives to convey its sense of the truth in terms of following the *Dao*.

The *Masters of Huainan* is a work focused on educating a ruler regarding the tasks before him. In the text, we find a theory of the fall of humanity from an original primitive harmony in the state of nature into human government and politics with its attendant disorder and violence. Instead of being the result of agreed contractual understandings between persons who find themselves in a "state of nature" where there is no law and the powerful can have their will over the weak, the text takes a completely reverse approach. Law and government, the emergence of the political state, are not a remedy to an originating situation of disharmony. The primal state is thought of as one of natural, spontaneous, peaceful existence. Government is the *source* of humanity's problems, not the answer to them. As *Masters of Huainan* 8.3 says:

The people of antiquity made their *qi* the same as that of heaven and earth; they wandered in an era of unity. At that time, there was no garnering advantage by praise and rewards, no intimidation by mutilations and punishments. Proprieties of conduct (*li*) and rightness (*yi*), purity and modesty, had not yet been established; slander and flattery, humaneness and contempt, had not yet been set up; and the myriad peoples had not yet begun to treat each other with fraud and oppression, cruelty and exploitation—it was as if they were still immersed in mystery (*hun ming* 混冥).

> (*Huainanzi*, Major et al. 2010, my changes).

In the age of utmost potency (*de*), [people] contentedly slept in boundless realms and moved [between] and lodged in indeterminate dwellings. They clasped heaven and earth and discarded the myriad things. They took primal chaos as their gnomon and floated freely in a limitless domain. For this reason, the sages [merely] inhaled and exhaled the *qi* of *yin* and *yang*, and none of the myriad living things failed to flourish as they acknowledged [the sages] ... When the age declined, in the reign of Fuxi, his way was obscure and indistinct. He contained potency (*de*) and embraced harmony, broadcasting them subtly and comprehensively, yet even so knowledge first stirred and sprouted. [The people] all wanted to part from their childlike and ignorant mind and awareness appeared in the midst of heaven and earth; thus their potency was vexed and could not be unified. Coming to the age of the Divine Farmer (i.e. Shennong) and the Yellow Emperor (i.e. Huangdi) ... The myriad things and hundred clans were each given structure and rule. At this, the myriad people all were alert and awake, and there were none who did not straighten up to listen and look. Thus they were orderly but could not be harmonized. Coming down to the age of Kun Wu and the descendants of the Xia, desires attached to things; hearing and sight were lured outward ...[10] Coming down to the house of Zhou, decadence dispersed simplicity; [people] deserted the Way (*Dao*) for artifice; they were miserly of potency in conduct; and cleverness and precedence sprouted. When the Zhou house declined, the kingly way was abandoned. The Confucians and Mohists thus began enumerating their way and debating, dividing up disciples, and reciting ... For this reason, the learning of the Sage seeks to return nature to its origin and restore the heart-mind to roaming emptiness. (Ibid., 2.10)

In the *Masters of Huainan* this theory of the fall from primitive harmony into human government and politics is developed in greater detail and brought down to the actual period of the formation of the work in 6.7.

Instructions to the ruler
The disciples of Confucius and Mozi all teach the techniques of humaneness and rightness to the age, yet they do not avoid destruction.

If they personally cannot practice [their teachings], how much less may those they teach? Why is this? Because their way is external. To ask the branches to return to the roots: if even Xu You could not do it, how much less the common people? If you genuinely break through to the basic tendencies of nature and destiny, so that humaneness and rightness adhere [to your actions], how then can choosing and discarding suffice to confuse your mind? (Ibid., 2.12)

Chapter Nine of the *Masters of Huainan* is entitled "The Ruler's Techniques" and is of particular interest to us as philosophers. The focus of this chapter is on the methods that a ruler should use to create a humane and orderly government. The first and certainly the most important technique for a ruler is to act in *wu-wei*. This does not mean the ruler should do absolutely nothing; it means that when he acts nothing comes from him personally (9.23), so his policies are neither biased by his private preferences (9.25) nor restricted by the limits of his own vision for the state (9.9–9.11). Instead, his actions implement the movement of the *Dao*. When this happens, the people find the policies suitable because they seem natural. In order to act in *wu-wei*, the ruler must refine his *qi*. In so doing he avails himself of the unlimited and mysterious Way (*Dao*) of Heaven (9.2).

> The Ruler's Techniques [consist of]
>   establishing non-active (*wu-wei*) management
>   and carrying out wordless instructions.
>   Quiet and tranquil, he does not move;
>   by [even] one degree he does not waver;
>   adaptive and compliant, he relies on his underlings;
>   dutiful and accomplished, he does not labor.
>   …
> Therefore,
>   his considerations are without mistaken schemes;
>   his undertakings are without erroneous content.
>   his words [are taken as] scripture and verse;
> his conduct [is taken as] a model and gnomon for the world. (Ibid., 9.1)

> Therefore,
>   the affairs of the world cannot be deliberately controlled.

> You must draw them out by following their natural direction.
> The alterations of the myriad things cannot be fathomed.
> You must grasp their essential tendencies and guide them to their
> homes. (Ibid., 1.5)

Actually, although the *Masters of Huainan* offers instructions in the technique of ruling, the ultimate basis of these is the ruler's internal spirit. If the ruler is one with the *Dao*, he can move in *wu-wei* and his action will be as efficacious as that of any of the Daoist heroes of the *Zhuangzi*.

As an example of its appropriation of the many other schools of thought, when discussing the response of the people to the ruler who is a "perfected person" (*zhenren*), *Masters of Huainanzi* cites Confucius's statement, "If the ruler himself is upright, even though he does not issue orders, they are carried out, if he is not upright, though he issue orders, they are not followed" (ibid., 9.23; this comes from *Analects* 13.6).

When we read about the *wu-wei* of the ruler, we may think this means that *Masters of Huainanzi* is recommending a state without law. But actually, this is not true. The perfected person (*zhenren*) as ruler is able to make law because he knows the wordless teaching and carries out the unalterable way (*dao*). His heart is one with the people, in the same way that a master chariot driver and the horses are coordinated.

> Now if the horses are matched to the chassis and the driver's heart is in
> harmony with the horses, a charioteer can travel perilous roads and go
> for long distances, advancing and retreating and turning circles, with
> nothing failing to accord with his will. [But if] even steeds as fine as
> Qiji and Lu'er were given to female bondservants to drive, they would
> revert to their own intractable ways, and the servants could not control
> them. Thus the ruler does not prize people being the way he wants
> them of their own accord but prizes there being no chance for them
> to go wrong. (Ibid., 9.24)

The ruler is the maker of laws and conversely, the quality of the law depends on the character of the ruler. "Law comes from rightness. Rightness comes from what is appropriate for the people. What is appropriate for the people accords with the human heart. This is the *sine qua non* of government" (ibid., 9.23).

Law is

not a gift of heaven,

not a product of earth.

It was devised by humankind but conversely is used [by humans] to
   rectify themselves ...

A country that can be said to be lost is not one without a ruler but one
   without laws. (Ibid., 9.23)

Since the *Masters of Huainan* holds that humans and the rest of nature are
interconnected, this certainly has implications for its view of rulership.

If there are punishments in cruelty, there will be whirlwinds.

If there are wrongful ordinances, there will be plagues of devouring
   insects.

If there are unjust executions, the land will redden with drought.

(Ibid., 3.3)

In order to get an answer to the question, what is the best form of
government? We may look in *Masters of Huainan* in several places. One
of these is 6.7, where the ideal rulers Fuxi and Nuwa, as well as the
Yellow Emperor (*Huangdi*), are described.

In ancient times, the Yellow Emperor ruled the world. Li Mu and
   Taishan Ji assisted him in

Regulating the movements of the sun and the moon,

setting in order the *qi* of *yin* and *yang*,

delimiting the measure of the four seasons, correcting the calculations
   of the pitch pipes and the calendar.

They

separated men from women,

differentiated female and male [animals],

clarified the high in the low,

ranked the worthy and the mean;

   they took steps [to ensure that]

the strong would not oppress the weak;

the many would not oppress the few.

People lived out their allotted lifespans and did not suffer early death;

crops ripened in season and were not subject to calamities.

All the officials were upright and not given to partiality.

High and low were in concord and did not find fault.
Laws and commandments were clear and there was no confusion.
Officials assisted the ruler and did not engage in flattery.

The *Masters of Huainan* does not hesitate to criticize the methods of government practiced under the philosophy of Han Fei and even mentions him by name.

Now take, for example, the methods of government [proposed by] Shen [Buhai], Han [Fei], and Shang Yang. They proposed to pluck out the stems [of disorder] and weed out the roots [of disobedience], without fully investigating where [those undesirable qualities] came from. How did things get to that point? They forcibly imposed the five punishments, employed slicing and amputations, and turned their backs on the fundamentals of the Way (*Dao*) and its potency (*de*) while fighting over the point of an awl. They mowed the common people like hay and exterminated more than half of them. Thus filled with self-admiration, they constantly took themselves as the model of government; but this was just like adding fuel to put out a fire or boring holes to stop water from leaking. (Ibid., 6.9)

In contrast, consider the description of the perfected person (*zhenren*) as a ruler.

His mind is coextensive with his spirit;
   his physical form is in tune with his nature.
   When he is still he embodies potency (*de*);
   when he acts, he patterns himself on penetration.
He follows his spontaneous nature and aligns himself with inevitable transformations.
He is profoundly non-active (*wu-wei*), and the world naturally becomes harmonious. (Ibid., 8.5)

Yan Fu (1854–1921): China Not Ready for Democracy

According to Fung Yulan, Yan Fu is not only the greatest authority on Western philosophy in China at the beginning of the twentieth century but also the first scholar to introduce Western philosophy to

China by translating a significant number of works, many of which have to do with political and social philosophy: Thomas Henry Huxley's *Evolution and Ethics* (1893), published in Chinese in 1898; Adam Smith's *The Wealth of Nations* (1776), published in Chinese in 1902; Herbert Spencer's *The Study of Sociology* (1872) and John Stuart Mill's *On Liberty* (1859), both translations published in Chinese in 1904; Charles de la Secondat de Montesquieu's *The Spirit of the Laws* (1748), J. S. Mill's *A System of Logic* (1843), translated in 1905; and William Stanley Jevons's *The Theory of Political Economy* (1878), all translated in 1909 (Fung 1948: 326).[11]

Yan tends to follow the lead of Herbert Spencer in applying Darwinism to society generally in the manner known as Social Darwinism. Although he translated both Huxley and Spencer, he was well aware of the conflict between them over the applicability of the concepts of "survival of the fittest" and "natural selection" to society and culture. Huxley thinks that society and culture represent the way of human beings, whereas Darwin has studied the way of nature. He does not think that Darwin's findings about nature can be transferred to human social and political constructs. Yan, however, agrees with Spencer in thinking that social organization is also a product of evolution and subject to its same laws and processes. Nonetheless, he does not allow his objections to Huxley to influence his translation of *Evolution and Ethics*. Instead, he puts his criticisms of Huxley in the commentary on the translation (Jiang 2009: 475).

In his commentary, Yan writes, "In natural evolution, the higher level a society has evolved to, the more liberty the society has" (1986: I, 133). He declares that both the Western powers and Japan, who had invaded and exploited China, are scientifically and socially superior. In his view, China has become inferior as a result of its inability to excel in the international competition of worldviews, technology and socio-political structure. He argues that if China does not fight for its own existence, it will succumb to Western domination because the West is more fitted for survival than the China of his day. As can be imagined, the translation itself, and especially Yan's positions, set off a heated debate among Chinese intellectuals over the social applications of the concept of "survival of the fittest" in general and its use with respect to China's place globally.

Although the purpose of Huxley's work is to show that the application of evolutionary theory to the social domain (Social

Darwinism) is inappropriate, nonetheless it constitutes, together with Spencer's work, an introduction to Social Darwinism in China. In his commentaries, Yan insists that China fares badly in conflict with the powers of the West and Japan because Chinese society is not rightly structured. He clearly thinks that for China to fare well in the global competition with other nations it must alter its societal structure (ibid., I, 12).

In search for why China is weaker and less able to compete compared to the Western nations, Yan claims the reason is China's lack of liberty for its people. He thinks this deficiency accounts for China's weakness and backwardness (ibid., I, 2). Yan not only accepts John Stuart Mill's (1806–73) view in *On Liberty* (1859) that the strength of a body politic lies in its commitment to the discovery of truth but also agrees with Mill that liberty of expression and inquiry is essential to the acquisition of truth. Moreover, Yan holds that freedom to choose one's own lifestyle creates the novelty and progress present in Western countries but absent in China. Accordingly, he claims that liberty is essential in order to produce a strong nation. When people lack liberty, they are not motivated to fight for the state or work hard in order to create a productive society. Yan writes:

> People in the West are respected and appreciated, even more than their kings or dukes, but the people in China are regarded as so low that they are all the property of their ruler. When the state needs people to fight for it, in the West people will naturally go to fight for their common interests and property, while in China slaves have to fight for their masters. When slaves fight against those who have been given human dignity, how can they not be defeated?
>
> (Ibid., I, 36)

Yan makes use of Mill's line of argument that a state will not prevail if its members are not invested in their own development by virtue of being free to choose their own life ends (Mill 1956: 143). However, Yan is forced to defend himself against conservative critics in China who think his call for greater liberty of thought and expression will lead to social instability. Yan's strategy is to claim that although society should not interfere with individual human liberty, neither should the individual do anything to harm society by his free expression. Yan extends Mill's "harm principle" beyond its use as a limitation on an individual's actions deterring harm to another person. He holds that it is legitimate to restrict freedom in the name of the protection of societal and communal integrity and value. For Yan, the concept of liberty does not mean unlimited expression or doing whatever one wants. Society has genuine interests that might be harmed by indiscriminate freedom of action. Society has a right to transmit a set of values and cultural practices that can limit freedom of the individual. In fact, it is significant that Yan's translation of Mill's *On Liberty* was published in full title as *On the Borderline between Society's and Individuals' Power.*

These factors lead some to believe that Yan Fu's translation does not capture the full intensity of Mill's commitment to liberty (Schwartz 1964: 131–48). However, Yan also holds that China's highly structured moral beliefs and social rituals can overwhelm liberty if not properly watched. He writes, "In Western countries, there is nothing that prohibits free speech more than religion. … In China, those moral norms for human relationships function in the same way. As far as those moral norms are concerned, no free discussion can be allowed. Chinese moral norms even do more than Western religions in prohibiting free discussion" (Yan 1986: I, 134).

We should not overlook the use Yan made of Mill's ideas. Xinyan Jiang reminds us that there had never before been an analysis of the nature and place of liberty in Chinese political philosophy (Jiang 2009: 477). While we can find some philosophical defences of remonstrance in the history of Chinese philosophy, the function of this concept is much different than what Mill means by liberty.[12] In remonstrance, a minister or even a citizen may sometimes protest that an action or policy of the ruler is unjust or unproductive and in this way influences a change. However, the life of the common person in China is often more restricted by the norms of custom and moral expectation than by law.[13] While we may certainly find examples of nonconformity in Chinese history, these are relatively few and far between. Accordingly, when Chinese intellectuals began to read Mill and especially Yan's commentaries on the translation of *On Liberty*, a new way of looking at society and a person's place within it came into view. Yan argues that even the beliefs and practices that hold a society together and make it stable cannot be placed outside of the realm of examination and critical scrutiny. This is the ultimate value of liberty of thought and discussion.

Yan holds that the well-being of a society depends on the liberty of the people, and liberty cannot be obtained in China without a critique of its traditional morality and its restriction on free expression, thought and discussion. Yan's conclusion becomes an impetus for the New Cultural Movement that begins in 1915.

Clearly, Yan believes the task of implementing liberty varies under different political systems. The challenges faced in Mill's England are not the same as those facing the Chinese coming out of a long history of imperial and despotic systems. Still, Yan recognizes that liberty is more fundamental than any political system humans have yet devised. It is more basic even than democracy. Yan thinks liberty can exist in systems that are not absolute democracies. In fact, he advocates that China move toward a constitutional monarchy, such as that found in the Britain of his day. He realizes that liberty might be achieved under more than one type of governmental structure, but he thinks such a model will optimize China's chances of creating a free society.

Nevertheless, Yan does not support China's 1911 revolution to create a Republic and disestablish the Qing dynasty. He insists on gradual reform and political change. Instead of active political overthrow of the government, Yan thinks improvement of the Chinese populous will gradually establish a new reality where freedom prevails and the Chinese people may pursue their own life projects. He offers a program of first enhancing the people's intellectual and education level, along with a re-creation and modification of Chinese cultural values, and an improvement of the people's physical health and well-being (Yan 1986: I, 27). In order for the people to reach these goals, China's education system has to be modernized and scientific methods of inquiry and research introduced.

As a philosopher, Yan believes the Chinese people at the turn of the twentieth century are not yet ready or capable of participatory government and responsible use of free expression. The extent and degree of liberty a society can tolerate and achieve is directly related to the capability and knowledge of the citizenry. Li Zhehou argues that Yan believes the imitation of Western democratic practice in the China of his own day, without enhancement of the people's knowledge, will lead to disaster (Li 2003: 259).

Kang Youwei (1858–1927)

Kang Youwei is a committed Chinese nationalist whose reformist ideas are despised by Empress Dowager Cixi (1835–1908) in the last years of the Qing dynasty. Kang wants to reform the Chinese government and establish a constitutional monarchy. He calls for an entirely new social order in China during the period when the Qing dynasty is withering away and revolution is in the wind. In Kang's utopian state, the government establishes socialist institutions to provide for the needs of the people. He thinks capitalism is a system that feeds on the greed and selfishness of persons and leads only to evil and injustice. Kang projects a Confucian utopian world free of political boundaries in his work *Book of Great Unity*, which was not published in its entirety until 1935, eight years after Kang's death.[14] This work may be compared to Plato's *Republic* and other utopias.

Kang wants to alter radically the traditional Chinese family structure and he is known as an advocate of women's independence and rights in China. Replacing the family will be state-run institutions, such as womb-teaching institutions, nurseries and schools, and retirement homes for the elderly. Marriage will be replaced by one-year contracts between a woman and a man. Kang considers the contemporary form of marriage known to him in China as oppressive. He believes in equality between men and women and believes there should be no social barrier barring women from employment, career advancement and leadership.

Liang Qichao (1873–1929): Emergent Chinese Nationalism

Xiao Yang calls Liang Qichao "the most widely read public intellectual during the transitional period from the late Qing dynasty (1644–1912) to the early Republican era (1912–49)" (Xiao 2002: 17).[15] The beginning of his philosophical career can be traced to his studies with Kang Youwei. Liang is only 22 years old when he and Kang organize the scholars' protest in Beijing in 1895, and he is instrumental in bringing about the "One Hundred Days Reform" in 1898.

For Liang Qichao, the central task of philosophy is to perfect the principles and rules necessary for social affairs within a political system. He thinks an authentic philosopher is not so much an ontologist or epistemologist as he is a *jingshi* (statesman or scholar who practices statesmanship). Liang's perceptive analysis of the relevance of new Western philosophical texts leads him to put aside the common distinction between Chinese learning and Western learning made by scholars of his day. He prefers to speak of *political* learning (*zheng xue*) that included *both* Chinese and Western thought.

Liang builds his early political philosophy (from 1896 to 1903) on the position that the myriad things of existence move continuously toward integration and grouping (*qun*). He reads Thomas Huxley's work *Evolution and Ethics* through the translation made by Yan Fu, and he interprets Huxley's findings to mean that higher evolutionary development always takes place when solidarity and group harmony become overriding intentions, whether in kinship lines, groups, tribes or emergent human societies. In his "A treatise on reform" and the first 17 sections of *New Citizens* (*Xinmin Congbao*, 1902), Liang advocates Western theories of government and he looks to constitutional forms to unite the citizenry of China, as well as to contain and channel competition.

This position leads Liang to distinguish between the moral virtues that relate to personal conduct (*side*) and civic or public virtues (*gongde*) that are necessary for the creation of a healthy and ideal society. Liang claims that Chinese philosophical reflection on the moral virtues is substantial and stretches over centuries of reflective analysis; however, China's history of political philosophy or public virtue is anemic and withered. In contrast, he feels Western political philosophy, especially since the eighteenth century, is robust and holds much of value.

Accordingly, Liang proposes to develop a modern Chinese political philosophy designed to produce what he calls a "new citizenry" (*xinmin*) for China (Liang 1999: I, 389). He elevates the nation above the individual in importance and considers it a civic virtue for the people of a state to possess a national consciousness and be ready to express loyalty and service to the state. More specifically, Liang does not think citizens of a particular nation state are capable of transforming their national loyalties into a commitment to a universal community of mankind. Rather, he insists citizens should be committed to their specific nation. Liang is one of the central philosophical figures in

China's shift away from privileging only culturalism to the creation of a strong nationalism. In fact, Liang holds that competitive nationalism is the most important reason for the rise of the West and joining this struggle will benefit China (Xiao 2002: 21).

Struggle between states, like that among individuals, is not something Liang wants to erase. In fact, he thinks struggle is the source of development and evolution. Probably he infers this principle from his reading of Huxley, but it is also quite compatible with what he also knows of the Western philosopher G. W. F. Hegel (1770–1831). With respect to internal reform and reconstitution of a political system, Liang is not shy at all. In fact, he holds that China's historical valorization of harmony and cooperation led to political authoritarianism and drained the people of their energy for innovation and diversity (Lee 1992: 243). He blames both Daoism and Confucianism for this cultural anemia. The Daoists value simplicity and do not recommend active change and shaping of society. The Confucians stress humaneness (*ren*) and harmony (*he*). Even the Mohists contribute to this mind-set by their stress on inclusive concern (*jian ai*).

Liang holds that there are three cultural assumptions among the Chinese that are the main causes of their civic weakness and inferior place among nations. He writes:

> First, there has been no awareness of the distinction between *guojia* (nation) and *tianxia* (the world). The Chinese have not been aware that their *guo* was one nation or state [among many]. For China has remained united since ancient time; it has been surrounded by "little barbarians", who do not have civilization or government and thus could not be called a nation or state. We Chinese people do not see them as equals. Therefore, for thousands of years, China has been isolated. We call China the world, not a nation. … Secondly, there has been no awareness of the distinction between a nation (or state) and a dynasty (or court). The biggest problem of the Chinese people is that we do not know what kind of thing a nation is and thus confuse the nation and the court, mistakenly believing that the nation is the property of the court. … Thirdly, there is no awareness of the relationship between the nation or state (*guo*) and the citizens (*guomin*). A nation consists of the people. Who is the master of the nation? The people of the nation. … The Western people regard the nation as being shared by the king and the people … This is not the case in China. One family owns the

nation and all the rest of the people are slaves of the family. This is why, although there are forty million people in China, there are actually only dozens of human beings (*ren*). When such a nation of dozens of human beings encounters the [Western] nations of millions of human beings, how can it not be defeated? (Liang 1999: 1, 413–14)

Liang argues that competition of ideas and lifestyles will bring the blood back into China's pale society. Accordingly, he is both an activist and an intellectual father of reform in China in the late Qing dynasty. He is involved in the new Republican government of China after 1911, holding several political positions. He freely appropriates many Western political ideas as answers to what he believes to be universal political quandaries all societies faced. "Regarding politics, there is no difference between China and the West. ... These [rules and laws] are the same in both the ancient and present time, in both the West and China. They are common principles for all nations" (ibid., I, 137). Liang turns the philosophical focus away from Western learning versus Chinese learning to "the universal laws of all nations" (*wanguo gongfa*) (Xiao 2002: 21). He holds that the preeminent place given to freedom of thought in the West leads to the exposure of the universal laws of political and social organization that all humans recognize as necessary to the pursuit of meaning and satisfaction in life.

Nonetheless, while Liang is an advocate for the state protection of freedom among its citizens, he also insists that freedom does not mean license and it must find its expression in laws that foster the integration of the people and the group (*qun*). The body politic in Liang's philosophy is not thought of as the result of a "social contract." While we might expect him to say that individuals group themselves into a state by agreeing to laws that govern their relationships, he moves nearer to Jeremy Bentham's (1748–1832) utilitarian ideal that the public interest is equivalent to what brings the greatest happiness to the greatest number. But, unlike Bentham, Liang's emphasis is on the public interest in a sort of inversion of Western utilitarianism. What benefits the greatest number is what the individual should submit himself to. In this way, Liang makes a clear difference between liberty and freedom as political principles and the maximization of human freedom on a personal level.

> Outside politics, one should not appeal to these [liberty and equality] as one's reasons for action. When they are applied to politics, they mean no more than that everyone has liberty protected by the law and that everyone is equal before the law. They should not be interpreted as going beyond this domain.
>
>   (Liang 1999: 5, 284; Xiao 2002: 27)

While this may sound like a formula for a repressive or censorist state, Liang's position must be understood in the context of his construction of the principle of popular sovereignty (*minquan*). As John Locke did in his two treatises on civil government, Liang uses the explanation of his political philosophy to offer a critique of the government then in power (the Qing imperial rule in Liang's case). He protests against arbitrary taxation that denies citizens their property, complains that the government spies on the free speech of the people, exposes the government's fabrication of evidence in order to deprive the citizens of their liberty and lives and manipulates the citizens, taking away their freedom of conscience (ibid.). For Liang, the people should express their right to self-mastery in the creation of a constitutional government. He even participates in the drafting of the Chinese constitution for the Republication government in 1912.

Liang takes the Chinese term *min* (people) that was used to mark the people who made up a population and replaces it with the concept *guomin* (citizens) in an intentional effort to tie identity and nationalism together. He believes a philosophically viable political body is not made up merely of a population. The people must be brought into being as citizens who express their powers and right to self-government, otherwise the nation itself ceases to exist and becomes something ultimately destructive to human flourishing (Liang 1999: 1, 273).

In his essay, "On the progress China has made in the last fifty years" (1922), Liang develops two principles. The first is "Anyone who is not Chinese has no right to govern Chinese affairs." The second is "Anyone who is Chinese has the right to govern Chinese affairs." The first of these Liang calls "the spirit of nation building" and the second he dubs "the spirit of democracy" (Liang 1999: 7, 4031).

By 1922, he moves toward advocating a strong government because he feels the Chinese people are not yet ready for self-governance. His *Travels in the New World* explains how he sees the differences between the American citizenry and the Chinese. He advocates the concept of

Enlightened Despotism to represent a gradualist program of liberty and change for a China led by a central ruler.[16]

Mao Zedong (1893–1976):
The Sinification of Marxism in China

Marx's socialist writings were part of the movement called "Western Learning" (*Xi xue*)[17] and no thinker is as important to the Sinification of Marxism in China of the twentieth century as Mao Zedong. He becomes the first Chairman of the Central Committee of the Communist Party of China, the founder of the "New China" (1 October 1949) and the "Father of the Nation."[18] For Mao, to be a Marxist is virtually equivalent to (1) rejecting China's traditional past with its social and economic oppression of women, workers and peasants by the landowners and (2) making a commitment that China will stand up to imperialist powers of the West and chart its own national destiny with a new pride (Zhou 2013).

While some question Mao's credentials as a philosopher, actually he did educate himself extensively on Chinese history and philosophy. Yet, Mao's true concerns are directed into a relatively narrow range of philosophical inquiry: social, political and economic thought. Still, few philosophers have had their writings distributed as widely and used in so many different ways as the book *Quotations from Chairman Mao* (a.k.a. the *Little Red Book*).[19] Of the early philosophers who engaged Western philosophy and Marxism in particular, Mao sends out a particular challenge when he writes the following:

> For Chinese Communists, we must learn how to apply the theories of Marxism–Leninism to concrete situations in China ... To make Marxism particularized, we must let it possess a nature that is necessarily and uniquely Chinese in all circumstances ... This means, use Marxism in accordance with Chinese distinctiveness. We must exchange slavish ideological doctrine with forms that are popular with common people and with Chinese styles of life and our historical endowments.
>
> (Mao 1968: 499–500).

Mao's call in October 1938 for the "Sinification of Marxism" results in a construction built around several fundamental concepts of political philosophy and is often called, simply, *Mao Zedong Thought* (*Mao Zedong Sixiang*).

Politics as Dialectics

When Mao recreates the Marxist understanding of Dialectical Materialism, the term *dialectical* is rendered into Chinese as *tongbian* or, literally, "continuity through change." This concept had been used before in Chinese tradition but Mao gives it a new meaning in his essay, "On Contradiction" (1937). He uses the terms *mao* (矛 spear) and *dun* (盾 shield) to express his understanding of dialectic.

> Once upon a time in the Chu state there was a man who made a living by selling both *mao* (spear) and *dun* (shield). He hawked in turn his spear and shield. Holding his shield, he bragged that it was so solid and hard that no spear could damage it. Then, picking up his spear, he resumed, boasting that it was so sharp and powerful that no shield could withstand it. He was not able to make any response, however, when someone from the crowd asked: "What would happen if you jabbed your shield with your spear?"

As this story was used in Chinese intellectual history, the compound of *mao* and *dun* came to indicate any statement or position that involved a contradiction, but as used by Mao in his appropriation of Marxism, it refers to the inevitability of the dynamic interaction of divergent views, classes or social processes. Mao observes:

> Changes in society are due chiefly to the development of the internal contradictions in society, that is, the contradiction between the productive forces and the relations of production, the contradiction between classes and the contradiction between the old and the new; it is the development of these contradictions that pushes society forward and gives the impetus for the suppression of the old society by the new.
> (Mao 1968: "On contradiction," August 1937)

In dialectics (*tongbian*), the oppositions are not lifted up to be intellectually reconciled in a synthesis, nor does one triumph over the other. Progress is revealed in actual practice as a dynamic interaction of views and voices; ideologies and philosophies. In this way, Mao's understanding of dialectics as contradiction refers both to the process of engagement of difference and the creative, even revolutionary, expression of novelty in actual practice. The outcome of dialectics cannot be explicated philosophically. Dialectics is embodied in life and political action.

Mao thinks several basic contradictions require dialectical engagement. These include the contradiction between imperialist and oppressed nations, the working class and the capitalists/land owners and, more broadly, between socialism and capitalism.

> Consider the contradiction between the exploiting and the exploited classes. Such contradictory classes coexist for a long time in the same society, be it a slave society, feudal society or capitalist society, and they struggle with each other; but it is not until the contradiction between the two classes develops to a certain stage that it assumes the form of open antagonism and develops into revolution. (Ibid., 45)

According to Mao, the emergence of political order is not as smooth as either the Chinese philosophers of his era or the Western social philosophers believe. The process is messy, transient and conflicted.

> A revolution is not a dinner party, or writing an essay, or painting a picture, or doing embroidery; it cannot be so refined, so leisurely and gentle, so temperate, kind, courteous, restrained and magnanimous. A revolution is an insurrection, an act of violence by which one class overthrows another. (Mao 1966: "Class and class struggle")

Political change in a revolutionary form is an expression of the dialectical character of history that Mao adapts from Marx. In his "Report on an investigation of the peasant movement in Hunan" (March 1927), Mao writes:

> The present upsurge of the peasant movement is a colossal event. In a very short time, in China's central, southern and northern provinces, several hundred million peasants will rise like a mighty storm, like a hurricane, a force so swift and violent that no power, however great, will be able to hold it back. They will smash all the trammels that bind them and rush forward along the road to liberation. They will sweep all the imperialists, warlords, corrupt officials, local tyrants and evil gentry

into their graves. Every revolutionary party and every revolutionary comrade will be put to the test, to be accepted or rejected as they decide. There are three alternatives: to march at their head and lead them; to trail behind them, gesticulating and criticizing; or, to stand in their way and oppose them. Every Chinese is free to choose, but events will force you to make the choice quickly. (Mao 1968)

New Democracy

Like Liang Qichao, Mao argues that China can only establish a new culture if there is a new nationalism as the point of departure. Although it was not delivered until 1940, Mao's essay "On New Democracy" reflects the passion for creating a new nation in China that he inherited from Liang Qichao, even though Mao criticized Liang for not really understanding the dialectical process, nor the need for revolution that it required. About his vision of New Democracy Mao states:

> The historical characteristic of the Chinese revolution lies in its division into the two stages, democracy and socialism, the first being no longer democracy in general, but democracy of the Chinese type, a new and special type, namely, New Democracy ... Clearly, it follows from the colonial, semi-colonial and semi-feudal character of present-day Chinese society that the Chinese revolution must be divided into two stages. The first step is to change the colonial, semi-colonial and semi-feudal form of society into an independent, democratic society. The second is to carry the revolution forward and build a socialist society. At present the Chinese revolution is taking the first step.
>
> (Mao 1968)

Mao's understanding of democracy is quite different than that articulated in Western philosophy. This is why he is careful to speak of "New" Democracy in order to underscore the unique philosophical constructions he is advocating.

First of all, there is the way in which Mao thinks political rulership comes to find expression.

> There is in China an imperialist culture which is a reflection of imperialist rule, or partial rule, in the political and economic fields. This culture is fostered not only by the cultural organizations run directly

by the imperialists in China but by a number of Chinese who have lost all sense of shame. Into this category falls all culture embodying a slave ideology. China also has a semi-feudal culture which reflects her semi-feudal politics[20] and economy, and whose exponents include all those who advocate the worship of Confucius, the study of the Confucian canon, the old ethical code and the old ideas in opposition to the new culture and new ideas ... This kind of reactionary culture serves the imperialists and the feudal class and must be swept away. Unless it is swept away, no new culture of any kind can be built up. There is no construction without destruction, no flowing without damming and no motion without rest; the two are locked in a life-and-death struggle. (Ibid.)

In China, it is perfectly clear that whoever can lead the people in overthrowing imperialism and the forces of feudalism can win the people's confidence, because these two, and especially imperialism, are the mortal enemies of the people. Today, whoever can lead the people in driving out Japanese imperialism and introducing democratic government will be the saviors of the people. History has proved that the Chinese bourgeoisie cannot fulfill this responsibility, which inevitably falls upon the shoulders of the proletariat ... The Chinese democratic republic which we desire to establish now must be a democratic republic under the joint dictatorship of all anti-imperialist and anti-feudal people led by the proletariat, that is, a new-democratic republic. (Ibid.)

Mao also advocates for a powerful governmental structure. Dealing with questions raised by members of his own party. He writes the following after the Anti-Japanese War (i.e., World War II) and the triumph of the Chinese communists in China's civil war in "On the People's Democratic Dictatorship" (30 June 1949).

[You ask], "Don't you want to abolish state power?" Yes, we do, but not right now. We cannot do it yet. Why? Because imperialism still exists, because domestic reaction still exists, because classes still exist in our country. Our present task is to strengthen the people's state apparatus—mainly the people's army, the people's police and the people's courts—in order to consolidate national defence and protect the people's interests. (Mao 1968)

Mao calls this state system a joint dictatorship of all the revolutionary classes, and he says it should be expressed in a democratic centralism. He defines the scope of the power of this dictatorship in "On the Correct Handling of Contradictions among the People" (27 February 1957):

> Our state is a people's democratic dictatorship led by the working class and based on the worker–peasant alliance. What is this dictatorship for? Its first function is to suppress the reactionary classes and elements and those exploiters in our country who resist the socialist revolution, to suppress those who try to wreck our socialist construction, or in other words, to resolve the internal contradictions between ourselves and the enemy. For instance, to arrest, try and sentence certain counterrevolutionaries, and to deprive landlords and bureaucrat–capitalists of their right to vote and their freedom of speech for a specified period of time—all this comes within the scope of our dictatorship. To maintain public order and safeguard the interests of the people, it is likewise necessary to exercise dictatorship over embezzlers, swindlers, arsonists, murderers, criminal gangs and other scoundrels who seriously disrupt public order. The second function of this dictatorship is to protect our country from subversion and possible aggression by external enemies. (Ibid.)

New Economy

If such a republic is to be established in China, it must also have a New Economy.

> It [the new government] will own the big banks and the big industrial and commercial enterprises. Enterprises, such as banks, railways and airlines, whether Chinese-owned or foreign-owned, which are either monopolistic in character or too big for private management, shall be operated and administered by the state, so that private capital cannot dominate the livelihood of the people: this is the main principle of the regulation of capital. (Mao 1968)

Mao insists that the New Democracy he is recommending should take the steps necessary to confiscate the land of the landlords and distribute it to those peasants having little or no land. Such dialectical activity will abolish what Mao called "feudal relations" between the peasants and the landowners in the rural areas and turn the land over to the private ownership of the peasants. He predicts this will result in a rich peasant economy and calls it the "equalization of landownership" as a principle of political philosophy (ibid.). Mao recalls the Chinese saying, "If there is food, let everyone share it," and writes:

> This old Chinese saying contains much truth. Since we all share in fighting the enemy, we should all share in eating, we should all share in the work to be done, and we should all share access to education. Such attitudes as "I and I alone will take everything" and "No one dare harm me" are nothing but the old tricks of feudal lords which simply will not work in the Nineteen Forties. (Ibid.)

Equalization of landownership eventually finds expression in agricultural collectives during the period 1949–58 as an implementation of Mao's political philosophy. Also developing from 1949 is a program designed to implement other economic aspects of the New Democracy known as the work unit or *danwei* employment model. Many work units are state owned enterprises, and they participate in what becomes known as the "iron rice bowl" (*tie fanwan*). The *iron rice bowl* comes into being as a program of guaranteed employment, steady income and a set of universal socio-economic benefits that continued to grow in number throughout the 1950s and 1960s.

New Culture

Mao argues that the emerging republic requires not only a new definition of democracy and a new economics but also a new culture. "As for the new culture, it is the ideological reflection of the new politics and the new economy which it sets out to serve" (Mao 1968). He continues in this way, "The New Democracy culture is one which belongs to the broad masses and not merely to an educated elite." The revolutionary leaders in the towns and villages known as cadres are charged with raising the cultural standards and educational level of the peasants. To attain this objective, Mao holds that written Chinese must be reformed and a more standardized spoken language be brought closer to that of the people. *Pinyin* simplified Romanization had its genesis in this philosophical commitment.

New Science

The New Democracy expresses a new science. It opposes all feudal cultural ideas and superstitious beliefs that substitute for material improvement and progress. New Science stands for seeking truth from facts, for objective truth and for the unity of theory and practice.

New Nationalism

According to Mao, this new democracy, economics, culture and science will give rise to a new Chinese nationalism.

> It [new Chinese nationalism] opposes imperialist oppression and upholds the dignity and independence of the Chinese nation. It belongs to our own nation and bears our own national characteristics. It links up with the socialist and new-democratic cultures of all other nations and they are related in such a way that they can absorb something from each other and help each other to develop, together forming a new world culture; but as a revolutionary national culture it can never link up with any reactionary imperialist culture of whatever nation. To nourish her own culture China needs to assimilate a good deal of foreign progressive culture, not enough of which was done in the past. We should assimilate whatever is useful to us today not only from the present-day socialist and new-democratic cultures but also from the earlier cultures of other nations, for example, from the culture of the various capitalist countries in the Age of Enlightenment. However, we should not gulp any of this foreign material down uncritically, but must treat it as we do our food—first chewing it, then submitting it to the working of the stomach and intestines with their juices and secretions, and separating it into nutriment to be absorbed and waste matter to be discarded—before it can nourish us. To advocate "wholesale westernization" is wrong. (Mao 1968)

Forms of Current Confucian Political Theory

Tu Weiming (1940–)

Western academic political philosophy has begun to pay some minor attention to non-Western models as is suggested by the inclusion of a section entitled, "Political theory in the world" in the 2006 *Oxford Handbook of Political Theory*. Indeed, in that same work, Daniel Bell's contribution is entitled, "East Asia and the West: the impact of Confucianism on Anglo-American political theory." But all this notwithstanding, we must admit that Confucianism as a political theory has received little attention by Western philosophers and what interest it has received is almost exclusively directed at the movement known as New Confucianism (*xin rujia*). This movement is a braided string of thought generated by scholars from mainland China to the U.S.A. According to John Makeham, the first generation of New Confucians includes scholars all based in mainland China after the May Fourth Movement (1919); the second includes those in either Hong Kong or Taiwan; and the third includes thinkers who principally base their work on engagement with the West.

One thinker who is contributing to the New Confucianism is Tu Weiming.[21] In his *Reinventing Confucianism: the New Confucian Movement*, Umberto Bresciani names Tu as the leader of the "third generation" of New Confucians (2001: 29).[22] Commenting in his "Response" to a special issue of *Dao: A Journal of Comparative Philosophy* devoted to his thought, Tu states his purpose clearly:

> Frankly, my intention is to show in both practical and normative terms what a modern society with Confucian characteristics might look like. I assume that if it is modern, it is inevitably under the influence of the modern West and, by implication, the Enlightenment mentality. Yet, as my edited collection of essays, *Confucian Traditions in East Asian Modernity* shows, the East Asian cultural forms—Chinese, Vietnamese, Korean, and Japanese—all share notably Confucian features that are significantly different from European and American cultural forms. My explanation is predicated on two assumptions: (1) the continuous presence of traditions in modernity, and (2) the likelihood that the modernizing process may assume different cultural forms (Tu 2008: 441).

A distinctive mark of Tu's writings and presentations on Confucianism is his understanding of politics as the "rectification" of social order undertaken to make possible the self-cultivation of the citizens. In taking this position, Tu appeals to Confucius's remark, "Politics is rectifying" (*Analects* 12.17). He takes this to mean that the work of government should extend beyond making laws and maintaining security. Instead, the purpose of politics is to monitor and constantly adjust social processes of communal life as well as the distribution of economic goods in order to bring about what he calls a "fiduciary community," in which the citizenry can trust the government to set up policies and structures that enable self-cultivation and even self-transcendence in each person.

The idea of a fiduciary community is first introduced by Tu in his writings from the late 1970s, but it is perhaps most clearly described in his recent work, *Centrality and Commonality: An Essay on Confucian Religiousness* (1989). In this book, Tu uses the English term "fiduciary," associated with the responsibility of a trustee in financial and legal interchanges, to render the Chinese concept *xinlai* (trust, trustworthiness) (Tu 1989a: 60).

For Tu, while the body politic may assume the form of family, clan, school, village, local government or central bureaucracy, if it fails to put into place and monitor the processes and structures required for the self-cultivation and humanization of its members, it will lose the trust and loyalty of the people. To keep that trust, the government must continuously be a self-correcting political system. Rectification of public policy is a value-laden concept. It means correction, implying that policies are constantly monitored and righted as needed.[23] An overarching purpose of civil libertarian politics in the West is preventing harm, while creating the greatest space for liberty of expression and freedom of lifestyle choice, generally in the pursuit of happiness as an end; whereas Tu holds that the goal in Confucian politics is creating the confidence within the citizenry that the government is pursuing policies designed for their development and flourishing as persons. Political institutions and actors are responsible for monitoring and constantly rectifying social processes of communal life in order to bring about an environment in which people are able to cultivate and humanize themselves.

While the new application of Confucian politics being recommended by Tu does not rest on the idea of a community as an aggregate of autonomous individuals, neither does it deny individuality. In fact, the fiduciary community's guiding purpose is the self-cultivation of individuals, not the homogenization of selves and loss of identity in the group (ibid., 56). Self-cultivation and humanization are not built on a monolithic conception of the good or the human. In the Confucian community Tu advocates, divergent interests and plural desires are dealt with differently than in social contract and civil libertarian adversarial systems where Tu fears the tyranny of the majority may be expressed in the ballot. In the fiduciary community, no political decision can be legitimate and just if it destroys the ethos of trustworthiness among the people or between the people and the government. Such a delimitation of power creates in the community what Tu calls a "convergence of orientations" (Tu 1984: 10).

Tu insists that the concept of a self-rectifying government always depends on having responsible leaders who are engaged in self-cultivation and avoid corruption and pride of power. The requirement for leader self-cultivation is expressed by Tu through the classical Confucian ideal "internally a sage, externally a ruler (*nei sheng wai wang*)" (Tu 1989b: 19). Engaged concern for the people, born of the ruler's personal self-cultivation, makes a leader into the sort of politically relevant person who is able to create and sustain the community of trust. Tu says that in the ideal Confucian community, leaders will have cultivated themselves to the point that their self-consciousness is able to represent the great interests (*da li*) of the entire community and their hearts are in tune with the hearts of the people (*min xin*). The resulting benefit is a fiduciary community of trust in which the citizens "exhort one another to do good (*bai xing quan*)."

Tu says that well-cultivated leaders demonstrate their knowledge by never relying exclusively on themselves, but always on the institutionalized authority of an interlocking system of other self-cultivating officials. Bureaucracy is not a bad thing in Tu's version of New Confucian political theory. Only bureaucrats who do not pay attention to their own rectification are undesirable. As for the qualifications of the ministers who make up this bureaucracy, Tu sums up his views on rulers by quoting Confucius who says simply that they should be "virtuous (good) and competent (*xian neng*)."

Speaking of the people's role in the new community, Tu says they should engage in a sort of "communal critical self-consciousness (*qunji de pipan de ziwo yishi*)." Communal critical self-consciousness goes beyond the personal individual and yet the individual is not absorbed into an amorphous collective interest. This is why Tu speaks of a fiduciary community as a "learning culture" (Tu 2002: 129). The learning represented by the activity of communal critical self-consciousness is not as simple as winning an election or succeeding in implementing a policy over conscientious objections of others. Its result is not the victory of an individual or a party, but the emergence of policies that both enhance the ongoing self-cultivation of each individual and reinforce trust among all. For Tu, this approach contrasts with those expressions of democracy that are not built on trust, but on a calculus of weighing interests and trade-offs.

Tu also distinguishes his notion of a learning culture from what he calls, "politicized Confucianism" (*zhengzhihua de ruxue*). Politicized Confucianism is the lineage of rule and politics often displayed in Chinese history and associated with authoritarianism and repression, closely related to what the mid-twentieth-century Chinese Communist Party objected to as "Confucian Feudalism." Tu recognizes that politicized Confucianism is an undeniable part of the historic tradition, but he considers it a perversion (Tu 1984: 105). He is particularly critical of the use of coerced and superimposed values and practices said to be Confucian in order to create uniformity and inhibit the cultivation and development of individual persons (ibid., 105, 106). For Tu, wherever forced conformity occurs, it is evidence of the sort of politicized Confucianism that destroys the trust that is essential to a community of self-cultivating persons.

A difficult task for Tu is to explain just how the communal critical self-consciousness can achieve trust and preserve individual self-cultivation apart from imposed prescriptions and laws. To account for how this occurs, Tu turns to the classical Chinese notion of the proprieties of conduct (*li* 禮). He radicalizes this idea by claiming that *li* consists of nothing more or less than learning how to become human alongside other humans (Tu 1979: 28). For Tu, it is not the moral rules or laws of a community that create trust, but *the process* of creating and recreating patterns of humanization that does so.

Tu argues that the Confucian concept of *li* can represent an alternative to the Western social contractual understanding of the function of law. *Li* is not an authoritarian imposition on a community but neither is it merely a calculus of agreed-upon rules designed to prevent one person from harming another. *Li* is a culture that bubbles up from the dynamism of a people committed to their own humanization. Tu believes that when coercion through law is used by a government on its people this practice runs the danger of becoming an overzealous attempt to force conformity and destroys the environment of trustworthiness. On the other hand, Tu holds that when *li* arises from the engaged processes of self-transcending humanization, imposition and coercion become unnecessary.

Since the goal of politics is the rectification of all the processes that advance humanization and self-cultivation, Tu thinks the government's reach must extend to care for the economic and material life of its people. He accepts the Confucian principle of distributive justice as "graded love" and interprets it to mean the consideration of need rather than an abstract equality. Here there is a grading or ranking of the distribution of social goods in such a way as to reinforce the ethos of trustworthiness. This approach to distributive justice differs starkly from the overriding Western justice values of impartiality and equality. While we may think primarily of justice as fairness in a Western political system, Tu argues that the Confucian model for social justice is not marked by impartiality, but by grading or ranking the distribution of social goods in such a way as to reach to the needs of the people and create trustworthiness between citizens and government.

We can see already that Tu's New Confucian construction of political theory surfaces numerous strategic and important differences from Western understandings of the nature and task of politics. For one thing, the webbing of the fiduciary community is mutual trust in each other and in one's governmental leadership. Such a view is in radical contrast to the kind of adversarial system that characterizes not only American but also many other democratic societies. To be candid, while democratic systems may ensure each person a vote, they do not necessarily have as their principal aim the creation of an ethos of trust. In Tu's version of Confucianism, the creation of a trustworthy community is paramount in the hierarchy of political values. We also cannot really claim that Western civil libertarian systems have as their overarching goal the creation of an environment that makes possible the self-cultivation of each individual. Liberty and freedom, while dominant and important values in Western political theory, may be preserved quite apart from both the realization of individual self-cultivation and the concomitant humanization of the citizens.

Other Current Confucian Models for Political Theory

Our survey of new Confucian models through Tu Weiming leaves out some other very deliberate and explicitly committed Confucian reconstructionists who are in full resistance to Western political theory as a possible model for China and who also feel that Chinese political thought after Mao has become a form of relatively free-floating pragmatism that has no firm cultural and historical anchorage. Accordingly, they are advocating for a much more explicit application of Confucianism to Chinese public policy.

Kang Xiaoguang (1963–) has taken up the challenge to offer a political philosophy for China's post-Mao years in several works (2003a, 2003b, 2005, 2006 and 2011). A good overview of his views in English is that of David Ownby (2009). Kang holds that the Chinese Communist Party must be Confucianized. He thinks Marxism should be replaced with the reconstituted and adapted philosophy of Confucius and Mencius. While the educational system will keep the party schools, their syllabi should be changed, listing the Confucian Four Books and Five Classics as required courses. There should be a return to the examination system for all political promotions, and Confucian philosophical teachings should be added to each examination. Moreover, he also maintains that the Chinese society must be Confucianized. Here the key is to introduce Confucianism into the national education system, adding courses in Chinese culture that Kang claims will impart a value system, a faith and soul for the culture. In the long term, this can be achieved only if Confucianism becomes the state's civil value system.

Fan Ruiping's project differs from Kang's. It is set out most clearly in his *Reconstructionist Confucianism* (2010). In this work, he calls for reclaiming and articulating resources from the Confucian tradition to address contemporary moral and public policy challenges. He sets his effort over against both Western civil libertarian democracies that conceive of morality by agreement and the New Confucianism of Tu Weiming and others. He holds that, while Western social philosophy is founded on abstract and general principles, Confucianism is defined by specific rules that identify particular practices leading to a virtuous mode of life developed in the forge of a properly harmonious Confucian family. Fan argues that in such families persons learn how to treat others as unequals and gain mastery of the push and pull of graded love, creating a sort of *virtuous familism* that is transferable to the society at large. Instead of Western language about rights, Fan holds that the goal in political policy is to *treat persons as relatives* and the nation and global community *as a household* drawing on the archetype of a traditional Chinese family that brought many persons into its circle of influence. Rather than norms such as "justice as fairness," Fan characterizes the Confucian model as "justice as harmony."

哲学

Guide to Philosophers
and Significant Works

The Chronicles of Zuo (Zuozhuan)

This text is a record of occurrences of the Spring and Autumn Period (*Chunqiu Shi Dai*) from *c.*771 to 468 BCE traditionally ascribed to a court writer in the State of Lu during the time of Confucius named Zuo Qiuming. The text is arranged as comments on the reign of various marquises and dukes. Although there are debates about the dating of some passages, current scholarship continues to hold that large sections of the text were completed no later than 389 BCE. This would mean that it dates to the period of Socrates (469–399 BCE) and Plato (427–347 BCE) in the West.

Confucius and the *Analects*

Confucius (a.k.a. Kongzi or personal name Kong Qiu, Kong Zhongni, 551–479 BCE) was born, lived and taught during the classical period of China. The traditions about Confucius were gathered and transmitted primarily in the *Analects*. This is a book composed of short texts and brief conversations in which Confucius is often, although not exclusively, the main teacher. Its Chinese title is *Lunyu*, meaning "selected sayings." The present *Analects* is divided into 20 books (roughly the size of chapters), that are further categorized into the sayings themselves with the convention of listing the book first, then the analects (i.e., 3.1 is Book Three, analect one). Recent textual critical studies of the received text of the *Analects* have identified various strata of analects in the text, some very likely traceable to the historical Confucius, others to his disciples, others to master teachers associated with him or a generation removed, and still others that may be several generations removed from Confucius himself.

Dai Zhen (1723–77)

Dai Zhen was born in Longfu City (Tunxi city) in Anhui Province, into the family of a poor cloth merchant. He attended local schools because his father could not afford private tutorials by Confucian scholars. However, he demonstrated remarkable scholarly accomplishments and won the backing of a literary scholar. According to Duan Yucai's *Bibliography of Dai* (*Dongyan Xiansheng*), Dai devoted himself to the study of the basic works of Chinese philosophy. His two most prominent philosophical works are entitled *On the Good* (*Yuanshan*) and *An Evidential Study of the Meaning and Terms of the Mencius* (*Mengzi ziyi shuzheng*). See *Works of Dai Zhen* (1980).

"Great Commentary" of the *Classic of Changes*

The *Classic of Changes* (*Yijing*) is the name for a complete work that includes two parts. One part is a quite ancient manual of divination known simply as the *Changes* (*Yi*), or, more correctly, as the *Zhouyi* because it is a handbook traceable to the period of the Western Zhou dynasty (*c*.1046–771 BCE). The other part is a set of seven commentaries (*zhuan*) attached to the *Yi*. Three of the commentaries are composed of two sections each, so taken as a whole, the commentary set is known as "The Ten Wings" (*Shiyi*). While there is a long-standing belief in Chinese intellectual history that Confucius knew and used the *Zhouyi* divination manual and that he was even the author of some or all of the "Ten Wings" commentaries, Richard Rutt has argued that there is no reliable evidence that Confucius either knew or used the book (Rutt 1999: 34).

One of the commentaries to the *Yi* (*Zhouyi*) is known by the various titles of the "Great Commentary" (*Dazhuan*) or "Appended Statements" (*Xici*). The "Great Commentary" is arguably the most important single text to study for an understanding of early Chinese ontology. Regrettably, we cannot fix for certain the date of the composition of the "Great Commentary." Edward Shaughnessy (1997) has done a recent translation of it based on the Mawangdui archaeological finds. He holds that there are reasons for thinking the work was written and edited most likely during the period from 320 to 168 BCE.

The "Great Plan" (*Hong Fan*) in the *Classic of History* (*Shujing*)

The "Great Plan" section of the *Classic of History* (*Shujing*) is constructed in the style of a dialogue between Wu Wang and a sage. The *Classic of History* had no single author and is a compilation of materials perhaps dating from as early as the time of Confucius (551–479 BCE). There were likely several versions of this work in circulation until and even after the infamous "Burning of the books and burial of the scholars" *fenshu kengru* (213–210 BCE). New light has been shed on the *Classic of History* by the recovery of a number of texts written on bamboo slips from tombs of the state of Chu in Jingmen, Hubei province during archaeological investigations from 1993 to 2008. These texts are believed to date from around 300 BCE. The Guodian slips are a subject of ongoing study and may help us date somewhat more confidently the emergence of various views in Chinese intellectual history.[1]

Han Fei (c.280–33 BCE)

Master Han Fei was a student of Xunzi, probably at the Jixia Academy. His essays, gathered into the work *Hanfeizi*, were probably written for the kings of the Han state, most likely King Huan-Hui (r. 272–239 BCE) or King An (r. 238–230 BCE). He shared a view of human nature somewhat similar to that of Xunzi. Although not a complete translation, Burton Watson's (1964) version of the *Hanfeizi* is still quite reliable. For a complete translation of Hanfeizi's work see Liao (1939) available in an online version.

Hu Shi (1891–1962)

Although influenced by Buddhism in his youth, Hu Shi studied in three schools known for the "New Education" or Western-style system in Shanghai. He did his doctorate in philosophy with John Dewey at Columbia University in the U.S.A. After completing his doctorate in 1917, he returned to China to become professor of Chinese and Western philosophy at Beijing National University where he taught until 1926. He was instrumental in the development of the New Culture Movement (1912–20) that was dedicated to the modernization of Chinese learning and social progress. He was also a key figure in introducing Pragmatism and scientific research methodology to China. There is no more succinct representation of the shift to Western science and ontology in China than Hu's "New credo," published in 1923. Among his representative works are "My tentative ideas of literature reform" (1917), *An Outline of Chinese Philosophy* (1919) and *The Development of Logical Method in Ancient China* (1922). Hu Shi was one of the few Chinese philosophers to publish widely in English. His English works are included in Chih-P'ing Chou's edition of *Collection of Hu Shih's English Writings* (3 volumes, 1995). He has been called the central figure in the history of Chinese academic thought in the twentieth century (Yu 1984: Preface).

Lao-Zhuang Tradition (c.350–139 BCE)

The long-standing tradition in China is that an individual philosophical master named Laozi was the author of a philosophical work known as the *Daodejing*, which means the "Classic of *Dao* (Way) and *De* (virtuous power)." The impact of the *Daodejing* has been monumental. According to one count, there are over 700 commentaries in Chinese on this work.[2] The *Zhuangzi* is the first text to use Laozi as a personal name. In that work, Laozi is often a character who is portrayed teaching and correcting Confucius, and Confucius is put in the role of giving Laozi great respect and honor. However, like many other names for persons in that text, Laozi was possibly a fictional name used to give a voice to ideas within an influential lineage of teachers. In Chinese, *lao* means "ancient, old" and *zi* means "teacher, master." So "Laozi" may stand in for "the ancient teachers" personified as one person. The present *Daodejing* represents a collection of teachings used across lineages of Daoist teachers and not the work of a single author.

On the other hand, most of what we know about Master Zhuang or Zhuangzi is taken from a work written by a historian named Sima Qian (*Records of the Historian*). According to his account, Master Zhuang's given name was Zhou. He lived during the reigns of King Hui of Liang (370–319 BCE) and King Xuan of Qi (319–309 BCE). He once served as an official in the "lacquer garden" in the Town of Meng (Mengcheng), believed to be in the State of Song (now Henan Province). Zhuangzi was a contemporary of Mencius (see below), and according to Sima Qian he was one of the masters who taught at the Jixia Academy. The present text of the *Zhuangzi* was edited by a scholar official named Guo Xiang (d. 312 CE) and contains 33 chapters. Most of these, like the *Daodejing*, contain many component text blocks (logia) put together by an editor.

Legalist School (*fa jia*)

Legalism refers loosely to Chinese philosophers of the classical period whose common conviction was that law rather than morality was the most reliable ordering mechanism for society. A number of philosophers associated with this school were, indeed, active in government and as imperial consultants. For example, Han Fei was advisor in the Han state, just prior to its annexation by the Qin in creating China's first empire in 221 BCE and a principal figure in this philosophical movement. Traditionally, Guan Zhong (d. 645 BCE) is called "the father of legalism." The *Guanzi*, compiled sometime in the later years of the Warring States Period or early Han dynasty (*c.*365–200 BCE), contains several chapters with Legalist content (Rickett 1985, 1998).

Liang Qichao (1873–1929)

Xiao Yang calls Liang Qichao "the most widely read public intellectual during the transitional period from the late Qing dynasty to the early Republican era" (Xiao 2002: 17). Liang was only 22 years old when he and Kang Youwei organized the scholars' protest in Beijing in 1895, and he was instrumental in bringing about the "One Hundred Days Reform" in 1898. Because of his political views, he was forced to flee China in 1898 and remained away for 14 years. During his exile years, Liang traveled to the U.S.A., England, Australia and many Western European countries, and he published a number of articles and edited the important newspapers *Qing Yi Bao* and *Xin Min Cong Bao*. He also wrote short treatises on Aristotle, Spinoza, Hobbes, Rousseau, Kant, Fichte, Montesquieu, Bacon, Bentham, Spencer and Darwin. After his return, he held various cabinet level positions in the new Republic of China government, taking on the role of a professor in the last decade of his life and becoming known as one of the "Four Great Masters" of Qinghua University.[3] Liang Qichao was a prolific writer. *The Collected Works of Liang Qichao* contains about 10 million words.

Lotus Sutra (i.e., The Sutra of the Lotus Blossom of the Subtle Dharma, Miaofa Lianhua Jing)

The *Lotus Sutra* is one of the most popular and influential Mahayana sutras and the basis for the Tiantai tradition of Buddhism in China. The oldest parts of the text (Chapters 1–9 and 17) were probably written down between 100 BCE and 100 CE, and most of the text had appeared by 200 CE. It was translated into Chinese for the use of Tiantai Buddhist teachers by Zhu Fahua (a.k.a. Dharmaraksa) in Chang'an (Xi'an) in *c*.286. The famous Buddhist translator Kumarajiva (334–413) made another translation, relying heavily on Zhu Fahua's in 406, and the text is now often simply called *Fahua jing* in Chinese. The *Lotus Sutra* presents itself as a discourse of Siddhartha Buddha.

Mao Zedong (1893–1976)

Mao Zedong was born in a village in Hunan province into a well-to-do farming family. He was influenced by Sun Yatsen's calls for a Republic of China and read widely from Western texts, including Darwin, Mill and Rousseau. He was a contributor to the newspaper *New Youth*. When the May Fourth Movement erupted in Beijing, Mao started a magazine in Changsha and called for a union of the popular masses, the liberation of women and new Chinese nationalism. When the Communist Party was founded in Shanghai in 1921, Mao started a branch in Changsha. From 1923 to 1925, Mao worked as a member of the Party Committee alongside KMT (Kuomintang/Nationalists) and even ran the activities in Hunan. From 1925 to 1927, Mao's support of the peasants, his urging of them to refuse to pay rent and stand against the gentry and corrupt officials were only partially implemented in KMT policy. After 1927, Mao became commander of the Red Army or People's Liberation Army. He later became the first Chairman of the Central Committee of the Chinese Communist Party of the People's Republic of China and the "Father of the Nation."

For English readers, the complete collected works of Mao from 1917 to 1945 are at the U.S. Government's Joint Publications Research Service, where all articles signed by Chairman Mao individually or jointly, as well as those unsigned but verified as his, are available. For works after 1945, *Selected Works of Mao Zedong* (1968) is a good source.

Masters of Huainan (Huainanzi)

According to his biography in the *Book of the Early Han* (*Hanshu*, 44.2145) Liu An, the king of Huainan (in modern Anhui province) and uncle of Han Emperor Wu, gathered a large number of philosophers, scholars, practitioners of esoteric techniques to Huainan in the period 160–140 BCE. The *Masters of Huainan* was a product of this interchange of ideas. Some traditions say the work was written collectively by the "Eight Gentlemen" (*bagong*) of Huainan and that Liu An was its general editor, rather than its sole author. It was presented to emperor Wu in 139 BCE.

Without going into great detail about all the sources used in the *Masters of Huainan*, we may say that it is a synthetic document meant to harmonize the thought of the so-called "Hundred Schools" (*baijia*) as a sort of universal encyclopaedia of knowledge, with an attempt to bring all the then-prevailing philosophies into a coherent body of work.[4]

As a collection of materials, the *Huainanzi* is a work of 21 essays ranging from cosmology and astronomy, to inner *qi* cultivation and spiritual transformation, and political rulership. The first complete English translation of the *Masters of Huainan* came out in 2010 from Columbia University Press (Major et al.).

Mencius (372–289 BCE)

According to Sima Qian's *Records of the Historian* text, Mencius was born in the small state of Zou, on the border of the state of Lu, not far from Confucius's home in present Shandong Province. Like Confucius, Mencius sought a position in government and is often pictured giving counsel to various rulers in the Mengzi, including those of the states of Liang and Qi. However, just as was the case with Confucius, the rulers would not follow his advice, and he too retired to teach. Mencius was also said to have been at the Jixia Academy.

The *Mengzi* is the text that contains virtually all of the significant teachings of Mencius. This work became one of the Four Books (*Sishu*) that formed the core of the Confucian examination and education system. It appears to have been collected by Mencius's disciples, some of whom are referred to in the text as "masters" themselves, indicating a later period of composition for those passages. The received text of the *Mengzi* was edited by Zhao Qi (d. 201 CE) into seven books, each in two parts, and each part with a number of passages. When scholars cite from the *Mengzi*, the form is always in this manner: book, section, passage (e.g., 3B9). This citation form enables the reader to locate the passage in any of the translations of the text.

Mozi (a.k.a. Mo Di, c.470–391 BCE)

Mozi was the originator of a far-reaching and influential school of philosophy in ancient China. According to the *Records of the Historian* (*Shiji*) by Sima Qian, Mo Di was an official of the state of Song and lived either at the same time as or just after Confucius. Our primary source for his thought is a collection of texts which form a large anthology simply called the *Mozi*, but this text contains materials much later in origin than the life of Mozi, thus representing more fully Mohism as a school or movement.

The *Mozi* is a collection of essays, short diagonal dialogues, anecdotes and compact philosophical discussions. Ian Johnston has provided a complete translation into English of the *Mozi* (2010). The second part of the text sets out the "Ten core doctrines" of Mohism in a triad of essays devoted to each. Just why there are three versions of each essay is not certain, but the prevailing theory is that the triads are probably versions of a common oral tradition as written down in the three different sects of Mohism. In addition to Johnston's, a full text of the *Mozi* in Chinese with an English translation is at "The Chinese text project" (online at http://chinese.dsturgeon.net/text.pl?node=101&if=en). Burton Watson's (1963) partial translation for Columbia Press is regarded as accurate and highly readable.

Mou Zongsan (1909–95)

Among Chinese philosophers, Mou Zongsan epitomized the development of New Confucianism in the contemporary era. Yet, what are sometimes overlooked are his extensive background and skill in Western philosophy. Refeng Tang observes, "His [Mou's] new Confucianism not only established a complete system of Chinese philosophy, but also provided grounds for the critical assessment of Western philosophy" (Tang 328).

In 1949, he left Beijing to teach in Taiwan and began to write on Chinese culture and politics. Mou admired Kant's work, especially his moral theory, writing, "All the ancient philosophies from Greek to Kant converge on Kant, and all kinds of philosophy after Kant develop from Kant" (Mou 1963:39). He thought Kantian moral philosophy was the only one that could engage in dialogue with Chinese philosophy, and he agreed with Kant that the highest good (*summum bonum*) is the one that brings virtue and happiness together.

Tu Weiming (1940–)

In his *Reinventing Confucianism: the New Confucian Movement*, Umberto Bresciani names Tu as the leader of the "third generation" of New Confucians (2001: 29). Tu is founding Dean of the Institute for Advanced Humanistic Studies at Peking University. A five-volume anthology of his works was published in Chinese in 2001.

Wang Chong (c.25–100 CE)

Wang studied at the imperial school in Luoyang, Henan province. After his training, he returned to his home near modern Shangyu, Zhejiang province in the position of Officer of Merit. However, he soon found dealing with judicial cases quarrelsome and stepped down. During the period after leaving his position, he wrote a number of tightly reasoned Confucian essays, including "On common morality," "Censures" and "On government." His essays on subjects ranging from morality, to government, to science and to technology were later compiled into the work *Critical Essays* (*Lunheng*). In fact, each of the essays in *Critical Essays* is meant to stand alone as a separate philosophical analysis, and there is no attempt to harmonize the contradictions apparent between the essays when they are read as a whole. However, Michael Nylan (2003) has argued that Wang's most critical and skeptical views often represent expansions of earlier critiques.

Wang Yangming (1472–1529)

Wang practiced Daoist "sitting in forgetfulness" (*zuowang*), grasped the realization of the unity of knowledge and action that Daoist thinkers stressed in *wu-wei*, and taught that the highest form of knowledge was *liangzhi*. The principal sources for Wang's ideas are his works, *Instructions for Practical Living* (1518, *Chuan Xilu*) and "Inquiry on the Great Learning" (1527) (see Chan 1963a and 1963b; and Neville 1977). Wang's stormy career was in large measure due to his opposition to the philosophy of Zhu Xi. He departed from Zhu in both his ontology and epistemology. In the Ming Dynasty, Wang Yangming became the most deliberative of Zhu Xi's critics.[5]

Xuanzang (c.596–664)

Xuanzang, born Chen Hui, was a Chinese Buddhist monk, scholar, traveler and translator in the early Tang dynasty. He was born in Chenhe village, near present-day Luoyang in what is now Henan province, in *c.*596, and his family was well educated. Although he received an orthodox Confucian education, he lived at Jingtu monastery (Jingtu si) in Luoyang with his brother for five years. He spent more than ten years traveling and studying in India. When he returned, he brought back 657 Buddhist texts and devoted the remainder of his life to a translation school he established in Chang'an (Xi'an). His travels in India are recorded in detail in the classic Chinese text *Great Tang Records on the Western Regions*, which in turn provided the inspiration for the fictitious religious novel *Journey to the West* written by Wu Cheng'en during the Ming dynasty, around nine centuries after Xuanzang's death.

Xuanzang's creation in China of the "Consciousness-only" School of Buddhism (*Weishi zong*) was greatly influenced by the writings of the Indian Yogacara master, Vasubandhu (Chinese name, Shi Qin). Xuanzang wrote an extensive commentary in ten volumes on Vasubandhu's text *Thirty Stanzas of Consciousness-Only* entitled, *A Treatise on the Establishment of Consciousness-Only* (*Cheng Wei-shi Lun*) and used it to set out his own views of this tradition of Buddhist teaching. The only English translation of Xuanzang's *Treatise* is by Tat Wei (1973). Chan's *Sourcebook* (1973: Chapter 23) has an excerpt.

Xunzi (c.310–220 BCE)

What little is known of the life of Xunzi, or Master Xun, is culled from evidence in his own writings and from the brief biography of him written by the historian Sima Qian some hundred years or so after his death. His personal name was Kuang, and he was a native of Zhao, a state situated in the central part of northern China. The date of his birth is unknown, but it was probably around 310 BCE. One source suggests that he lived to see the establishment of the empire of Qin (220 BCE), but we cannot be certain. Xunzi, unlike Confucius and Mencius, has no Romanized name probably because when the Western missionaries arrived in China they heard little about him.

If we are right about Xunzi's year of birth, he would have been around 20 when Mencius died. Sima Qian reports that Xunzi studied at the Jixia Academy and it is not impossible that he could have been well acquainted with Mencius's ideas directly or through first-generation disciples. He and his disciples seem to have been highly regarded by the rising Qin rulers. In fact, two of his students, Han Fei and Li Si (280?–208 BCE) were instrumental in developing the theory of law and justice used in the Qin dynasty and known simply as Legalism.

The primary source for Xunzi's thought is simply called the *Xunzi*. This book in its received form is 32 chapters that are essentially well-crafted, self-contained essays. The *Xunzi* was not a part of any of the later lists of Confucian classics in the canon, very much unlike the *Mengzi* that became part of the Four Books and occupied a central place in Confucian learning. For years, the standard English translation with interpretive comments of *Xunzi* in three volumes was that by John Knoblock (1988, 1990, 1994), but in 2014 a new translation done by Eric Hutton appeared. Burton Watson's version (1963) is not a translation of the complete text, but it is quite readable.

Yan Fu (1854–1921)

Prior to Yan's translations of Western texts (see Chapter IV), the philosophers of China worked with Japanese versions. To the translations, Yan added his own commentaries and philosophical criticisms. After 1896, he supervised several translation institutes operating under central and local government authority. He went on to become President of Fudan University in Shanghai and Beijing (Peking) University, and was instrumental in the creation of a department for the study of Western philosophy at that university in 1919.

Zhang Dongsun (1886–1973)

Zhang Dongsun came from a prominent Zhejiang family and became a lay Buddhist practitioner before leaving China to study philosophy at Tokyo University. Upon his return to China in 1911, he taught at various universities, including Beijing University, and he enjoyed a distinguished academic career. He published a number of works in Chinese devoted to important fields of philosophical inquiry, many of which have not yet been translated into English or other languages. Some of these works are: *Science and Philosophy* (*Kexue yu Zhexue*, 1924), *Moral Philosophy* (*Daode Zhexue*, 1931), *Epistemology* (*Renshi Lun* (1934a), *The Restatement of Pluralistic Epistemology* (*Duoyuan Renshi Lun Chongshu*, 1937), *Knowledge and Culture* (*Zhishi yu Wenhua*, 1946a) and *Rationality and Democracy* (*Lixiang yu Minzhu*, 1946b). After the founding of the People's Republic of China in 1949, Zhang became a member of the Central Committee of the People's Government. In 1951, he was censured by the government and removed from his post on the faculty at Yenjing University. He later suffered several episodes of self-criticism and was even accused of spying for the U.S. government. Eventually, during the Cultural Revolution he was placed under hospital confinement from 1968 until his death in 1973 (Yap 2003: 857). There is very little philosophical discussion of Zhang Dongsun in English, however Chinese intellectuals have written a considerable amount on his thought. In 1998, a complete biography of Zhang was published by Zuo Yuhe.

Zhu Xi (1130–1200)

Zhu Xi was born in Youqi in Fujian province, China in 1130.[6] Showing himself to be an intellectual prodigy, Zhu passed the top-level *jinshi* exam at the young age of 19 in 1148. From 1151 to 1156, he held minor posts in the government. Zhu's early interests were in Daoism and Buddhism, but he became the student of Li Tong (1093–1163) in 1160. Li had worked within the philosophical tradition of the Cheng brothers (Cheng Yi [1033–1107] and Cheng Hao [1032–85]), who became prominent influences on Zhu. Zhu Xi compiled an anthology of these thinkers known as *Reflections on Things at Hand* that was the primer for Neo-Confucianism for generations. His oral teachings to students are preserved in *Conversations of Master Zhu, Arranged Topically* (1270). One of Zhu Xi's greatest accomplishments was collecting and compiling the Four Books (*sishu*), which were made the foundation of the all-important imperial examinations.

If we were to compare him to Western philosophers of the same stature we would take note of Aristotle's influence in the classical period, Thomas Aquinas in the medieval period, and Immanuel Kant in the Enlightenment period. His systematization of the Confucian Way (*Dao*) into a coherent program of education became the foundation for educational systems in China, Korea and Japan for centuries. In terms of his impact on Confucian thought and upon Chinese intellectual history in general, Zhu Xi ranks along with Confucius and Mencius as one of the three preeminent thinkers of China.

哲学

Quick Guide to Pronunciation

Adapted from Terry Kleeman and Tracy Barrett (2005: 171)

ai	the y in fry	ia	the ca in caveat
an	the on in on	iang	ee, plus the yang in yang
ang	the ong in gong	ie	ee, plus the yeah in yeah
ao	the ow in cow	in	the ee in been
c	the ts in fits	iu	ee, plus the ow in blow
cao	is pronounced tsaow	jiu	is pronounced jeeoh
chiang	is pronounced cheeahng	men	is pronounced muhn
e	the oo in foot	meng	is pronounced muhng
ei	the ay in bay	mo	is pronounced mwho
en	the un in fun	mu'er	is pronounced moo-er
eng	the ung in fungus	o	the aw in awful
er	the are in are	ou	oh
fan	is pronounced fahn	q	the ch in child
fang	is pronounced fahng	qi	is pronounced chee
fei	is pronounced fay	qie	is pronounced cheeyeh
g	the g in girl	qin	is pronounced cheen
gao	is pronounced gaow	quan	is pronounced chooen
gao	is pronounced haow	que	is pronounced chooeh
gu	is pronounced goo	se	is pronounced suh
guo	is pronounced gwoh	shi	is pronounced shur
hai	is pronounced hi	sun	is pronounced swun
hua	is pronounced hwah	u	the ew in few
huan	is pronounced hwahn	u	the oo in boo
huang	is pronounced hwahng	ua	the wa in water
i	the ee in glee	uan	the wan in wander

uan	oo, plus the en in men	xing	is pronounced shing
uang	the wan in wander plus ng	yu	is pronounced yew
		yuan	oo, plus the en in went
ue	oo, plus the e in went	yuan	is pronounced yuwen
un	the won in won	z	the ds in yards
uo	the awe in awful	zeng	is pronounced dzeng
x	the sh in should	zh	the j in juice
xia	is pronounced sheeah	zhou	is pronounced jo
xin	is pronounced sheen		

哲学

Comparative Chronology
of Philosophers

Adapted from Bo Mou (ed.), *History of Chinese Philosophy*, 609–12

Chinese Philosophy	Western Philosophy
2200 BCE	
Xia dynasty (2070–1600 BCE)	
2000 BCE	
Shang dynasty (1600–1046 BCE)	
Zhou dynasty (1046–256 BCE)	
800 BCE	
Spring and Autumn Period (722–481 BCE)	Thales (640–546 BCE)
Confucius (Kong Qiu/Kongzi, 551–479 BCE)	Founding of Rome (508 BCE)
	Heraclitus (535–475 BCE)
500 BCE	
Warring States Period (480–222 BCE)	Parmenides (515–450 BCE)
Mozi (Mo Di, 470–391 BCE)	Anaxagoras (500–428 BCE)
Yangzi (5th century BCE)	Empedocles (*c.*495–435 BCE)
Laozi ? (before 4th century BCE)	Protagoras (485–415 BCE)

Chinese Philosophy	Western Philosophy
	Zeno of Elea (*c.*470 BCE)
	Socrates (470–399 BCE)
	Democritus (460–370 BCE)
	Plato (427–347 BCE)
400 BCE	
Zhuangzi (Zhuang Zhou, 375–300 BCE)	Aristotle (384–322 BCE)
Mencius (Mengzi, 371–289 BCE)	
Hui Shi (350–280 BCE)	
Gongsun Long (320–250 BCE)	
300 BCE	
Xunzi (Xun Kuang, 310–220 BCE)	
Han Fei (*c.*280–233 BCE)	
Qin dynasty (221–206 BCE)	
Han dynasty (206 BCE–220 CE)	
200 BCE	
Dong Zhongshu (179–104 BCE)	
Masters of Huainan (*Huainanzi*, 139 BCE)	
CE	
Wang Chong (*c.*25–100)	
100	
200	
The Three Kingdoms Period (220–80)	Sextus Empiricus (early 3rd century)
He Yan (*c.*204–49)	Plotinus (204–70)
Wang Bi (226–49)	
Jin dynasty (265–420)	
300	

Chinese Philosophy	**Western Philosophy**
Guo Xiang (d. 312)	
Dao An (312–85)	
Hui Yan (336–416)	Augustine (354–430)

400

Northern and Southern dynasties (420–589)	
Seng Zhao (384–414)	Fall of Roman Empire (476)
Bodhidharma (f. 460–534)	Boethius (*c.*480–c.526)

500

Sui dynasty (581–618)

Zhiyi (538–97)

600

Xuanzang (Xuan Zang, 596–664)

Shen Xiu (*c.*605–706)

Tang dynasty (618–907)

Hui Neng (638–713)

Fa Zang (643–712)

700

900

The Five Dynasty Period (907–60)

Song dynasty (960–1279)

1000

Shao Yong (1011–77)	
Zhou Dunyi (1017–73)	
Zhang Zai (1020–77)	
Cheng Hao (1032–85)	
Cheng Yi (1033–1107)	Anselm of Canterbury (1033–1109)

Chinese Philosophy	Western Philosophy
1100	
Zhu Xi (1130–1200)	
Lu Jiuyuan (1139–93)	
1200	
Yuan dynasty (1206–1368)	Renaissance begins in Italy (1215)
	Thomas Aquinas (1224–74)
	William of Ockham (1285–1347)
1300	
Ming dynasty (1368–1644)	
1400	
Wang Yangming (1472–1529)	Copernicus (1473–1543
1500	
	Francis Bacon (1561–1626)
	Galileo Galilei (1564–1642)
	Thomas Hobbes (1588–1679)
	René Descartes (1596–1650)
1600	
Qing dynasty (1616–1911)	Baruch Spinoza (1632–77)
Huang Zongxi (1610–95)	John Locke (1632–1704)
Wang Fuzhi (1619–92)	Gottfried Leibniz (1646–1716)
	George Berkeley (1685–1753)
1700	
Dai Zhen (1723–77)	David Hume (1711–76)
	Immanuel Kant (1724–1804)
	French Revolution (1789–91)
	G. W. F. Hegel (1770–1831)
	Arthur Schopenhauer (1788–1860)

Chinese Philosophy	Western Philosophy
1800	
Opium Wars (1839–43)	John Stuart Mill (1806–73)
Taiping Revolution Civil War (1851–64)	Soren Kierkegaard (1813–55)
Yan Fu (1854–1921)	Karl Marx (1818–83)
Liang Qichao (1873–1929)	Friedrich Engels (1820–95)
Wang Guowei (1877–1927)	William James (1842–1910)
Xiong Shili (1885–1968)	Friedrich Nietzsche (1844–1900)
Zhang Dongsun (1886–1973)	Edmund Husserl (1859–1938)
Hu Shi (1891–1962)	John Dewey (1895–1952)
Mao Zedong (1893–1976)	American Civil War (1861–5)
Liang Shuming 1893–1988)	Alfred North Whitehead (1861–1947)
	Ludwig Wittgenstein (1889–1951)
	Martin Heidegger (1889–1976)
	World War II (1939–45)
1900	
The Boxer Movement (1900)	Gilbert Ryle (1900–76)
He Lin (1902–92)	Hans Georg Gadamer (1900–2002)
Xu Fuguan (1903–82)	Jean-Paul Sartre (1905–80)
Hong Qian (1909–92)	Willard V. Quine (1908–2000)
Tang Junyi (1909–78)	World War I (1914–18)
Republic of China (1912–)	Russian Revolution (1917)
Mon Zongsan (1909–95)	Donald Davidson (1917–2003)
May Fourth Movement (1919)	John Rawls (1921–2002)
Tu Weiming (1940–)	Jacques Derrida (1930–2004)
People's Republic of China (1949–)	Richard Rorty (1931–2007)
Kang Xiaoguang (1963–)	
Great Proletarian Cultural Revolution (1966–76)	

哲学

Notes

Chapter I: Ontology

1. Cheng sets out his view in several places. The essays he contributed to *Philosophy of the Yi: Unity and Dialectics* (2010) are good examples of the way he works with this concept.

2. Tradition says that King Wen of the Zhou dynasty (*c.*1150 BCE) created the hexagrams. Actually, each of these heuristics is also in continual transition as well. In the actual divination process using milfoil sticks, there was a mechanism for what was known as the "moving line" which meant that the *yin* and *yang* aspects of a situation were changing even as the divination was being done. While it is not in the scope of our present introduction to go into the layers of how a hexagram itself reflects change, we may say that the practitioners had an elaborate numerology for making this point and a vocabulary of "old" and "new" *yin* or *yang* in addition to the idea of "moving line." In this respect, the purpose of the *Zhouyi* is not simply a text taking the position that reality is in process, but it means to help its readers reflect on how the world changes and how things change the world, thereby enabling its reader to engage in penetrating self-introspection, considering the outer world, and creatively engaging in the processes of the future.

3. John Major (1993) provides evidence that *yin/yang* categories can be documented as explanatory mechanisms as far back as the Shang dynasty (*c.*1600–1046 BCE).

4. The classic exposition and description of what it is to make a "category mistake" is in Gilbert Ryle (1949).

5. These are long life, riches, soundness of body and serenity of mind, love of virtue, and fulfilling the will of Heaven (2.11).

6. These are misfortune, early death, sickness, distress and confusion of mind, corrupt character, and weakness (2.11).

7. See Chapters 1, 4, 8, 9, 14, 16, 18, 21, 23, 24, 25, 30, 31, 32, 34, 35, 37, 38, 40, 41, 42, 46, 47, 48, 51, 53, 54, 55, 56, 59, 60, 62, 65, 67, 77, 79 and 81. Unless noted, translations from *DDJ* are from Philip Ivanhoe (2002).

8. This is the only instance in the *Daodejing* of the character *di*, a name for the high god of ancient Shang dynasty Chinese religion.

9. The term *ao* is used in Chinese religion for the southwest corner of one's home where the household gods are lodged and worshipped; a sacred space where they are present, even if not visible.

10. Although it is impossible to say for sure whether he is correct, nevertheless, in the Preface to his commentary on the work, Han dynasty scholar Gao You says, "Many of the empire's masters of esoteric techniques journeyed [to Huainan] and made their home [at Liu An's court]. Subsequently [Liu An], with the following eight men, Su Fei, Li Shang, Zuo Wu, Tian You, Lei Bei, Mao Beig, Wu Bei and Jin Chang, and various Confucians who were disciples of the Greater and Lesser Mountain [traditions], together discoursed upon the Way and its Potency [*Dao de*] and synthesized and unified Humaneness [*ren*] and Rightness [*yi*] to compose this work" (quoted in Shuangdi Zhang 1997: 1, 1–2).

11. See John Major et al. 2010: 27–32. Harold Roth (1991, 1994) argues specifically in favor of the Yellow Emperor-Laozi (*Huang-Lao* 黄老) version of Daoism as the primary influence on *Masters of Huainan*.

12. The "four binding cords" (*si wei* 四维) are the "corners" of the compass-circle: Northeast, Southeast, Southwest and Northwest.

13. This is not to say that there were no attempts to make predictions based on the Five Phase physics. There is in Chapter 5 ("Seasonal Rules") of the *Masters of Huainan* a kind of almanac that tells rulers and the people generally what would most likely happen each month and what they should do accordingly in order to obtain harmony with Heaven and *Dao*. What is interesting is that as applied in various ways the recommendations actually yield a kind of rudimentary ecology and environmental balance by protecting natural resources and balancing supply and demand.

14. Introductions to the nature of Buddhism and the challenges it faced in the Chinese context include the following: Karyn Lai (2008: 235–68); JeeLoo Liu (2006: 209–20); Wing-Tsit Chan (1957–8); Leon Hurvitz (1999); Kenneth Ch'en (1964); John Kieschnick (2003) and Arthur Wright (1959).

15. We can compare this argument to George Berkeley's approach to proving the incoherence of the notion of matter as a substratum or the stuff from which objects are made in the third dialogue of his *Three Dialogues between Hylas and Philonous* (1713).

16. Shu-shien Liu tries to make a case that the most prominent of these new philosophers, Zhu Xi, did not borrow concepts or vocabulary from Daoism or Buddhism (Shu-Shien Liu 1998: Chapter 10).

17. Some basic studies of Neo-Confucian thought include Percy Bruce (1923) and Carsun Chang Chang (1957, 1962), Wm. Theodore De Bary (1975), and Shu-shien Liu (2009a and 2009b).

18. The *Zhu Xi Xing Chuang* is the primary source of information on the life of Zhu Xi. It was written by his pupil and son-in-law, Huang Kan (1152–1221).

19. An important historical study on the various uses of Principle(s) (*li*) in Neo-Confucianism is Chan (1964). The centrality of the concept of li (理, pattern, principle) to Zhu Xi's thought is confirmed by the fact that his thought is still sometimes referred to as the School of Li (*Lixue*). See also Philip Ivanhoe (1998).

20. Kirill Thompson (1998) offers a different point of view.

21. Tu Wei-ming (1976) is a spiritual biography of Wang Yang-ming's early life.

22. For an extended discussion of the characteristics of Dai Zhen's naturalism see David S. Nivison (1996).

23. Italian (Fathers: Matteo Ricci; Longobardi; De Urbsis, Aleni and Rho); Portuguese (Francis Furtado); Swiss (Jean Terrenz, Polish (Jean Nicolas Smogolenshi), and French (Ferdinand Verbiest, Nicolas Trigaut).

24. Xu Guangqi and Li Zhizao were two of the "Three Pillars of Chinese Catholicism," along with Yang Tingyun, who was the third.

Chapter II: Epistemology

1. There has been considerable discussion whether *ming* is anything like an equivalent to "fate," if by that we mean that events are fixed and destined to occur as they do. For two essays addressing this topic in the context of Mencius's thought, see Chen Ning (1997) and Ronnie Littlejohn (2001).

2. The modern Chinese philosopher Hu Shi classifies the *mingjia* and *bianshi* thinkers together in the category of Later Mohists (Hu Shi 1928). Angus Graham (1978) provides an important study of the later Mohist texts.

3. This particular *bian* 辨 includes in the Chinese character a component (called a radical) for "knife" (刀). The character is also used for "investigate," "resolve" and is used in the idiom, "This person cannot distinguish beans from wheat" *bubian shu mai* (不辨菽麦)," meaning that such a person is of no use in practical matters.

4. Ian Johnston (2010: 372–4) has an overview of these problems and how various scholars have dealt with them. In the approach taken in this current overview, I generally follow Johnston but with some revisions which the reader can identify by comparing directly my rendering of the text with his.

5. My reconstructions here depend, of course, on my own interpretations of the reconstructed text and A1 is one of the most badly mutilated of the entire canons of later Mohism in the *Mozi*.

6. In my view, it was actually this kind of epistemological insight that led to what some scholars take to be the logic chopping of the *mingjia* and *bianshi* and of course to the famous discussion of what is known as the White Horse Debate (i.e., "a white horse is not a horse") in the text *Gongsun Longzi* attributed to Gongsun Long (b. 380 BCE). For an English translation see Yi-Pao Mei (1953). On the nature of this text see Jianguo Liu (2004), Karyn Lai (2008: 118–23) and Angus Graham (1989).

7. I do not include in this group the philosopher or the text of *Deng Xi*, which is almost certainly a forgery.

8. In the Watson translation of *Zhuangzi* these five passages are pages 132–3; 149–50; 161–2; 162–3; 165–6. See also Ronnie Littlejohn (2010: 35–6).

9. In Western philosophy, the example of Edmund Husserl's (1931) procedure of bracketing may be offered as a point of comparison.

10. For further discussion of Xunzi's philosophy of religion see Edward Machle (1976, 1993).

11. Some recent studies of Wang Chong's *Lunheng* include Guidian Zhou (1994), Michael Puett (2005–6); and Alexus McLeod (2011).

12. A study of Wang's method of pursuing truth which is specifically directed at a chapter from the *Lunheng* that is concerned with Confucius is Alexus McLeod (2007).

13. Huan Tan (43 BCE–28 CE) was admired by Wang Chong. His major work was the "New Discussions" (*Xinlun*). He is reported to have said that the Han fascination with the Daoist immortals (*xian* 仙) was owing to fabricated stories told by the lovers of the strange.

14. Antonio Cua specifically suggests the affinities between Wang Yangming's views of *liangzhi* and Francis Hutcheson's theory of a moral sense (2003: 771). For an interpretation of Hutcheson's position, see D. D. Raphael (1969: I, 269–71).

15. Michael Tophoff (2007) is perhaps one of the most ardent supporters of the position that Wang Yangming was influenced by Chan Buddhism.

16. I refer to the question of what an object is itself as distinguished from its attributes. Many examples could be given of how Russell and Wittgenstein wrested with this problem, I mention only these: Russell's *The Problems of Philosophy* (1912), esp. Chapters 1–5 and *Our Knowledge of the External World* (1914), esp. Chapters 3 and 4, and Wittgenstein's *Tractatus Logico-Philosphicus* (1922), esp. 2.02, 2.021, 2.0272, 2.04, 2.05, 3.203, 3.221 and 3.26.

Chapter III: Value Theory

1. Consider that Yan Lingfeng edited hundreds of volumes of commentaries on the *Analects* that filled a 408-volume edition.

2. A place to begin with a study of the approaches to virtue taken in Confucius and Aristotle is Jiyuan Yu (1998). For an extended discussion of the relationship between Aristotle and Confucius on a number of philosophically significant issues see May Sim (2007).

3. Some Western philosophers have also questioned the appropriateness of the concept of moral saint as an ethical ideal in any morality. See Susan Wolf (1982).

4. An exception to this statement is the work of Chris Fraser (2014).

5. As a test case, consider the famous exchange between Confucius and the Governor of She about whether a son should report his father for stealing a sheep. Confucius insists he should not. He should cover for his father (*Analects* 13.18). I recommend Tim Murphy and Ralph Weber (2010) for further discussion.

6. I am following Angus Graham's translation of *jian ai* as "inclusive concern" and I recommend reading his defense of this translation (1989: 41–2).

7. Karyn Lai discusses this matter of *tui* (2008: 60–3).

8. The *Masters of Huainan* (see Chapter IV) also develops the idea of inborn nature. That text calls on its readers to "return to their nature" (*fan xing*). In both of these sets of materials, becoming a "perfected person" (*zhenren*) means not straying from one's inborn nature.

9. There is a wide divergence in the claims of moral ethologists. As a place to begin, I recommend Frans De Waal (1996) and Steven Pinker (2006). Works that generally lack De Waal's empirical rigor, but build upon his research and that of other ethologists include Marc Hauser (2007). For a general argument against the modernist idea in Western tradition that the human being is born as a completely blank slate see Steven Pinker (2003).

10. A good bit of what I say here and in what follows draws its inspiration from the really fine analysis of Mencius on self-cultivation in Philip Ivanhoe (2000).

11. I wish to acknowledge the work of Peter Gregory that has influenced my assessment of these comparisons between Confucianism and Buddhism.

12. We may think here of Kant's *Critique of Practical Reason* and also *Metaphysics of Morals* as but two such examples.

13. Zhu Xi objected to Buddhism because he believed it undervalued the Five Relationships and encouraged persons to abandon them (Joseph Adler 2008: 60).

14. A thorough discussion of "harmony" in Confucian thought is Chenyang Li 2014.

15. Julia Ching (1976) is a full-scale study of Wang's thought.

16. See Kwong-loi Shun (2002) and Justin Tiwald (2009) for extended discussions.

17. The formulation I use here is only one of three different versions Kant employs. It is basically the universality test and a good place to find it discussed in isolation is "Kant and the German Enlightenment" (Paul Edwards 1972).

Chapter IV: Political Philosophy

1. A substantial and thorough overview of classical Chinese political thought is Roger Ames (1993) and an ambitious effort at a survey of the entire scope of Chinese political philosophy is Gongquan Xiao's two-volume work (1945).
2. See Stephen Angle (2012) and Sor-hoon Tan (2011) for discussions of the relationship of morality and government in Confucius.
3. See Liang Tao (2010) for an overview of early Confucian political thought.
4. For a much fuller discussion of Confucian political philosophy with suggestions for its application in current times see Joseph Chan (2013) and the quite different alternatives held up by Qing Jiang (2013) and Ruiping Fan (2010).
5. That is, Yao, Shun and Yu, the great dynasties of Chinese antiquity.
6. See Justin Tiwald (2008) for an extended discussion of the issue of revolution in Mencius.
7. Shang Yang called his political model "governing by punishment" (*xingzhi* 刑治 or *xingzheng* 刑政) (*Shang Jun Shu*, 77/229, 136/284).
8. JeeLoo Liu (2006: 187–94) has a very clear discussion of the profound difference between Han Fei and Confucius on the relation of morality and politics.
9. I am indebted to Bryan Van Norden (2011: 190–6) for this categorization of Han Fei's techniques of government.
10. *Masters of Huainan* provides us a horrifying picture of the excesses and violence of the Xia period including trying to govern by tortuous punishments such as cooking people alive, forcing persons to walk across fire on hot metal beams and laughing when they fell in, removing hearts from living persons, and grinding persons into meat jam between massive stones (John Major et al. 2010: 2.14).
11. For key thinkers in the development of Chinese political thought in the twentieth century see Chester Tan (1971).
12. For political dissent in China, one can begin with Irene Bloom (2004) and William Jones (2004).
13. See Alan T. Wood (1995) for an argument defending this claim.
14. Laurence Thompson (1958), Richard Howard (1962) and Kung-Chuan Hsiao (1975) are key studies of Kang Youwei in English.
15. Some helpful studies of Liang Qichao's thought in English include Hao Chang (1971) and Joseph Levenson (1970).
16. The periodization of Liang Qichao's thought which I am following is informed by Alison Adcock Kaufman (2007).
17. The first reference to Western socialism seems to be in an essay by Yan Fu (Yuning Li 1971). Ma Zuyi holds that Zhao Bizhen's translation of Fukui Junzo's *Modern Socialism* in 1903 was the first comprehensive introduction of Marxism into China (Ma 1984: 277). The monumental work *Das Kapital*

(1859), the fundamental text of Marxist economics, was translated by Chen Qixiu in 1931. For an overview of Marxism in China 1922–45, see Nick Knight (2010).

18. There are many studies of Mao's thought. Readers may find helpful Nick Knight (2007). Among the great number of biographies, Jonathan Spence (1999) is both reliable and readable. For English readers, the complete collected works of Mao from 1917 to 1945 are at the U.S. Government's Joint Publications Research Service, where all articles signed by Chairman Mao individually or jointly, as well as those unsigned but verified as his, are available. For works after 1945, *Selected Works of Mao Zedong* (1968) is a good source.

19. A delightfully interesting study of the uses and forms of Mao's *Quotations* from the handbook of the Red Guards of the Cultural Revolution (1966–76), to art and song, and many others is Alexander Cook (2014).

20. "Semi-feudalism" is a euphemism for the kind of social structure that evolved over several hundred years and co-opted Confucian texts and thinkers into its intellectual justification of class and gender repression.

21. Eske Mollgaard (2007) explores the argument surrounding whether Tu may be considered a Confucian.

22. A blog site with considerable information about the publications and activities of Tu Weiming is http://tuweiming.net/.

23. John Berthrong interprets Tu's fiduciary society on the analogy of the Christian concept of "the beloved community" and compares both of these to the model of Alfred North Whitehead's "vision of a civilized society" (1994: 104, 130).

Guide to Philosophers and Significant Works

1. See Cook (2013) and Holloway (2009).

2. Julia Hardy (1998) provides a helpful overview of Western interpretations of the *Daodejing*. Judith Boltz (1987) provides us with a survey of Daoist literature.

3. The other three were Wang Guowei, Chen Yike and Zhao Yuanren.

4. Here I am accepting with some modification the characterizations of Mark Csikszentmihalyi (2006) and Mark Lewis (1999).

5. Tu Wei-ming (1976) is a spiritual biography of Wang Yang-ming's early life.

6. A general study that sets Zhu Xi in his intellectual context is Tillman (1992). Works devoted to Zhu's philosophy specifically include Gardner (1990) and Chan (1987).

哲学

References

Adler, Joseph (2008). "Zhu Xi's spiritual practice as the basis of his central philosophical concepts," *Dao: A Journal of Comparative Philosophy* 7.1, pp. 57–79.

Ames, Roger (1986). "Tao and the nature of nature," *Environmental Ethics* 8, pp. 317–50.

——— (1993). *The Art of Rulership: A Study of Ancient Chinese Political Thought* (Albany: State University of New York Press).

——— (2011). *Confucian Role Ethics* (Honolulu: University of Hawaii Press).

Ames, Roger and Henry Rosemont (1998). *The Analects of Confucius: A Philosophical Translation* (New York: Ballantine Books).

Angle, Stephen C. (2009). *Sagehood: The Contemporary Significance of Neo-Confucian Philosophy* (New York: Oxford University Press).

——— (2012). *Contemporary Confucian Political Philosophy* (Oxford: Polity Press).

Arjo, Dennis (2011). "*Ren Xing* and what it is to be truly human," *Journal of Chinese Philosophy* 38, pp. 455–73.

Bell, Daniel (1999). "Democracy with Chinese characteristics: a political proposal for the post-communist era," *Philosophy East and West* 49.4, pp. 451–93.

——— (2006). "East Asia and the West: the impact of Confucianism on Anglo-American political theory," in John Dryzek, Bonnie Honig and Anne Phillips (eds), *The Oxford Handbook of Political Theory* (Oxford: Oxford University Press), pp. 262–81.

——— (2008). *China's New Confucianism: Politics and Everyday Life in a Changing Society* (Princeton: Princeton University Press).

Bersciani, Umberto (2001). *Reinventing Confucianism: The New Confucian Movement.* (Taipei: Taipei Ricci Institute for Chinese Studies).

Berthrong, John (1994). *All Under Heaven: Transforming Paradigms in Confucian-Christian Dialogue* (Albany, NY: SUNY Press).

Bishop, Donald (ed.) (1985). *Chinese Thought: An Introduction* (Delhi: Motilal Banarsidass Publishers).

Blakeley, Donald (2004). "The lure of the transcendent in Zhu Xi," *History of Philosophy Quarterly* 21.3, pp. 223–40.

Bloom, Irene (2004). "The moral autonomy of the individual in Confucian tradition," in William C. Kirby (ed.), *Realms of Freedom in Modern China* (Stanford: Stanford University Press), pp. 19–44.

Boltz, Judith (1987). *A Survey of Taoist Literature, Tenth to Seventeenth Centuries* (Berkeley: Institute of East Asian Studies).

Brooks, E. Bruce and A. Taeko Brooks (1998). *The Original Analects: Sayings of Confucius and His Successors* (New York: Columbia University Press).

Bruce, Percy (1923). *Chu Hsi and His Masters: An Introduction to Chu Hsi and the Sung School of Chinese Philosophy* (London: Probsthain & Co).

Carr, Karen and Philip J. Ivanhoe (2000). *The Sense of Antirationalism: The Religious Thought of Zhuangzi and Kierkegaard* (New York: Seven Bridges).

Chan, Joseph (2013). *Confucian Perfectionism: A Political Philosophy for Modern Times* (Princeton: Princeton University Press).

Chan, Wing-Tsit (1957–8). "Transformation of Buddhism in China," *Philosophy East and West* 7, pp. 107–16.

—— (trans.) (1963a). *Instructions for Practical Living and Other Neo-Confucian Writings by Wang Yang-Ming* (New York: Columbia University Press). Available at https://archive.org/details/instructionsforp00wang.

—— (trans.) (1963b). *A Sourcebook in Chinese Philosophy*, 4th ed. (Princeton: Princeton University Press).

—— (1964). "The evolution of the Neo-Confucian concept Li 理 as principle," *The Tsing Hua Journal of Chinese Studies*. New Series 4, no. 2, pp. 121–48. Available at http://nthur.lib.nthu.edu.tw/retrieve/73262/JA01_1964_p123.pdf.

Chang, Carsun Chang (1957, 1962). *The Development of Neo-Confucian Thought*, 2 vols (New York: Bookman Associates).

Chang, Hao (1971). *Liang Ch'i-Ch'ao and Intellectual Transition in China* (London: Oxford University Press.

Chang, Ruth (2000). "Understanding *Di* and *Tian:* deity and heaven from Shang to Tang," *Sino-Platonic Papers* 108, pp. 1–54.

Ch'en, Kenneth (1964). *Buddhism in China: A Historical Survey* (Princeton: Princeton University Press).

Chen, Junmin (ed.) (2000). 《朱子文集》(*Zhuxi Wenji, The Collected Writings of Zhu Xi) (Defu Wenjiao Jijinhui Chuban*).

Chen, Ning (1997). "The concept of fate in Mencius," *Philosophy East and West* 47.4, pp. 495–520.

Cheng, Chung-ying (2009a). "Philosophical development in late Ming and early Qing," in Bo Mou (ed.), *History of Chinese Philosophy* (New York: Routledge), pp. 429–69.

—— (2009b). "The Yi-jing and Yin-Yang way of thinking," in Bo Mou (ed.), *History of Chinese Philosophy* (New York: Routledge), pp. 71–106.

Cheng, Chung-ying and Nicholas Bunnin (eds) (2002). *Contemporary Chinese Philosophy* (Oxford: Blackwell Publishing).

Cheng, Chung-ying and On-cho Ng (eds) (2010). *Philosophy of the Yi: Unity and Dialectics* (Oxford: Wiley-Blackwell).

Chin, Ann-ping and Mansfield Freeman (1990). *Tai Cheng on Mencius: Explorations in Words and Meaning* (New Haven: Yale University Press).

Chin, Yajun (2010). "Pragmatism in China and Chinese philosophy." Available at http://brown.edu/Programs/Nanjing/content/documents/Pragmatism_in_China_ChenYajun.pdf.

Ching, Julia (1976). *To Acquire Wisdom: The Way of Wang Yang-ming* (New York: Columbia University Press).

Chou, Chih-P'ing (ed.) (1995). *Collection of Hu Shih's English Writings*, 3 vols (Heidelberg: Foreign Language Teaching and Research Publishing Co.).

Chou, Min-chih (2003). "Liang Qichao (Liang Chi'i-ch'ao)," in Antonio S. Cua (ed.), *Encyclopedia of Chinese Philosophy* (New York: Routledge), pp. 388–94.

Classic of History, The Chinese Text Project, http://ctext.org/shang-shu/great-plan.

Cook, Alexander (2014). *Mao's Little Red Book: A Global History* (Cambridge: Cambridge University Press).

Cook, Scott (2013). *The Bamboo Texts of Guodian: A Sudy and Complete Translation* (Cornell East Asia Series).

Csikszentmihalyi, Mark (2006). *Readings in Han Chinese Thought* (Indianapolis: Hackett).

Cua, Antonio S. (1982). *The Unity of Knowledge and Action: A Study in Wang Yang-ming's Moral Psychology* (Honolulu: University of Hawaii Press).

—— (2003). "Wang Yangming," in Antonio S. Cua (ed.), *Encyclopedia of Chinese Philosophy* (New York: Routledge), pp. 760–81.

Davis, Edward (2001). *Society and the Supernatural in Song China* (Honolulu: University of Hawaii Press).

Dai, Zhen (1980).《戴震文集》(*Dai Zhen Wenji, Works of Dai Zhen*) (Beijing: Zhonghua).

Devlin, Patrick (1965). *The Enforcement of Morals* (Oxford: Oxford University Press).

Dennett, Daniel (1976). "The conditions of personhood," in Amelie Rorty (ed.), *Identities of Persons* (Berkeley: University of California Press), pp. 175–96.

De Bary, Wm. Theodore (ed.) (1975). *The Unfolding of Neo-Confucianism* (New York: Columbia University Press).

De Waal, Frans (1996). *Good Natured: The Origins of Right and Wrong in Humans and Other Animals* (Harvard: Harvard University Press).

Dirlik, Arif (1997). "Mao Zedong and 'Chinese Marxism'," in Brian Carr and Indira Mahalingam (eds), *Companion Encyclopedia of Asian Philosophy* (New York: Routledge), pp. 75–104.

Donner, Neal and Daniel Stevenson (1993). *The Great Calming and Contemplation: A Study and Annotated Translation of the First Chapt of Chih-I's Mo-ho chih-kuan* (Honolulu: University of Hawaii Press).

Dryzek, John S., Bonnie Honig and Anne Phillips (eds) (2006). *The Oxford Handbook of Political Theory* (Oxford: Oxford University Press).

Edwards, Paul (ed.) (1972). "History of ethics," *Encyclopedia of Philosophy*, 8 vols (New York: Macmillan).

Eno, Robert (1996). "Cook Ding's Dao and the limits of philosophy," in Paul Kjellberg and Philip J. Ivanhoe (eds), *Essays on Skepticism, Relativism, and Ethics in the Zhuangzi* (Albany: State University of New York Press), pp. 127–51.

Fan, Ruiping (2010). *Reconstructionist Confucianism: Rethinking Morality after the West* (Heidelburg: Springer).

——— (ed.) (2011). *The Renaissance of Confucianism in Contemporary China* (Heidelburg: Springer).

Fang, Qiang and Roger Des Forges (2008). "Were Chinese rulers above the law: toward a theory of the rule of law in China from early times to 1949 CE," *Stanford Journal of International Law* 44. Available at http://www.thefreelibrary. com/Were+Chinese+rulers+above+the+law%3f+Toward+a+theory+of+th e+rule+of+law...-a0182200366.

Forke, Alfred (trans.) (1907). *Philosophical Essays of Wang Ch'ung* (London: Luzac).

Fraser, Chris (2011). "Knowledge and error in early Chinese thought," *Dao: A Journal of Comparative Philosophy* 10.2, pp. 127–48.

——— (2012). "Language and logic in the *Xunzi*." Available at http://cjfraser. net/publications/language-and-logic-in-xunzi/.

——— (2013). "Distinctions, judgment, and reasoning in classical Chinese thought," *History and Philosophy of Logic* 34.1, pp. 1–24.

——— (2014). "The Mohist conception of reality." Available at http://cjfraser. net/2013/02/21/chinese-metaphysics-conference/.

Fung, Yiu-ming (2009). "Philosophy in the Han Dynasty," in Bo Mou (ed.), *History of Chinese Philosophy* (New York: Routledge), pp. 296–302.

Fung, Yulan (1948). *A Short History of Chinese Philosophy* (New York: Macmillan).

——— (1953). *A History of Chinese Philosophy*, 2 vols (Princeton: Princeton University Press).

Gardner, Daniel (1990). *Learning to be a Sage: Selections from the Conversations of Master Chu, Arranged Topically* (Berkeley: University of California Press).

——— (1995). "Ghosts and spirits in the Sung Neo-Confucian world: Chu Hsi on Kuei-shen," *Journal of the American Oriental Society* 115, pp. 598–611.

Goldin, Paul (trans.) (2005). "Xunzi and the Confucian way," in Victor Mair, Nancy Steinhardt and Paul Goldin (eds), *Hawai'i Reader in Traditional Chinese Culture* (Honolulu: University of Hawaii Press), pp. 121–30.

Graham, A. C. (1978). *Later Mohist Logic: Ethics and Science* (Hong Kong: Chinese University Press).

——— (1989). *Disputers of the Tao: Philosophical Argument in Ancient China* (La Salle, IL: Open Court).

—— (1990). *The Book of Lieh-tzu* (New York: Columbia University Press).

Hansen, Chad (1985). "Chinese language, Chinese philosophy, and 'truth'," *Journal of Asian Studies* 44.3, pp. 491–519.

Hardy, Julia (1998). "Influential Western interpretations of the Taote-ching," in Livia Kohn and Michael LaFargue (eds), *Lao-tzu and the Tao-te-ching* (Albany: State University of New York Press), pp. 165–88.

Hauser, Marc (2007). *Moral Minds: The Nature of Right and Wrong* (New York: Harper).

Holloway, Kenneth (2009). *Guodian: The Newly Discovered Seeds of Chinese Religion and Political Philosophy* (Oxford: Oxford University Press).

Howard, Richard (1962). "K'ang Yu-wei: his intellectual background and early thought," in A. F. Wright and Denis Twitchett (eds), *Confucian Personalities* (Stanford: Stanford University Press), pp. 294–316.

Hsiao, Kung-Chuan (1975). *A Modern China and a New World—K'ang Yu-Wei, Reformer and Utopian, 1858–1927* (Seattle: University of Washington Press).

Hsu, Sung-Peng (1995). "Hu Shih," in Donald Bishop (ed.), *Chinese Thought: An Introduction* (Delhi: Motilal Banarsidass Publishers), pp. 364–91.

Hu Shi (1921). "Mr. Dewey and China," *Enlightenment, Supplement of Republic Daily*, July.

—— (1928). *The Development of the Logical Method in Ancient China* (Shanghai: The Oriental Book Co.).

—— (1931). "My credo and its evolution," in *Living Philosophies: A Series of Intimate Credos* (New York: Simon and Schuster), pp. 235–63.

Hu, Xinhe (2002). "Hu Shi's enlightenment philosophy," in Chung-ying Cheng and Nicholas Bunnin (eds), *Contemporary Chinese Philosophy* (Oxford: Blackwell Publishing), pp. 82–102.

Hurvitz, Leon (1999). "Schools of Buddhist doctrine," in W. T. DeBary and Irene Bloom (eds), *Sources of Chinese Tradition: From Earliest Times to 1600*, vol. 1 (New York: Columbia University Press), pp. 433–80.

Husserl, Edmund (1931). *Cartesian Meditations*, D. Cairns (trans.) (Dordrecht: Kluwer).

Hutton, Eric (trans.) (2001). "Xunzi," in P. J. Ivanhoe and Bryan Van Norden (eds), *Readings in Classical Chinese Philosophy*, 2nd ed. (Indianapolis: Hackett Publishing), pp. 255–311.

—— (trans. and ed.) (2014). *Xunzi: The Complete Text* (Princeton: Princeton University Press).

Irwin, Terence (trans.) (1985). *Nicomachean Ethics* (Indianapolis: Hackett Publishing).

Ivanhoe, Philip J. (1998). "*Li*," in Edward Craig (ed.), *Routledge Encyclopedia of Philosophy* (New York: Routledge).

—— (2000). *Confucian Moral Self-Cultivation*, 2nd ed. (Indianapolis: Hackett Publishing Co.).

—— (trans.) (2002). *The Daodejing of Laozi* (New York: Seven Bridges).

————— (2007). "Heaven as a source for ethical warrant in early Confucianism," *Dao: A Journal of Comparative Philosophy* 6.3, pp. 211–20.

————— (2011). "McDowell, Wang Yangming, and Mengzi's contributions to moral perception," *Dao: A Journal of Comparative Philosophy* 10, pp. 273–90.

James, William (2000). *Pragmatism and Other Writings* (New York: Penguin).

Jiang, Qing (2013). *A Confucian Constitutional Order: How China's Ancient Past Can Shape Its Political Future* (Princeton: Princeton University Press).

Jiang, Xinyan (2002). "Zhang Dongsun: pluralist epistemology and Chinese philosophy," in Chung-ying Cheng and Nicholas Bunnin (eds), *Contemporary Chinese Philosophy* (Oxford: Blackwell Publishing), pp. 57–81.

————— (2009). "Enlightenment movement," in Bo Mou (ed.), *History of Chinese Philosophy* (New York: Routledge), pp. 473–511.

Johnston, Ian (trans.) (2010). *The Mozi: A Complete Translation* (New York: Columbia University Press).

Jones, William C. (2004). "Chinese law and liberty in comparative historical perspective," in William C. Kirby (ed.), *Realms of Freedom in Modern China* (Stanford: Stanford University Press), pp. 19–44.

Kalupahana, David (1976). *Buddhist Philosophy: A Historical Analysis* (Honolulu: University of Hawaii Press).

Kang, Xiaoguang (2003a). "Outline of a theory of cultural nationalism" (*Wenhua minzu zhuyi ganglun*)," *Zhanlüe et guanli* 2, pp. 9–27.

————— (2003b). "Searching for a political development strategy for China's new decade" (*Weilai shinian Zhongguo zhengzhi fazhan celüe tansuo*)," *Zhanlüe et guanli* 1, pp. 75–81.

————— 2005. *Benevolent Government: The Third Path for China's Political Development.* (*Renzheng: Zhongguo zhengzhi fazhan de disan tiao daolu*) (Singapore: Shijie keji chubanshe).

————— (2006). "Confucianization: a future in the tradition," *Social Research* 73.1, pp. 77–121.

————— (2011). *The Renaissance of Confucianism in Contemporary China* (Heidelburg: Springer).

Kant, Immanuel (1993, 1788). *Critique of Practical Reason*, Lewis White Beck (trans.), 3rd ed. (Upper Saddle River: Prentice Hall).

Kaufman, Alison Adcock (2007). *One Nation among Many: Foreign Models in the Constitutional Thought of Liang Qichao.* PhD dissertation, University of California, Berkeley. UMI: 3306191.

Keenan, Barry (2011). *Neo-Confucian Self-Cultivation* (Honolulu: University of Hawaii Press).

Kieschnick, John (2003). *The Impact of Buddhism on Chinese Material Culture* (Princeton: Princeton University Press).

Kim, Sungmoon (2012). "A pluralist reconstruction of Confucian democracy," *Dao: A Journal of Comparative Philosophy* 11.3, pp. 315–36.

Knight, Nick (2007). *Rethinking Mao: Explorations in Mao Zedong's Thought* (Lanham: Lexington Books).

———— (2010). *Marxist Philosophy in China: From Qu Qiubai to Mao Zedong* (Heidelburg: Springer).

Knoblock, John (trans. and ed.) (1988, 1990, 1994). *Xunzi: A Translation and Study of the Complete Works*, 3 vols (Stanford: Stanford University Press).

Lai, Karyn (2008). *An Introduction to Chinese Philosophy* (Cambridge: Cambridge University Press).

Lau, D. C. (trans.) (2003). *Mencius* (New York: Penguin Books), revision of 1970 ed.

Lee, Seung-Hwan (1992). "Was there a concept of rights in Confucian-based morality?" *Journal of Chinese Philosophy* 19, pp. 241–61.

Legge, James (trans.) (1885). "*The Li Ki or Collection of Treatises on the Rules of Propriety or Ceremonial Usages*. Chinese Text Project. Available at http://ctext. org/liji/li-yun.

Levenson, Joseph (1970). *Liang Ch'i-Ch'ao and the Mind of Modern China* (Los Angeles: University of California Press).

Lewis, Mark (1999). *Writing and Authority in Early China* (Albany: State University of New York Press).

Li, Chenyang (2014). *The Confucian Philosophy of Harmony* (New York: Routledge).

Li, Yuning (1971). *The Introduction of Socialism into China* (New York: Columbia University Press).

Li, Zhehou (2003).《中国近代思想史論》(*Zhongguo Jindai Sixiang Shilun, A Study of the Modern History of Chinese Thought*) (Tianjing: Tianjing Academy of Social Science Press).

Liang, Qichao (1999).《梁啟超全集》(*Liang Qichao Quanji, The Collected Works of Liang Qichao*), 10 vols (Beijing: Beijing Publishing House).

Liao, W. K. (trans.) (1939). *Complete Works of Hanfeizi* (London: Arthur Probsthain). Available at http://www2.iath.virginia.edu/saxon/servlet/Saxon Servlet?source=xwomen/texts/hanfei.xml&style=xwomen/xsl/dynaxml. xsl&chunk.id=d1.1&toc.depth=1&toc.id=0&doc.lang=bilingual.

Littlejohn, Ronnie (2001). "The received tradition on Ming 命 in the Mencius 孟子," *The Southeast Review of Asian Studies* 23, pp. 33–45.

———— (2006). "Kongzi on religious experience," presented at the American Academy of Religion, Washington, DC, 18–21 November.

———— (2008). "Did Kongzi teach us how to become gods?" in Marthe Chandler and Ronnie Littlejohn (eds), *Polishing the Chinese Mirror: Essays in Honor of Henry Rosement, Jr.* (New York: Global Scholarly Publications), pp. 188–212.

———— (2009). *Daoism: An Introduction* (London: I.B. Tauris).

———— (2010). "Kongzi in the Zhuangzi," in Victor Mair (ed.), *Experimental Essays on Zhuangzi* (Dunedin, FL: Three Pines Press), pp. 175–95.

———— (2011). *Confucianism: An Introduction* (London: I.B. Tauris).

Liu, JeeLoo (2006). *An Introduction to Chinese Philosophy: From Ancient Philosophy to Chinese Buddhism* (Oxford: Blackwell Publishing).

Liu, Jianguo (2004). *Distinguishing and Correcting the Pre-Qin Forged Classics* (Xi'an: Shaanxi People's Press).

Liu, Shu-Shien (1998). "Background for the emergence of Confucian philosophy," in Shu-Shien Liu (ed.), *Understanding Confucian Philosophy: Classical and Sung-Ming* (Westport, CT: Praeger).

———— (2009a). "Neo-Confucianism (1): from Cheng Yi to Zhu Xi," in Bo Mou (ed.), *History of Chinese Philosophy* (New York: Routledge), pp. 365–95.

———— (2009b). "Neo-Confucianism (II): from Lu Jiu-Yuan to Wang Yang-Ming," in Bo Mou (ed.), *History of Chinese Philosophy* (New York: Routledge), pp. 396–428.

Liu, Xiaogan (1994). *Classifying the Chuang-tzu Chapters* (Ann Arbor: Center for Chinese Studies, University of Michigan).

Loy, Hui-Chieh (2010). "Mozi," in *The Internet Encyclopedia of Philosophy*. Available at http://www.iep.utm.edu/mozi/.

Ma, Junwu (trans.) (1920). 《達爾文物種原始》 (*Daerwen Wuzhong Yuanshi, Darwin's Origin of Species*) (Shanghai: Zhonghua Bookstore).

Ma, Zuyi (1984). 《中国翻懿簡史》 (*Zhongguo Fanyi Jianshi, An Outline History of Chinese Translation of Foreign Literature*) (Beijing: China Foreign Translation Publishing Co.).

Machle, Edward (1976). "Hsun Tzu as a religious philosopher," *Philosophy East and West* 26.4, pp. 443–61.

———— (1993). *Nature and Heaven in the Xunzi* (Albany: State University of New York Press).

Major, John (1993). *Heaven and Earth in Early Han Thought* (Albany: State University of New York Press).

Major, John, Sarah Queen, Andrew Set Meyer and Harold Roth (trans.) (2010). *The Huainanzi: A Guide to the Theory and Practice of Government in Early Han China* (New York: Columbia University Press).

Mao, Zedong (1917–45). *Collected Works of Mao Zedong*. U.S. Government's Joint Publications Research Service. Available at http://marxists.org/reference/archive/mao/works/collected-works-pdf/index.htm.

———— (1966). *Quotations from Mao Tse Tung* (Beijing: Peking Foreign Languages Press). *Mao Tse Tung Internet Archive*, 2000. Available at http://www.marxists.org/reference/archive/mao/works/red-book/index.htm.

———— (1968). 《毛泽东選集》 (*Mao Zedong Xuanji, Selected Works of Mao Zedong*) (Beijing: Renmin Press). Available at http://www.marxists.org/reference/archive/mao/selected-works/index.htm.

Marx, Karl (1842). *Theses on Feuerbach*, Cyril Smith and Don Cuckson (trans.). *Marxists Internet Archive*, 2002. Available at http://www.marxists.org/archive/marx/works/1845/theses/theses.htm.

McLeod, Alexus (2007). "A reappraisal of Wang Chong's critical method through the Wenkong Chapter," *Journal of Chinese Philosophy* 34:4, pp. 581–96.

——— (2011). "Pluralism about truth in early Chinese philosophy: a reflection on Wang Chong's approach," *Comparative Philosophy* 2:1, pp. 38–60.

Mei, Yi-Pao (1953). "The Kung-sun Lung Tzu with a translation into English," *Harvard Journal of Asiatic Studies* 16, pp. 404–37.

Metzger, Thomas (1977). *Escape from Predicament: Neo-Confucianism and China's Evolving Political Culture* (New York: Columbia University Press).

Mill, John Stuart (1956). *On Liberty* (Englewood Cliffs: Prentice Hall), first published 1859.

Mollgaard, Eske (2007). "Is Tu Wei-ming Confucian?" *Dao: A Journal of Comparative Philosophy* 6, pp. 397–411.

Mou, Bo (ed.) (2009). *History of Chinese Philosophy* (New York: Routledge).

Mou, Zongzan (1968). "Metaphysical mind and metaphysical nature (*Xinti yu xingti*)," in *Mou Zongsan's Complete Works*, Vol. 5 (Taipei: Lianjing).

——— (1971). *Intellectual Intuition and Chinese Philosophy* (*Zhide zhijue yu zhongguo zhexue*) in *Mou Zongsan's Complete Works*, Vol. 20 (Taipei: Lianjing).

——— (1985). *On the Perfect Good* (*Yuan shan lun*), in *Mou Zongsan's Complete Works*, Vol. 22 (Taipei: Lianjing).

Murphy, Tim and Ralph Weber (2010) "Confucianizing Socrates and Socratizing Confucius—on comparing *Analects* 13:18 and the *Euthyphro*," *Philosophy East and West* 60, pp. 187–206.

Muzumdar, Haridas (1956). "A Chinese philosopher's theory of knowledge," *The Midwest Sociologist* 19.1, pp. 12–17.

Neville, Robert (1977). "Wang Yang-Ming's *Inquiry on the Great Learning*," *Process Studies* 7.4, pp. 217–37. Also available at Religion-Online, Claremont School of Theology. Available at http://www.religion-online.org/showarticle. asp?title=2435.

Ning, Chen (1997). "The concept of fate in Mencius," *Philosophy East and West* (October), pp. 495–520.

Ng, Yu-kwan (1993). *T'ien-t'ai Buddhism and Early Madhyamika* (Honolulu: University of Hawaii Press).

Nivison, David S. (1996). "Two kinds of 'Naturalism': Dai Zhen and Zhang Xuecheng," in Bryan Van Norden (ed.), *The Ways of Confucianism: Investigations in Chinese Philosophy* (Chicago: Open Court), pp. 261–82.

Nylan, Michael (2003). "Wang Chong," in Antonio S. Cua (ed.), *Encyclopedia of Chinese Philosophy* (New York: Routledge), pp. 745–48.

Ownby, David (2009). "Kang Xiaoguang: social science, civil society, and Confucian religion," *China Perspectives* 4. Available at http://chinaperspectives.revues. org/4928.

Peerenboom, Randall P. (1993). *Law and Morality in Ancient China: The Silk Manuscripts of Huang-Lao* (Albany: State University of New York Press).

Pinker, Steven (1994). *The Language Instinct* (New York: William Morrow Co.).

——— (2003). *The Blank Slate: The Modern Denial of Human Nature* (New York: Penguin).

——— (ed.) (2006). *Primates and Philosophers: How Morality Evolved* (Princeton: Princeton University Press).

Puett, Michael (2005). "Listening to sages: divinations, omens, and the rhetoric of antiquity in Wang Chong's Lunheng," *Oriens Extremis* 45, pp. 271–81.

Raphael, D. D. (ed.) (1969). *British Moralists: 1650–1800*, Vol. 1 (Oxford: Clarendon Press).

Rahula, Walpola (1974). *What the Buddha Taught: Revised and Expanded Edition with Texts from Suttas and Dhammapada* (New York: Grove Press).

Rickett, W. Allyn (1985, 1998). *Guanzi: Political, Economic, and Philosophical Essays from Early China*, 2 vols (Princeton: Princeton University Press).

Robins, Dan (2007). "Xunzi," in Edward Zalta (ed.) *The Stanford Encyclopedia of Philosophy*. Available at http://plato.stanford.edu/entries/xunzi/.

Rosemont, Henry (2002). "Is there a universal path of spiritual progress in the texts of early Confucianism?" in Tu Weiming and Mary Evelyn Tucker (eds), *Confucian Spirituality*, Vol. 1 (New York: New Crossroads Publishing Co.), pp. 183–96.

Rosker, Jana (2008). *Searching for the Way—Theory of Knowledge in Premodern and Modern China* (Hong Kong: Chinese University Press).

——— (2010). "The concept of structure as a basic epistemological paradigm of traditional Chinese thought," *Asian Philosophy* 20.1, pp. 79–96.

Roth, Harold (1991). "Who compiled the Chuang-tzu?" in Henry Rosemont, Jr. (ed.), *Chinese Texts and Philosophical Contexts* (La Salle: Open Court), pp. 79–128.

——— (1992). *The Textual History of the Huai-nan Tzu* (Ann Arbor: Association for Asian Studies Monograph No. 46).

——— (1994). "Redaction criticism and the early history of Taoism," *Early China* 19, pp. 1–46.

Ryle, Gilbert (1949). *The Concept of Mind* (London: Hutchinson).

——— (1951). "Systematically misleading expressions," in Gilbert Ryle and Antony Flew (eds), *Logic and Language (First Series) Essays* (Oxford: Basil Blackwell), pp. 11–37.

Russell, Bertrand (1912). *The Problems of Philosophy* (London: Williams and Norgate).

——— (1914). *Our Knowledge of the External World as a Field for Scientific Method in Philosophy* (London: George Allen and Unwin).

Rutt, Richard (trans.) (1996). *Zhouyi: The Book of Changes* (New York: Routledge/ Curzon).

Schwartz, Benjamin (1964). *In Search of Wealth and Power: Yen Fu and the West* (Cambridge: Harvard University Press).

Shaughnessy, Edward (trans.) (1997). *The I Ching: The Classic of Changes* (New York: Ballatine Books).

Shen, Tsing Song (Shen, Vincent) (2015). "Evolutionism through Chinese eyes: Yan Fu, Ma Junwu and their translations of Darwinian evolutionism," *ASIANetwork Exchange*, Spring.

Shun, Kwong-loi (2002). "Mencius, Xunzi, and Dai Zhen: a study of the *Mengzi ziyi shuzheng*," in Alan Chan (ed.), *Mencius: Contexts and Interpretations* (Honolulu: University of Hawaii Press), pp. 216–41.

——— (2005). "Zhu Xi on *Gong* (impartial) and *Si* (partial)," *Dao: A Journal of Comparative Philosophy* 5.1, pp. 1–9.

Sim, May (2007). *Remastering Morals with Aristotle and Confucius* (Cambridge: Cambridge University Press).

Spence, Jonathan (1999). *Mao Zedong: A Life* (New York: Penguin).

Sprague, Elmer (1962). *What Is Philosophy?* (New York: Oxford University Press).

Suzuki, D. T. (1956). *Zen Buddhism: Selected Writings of D. T. Suzuki*, William Barrett (ed.) (New York: Doubleday).

Swanson, Paul L. (1989). *Foundations of T'ien-t'ai Buddhism: The Flowering of the Two Truths Theory in Chinese Buddhism* (Berkeley: Asian Humanities Press).

Tan, Chester (1971). *Chinese Political Thought in the Twentieth Century* (Garden City: Anchor Books).

Tan, Sor-hoon (2007). "Confucian democracy as pragmatic experiment: uniting love of learning and love of antiquity," *Asian Philosophy* 17.2, pp. 141–66.

——— (2009). "Contemporary Neo-Confucian philosophy," in Bo Mou (ed.), *History of Chinese Philosophy* (New York: Routledge), pp. 539–70.

——— (2011). "The Dao of politics: *Li* (rituals/rites) and laws as pragmatic tools of government," *Philosophy East and West* 61.3, pp. 468–91.

Tao, Liang (2010). "Political thought in early Confucianism," *Frontiers of Philosophy in China* 5.2, pp. 212–36.

Thompson, Kirill (1998). "*Li* and *Yi* as immanent: Chu Hsi's thought in practical perspective," *Philosophy East and West* 28.1, pp. 30–46.

Thompson, Laurence (1958). *Ta t'ung shu: The One-world Philosophy of K`ang Yu-wei* (London: George Allen and Unwin).

Tian, Chenshan (2002). "Development of dialectical materialism in China," in Bo Mou (ed.), *History of Chinese Philosophy* (New York: Routledge), pp. 516–38.

Tillman, Hoyt (1992). "A new direction in Confucian scholarship: approaches to examining the differences between Neo-Confucianism and Tao-hsueh," *Philosophy East and West* 42.3, pp. 455–74.

Tiwald, Justin (2008). "A right of rebellion in the *Mengzi*?" *Dao: A Journal of Comparative Philosophy* 7.3, pp. 269–82.

——— (2009). "Dai Zhen on human nature and moral cultivation," in John Makeham (ed.), *The Dao Companion to Neo-Confucian Philosophy* (Heidelburg: Springer), Ch. 20.

———— (2010). "Dai Zhen," *Internet Encyclopedia of Philosophy*. Available at http://www.iep.utm.edu/dai-zhen.

———— (2012). "Xunzi on moral expertise," *Dao: A Journal of Comparative Philosophy* 11, pp. 275–93.

Tophoff, Michael W. (2007). "The ethics of knowledge and action in postmodern organizations," *Journal of Buddhist Ethics* 14, pp. 181–200.

Tu, Wei-ming (1976). *Neo-Confucian Thought in Action: Wang Yang-ming's Youth (1472–1509)* (Berkeley: University of California Press).

———— (1979). *Humanity and Self-Cultivation: Essays in Confucian Thought* (Berkeley: Asian Humanities Press).

———— (1984). *Confucian Ethics Today: The Singapore Challenge* (Singapore: Federal Publications).

———— (1989a). *Centrality and Commonality: An Essay on Confucian Religiousness* (Albany: SUNY Press).

———— (1989b). *Way, Learning and Politics: Essays on the Confucian Intellectual* (Singapore: The Institute of East Asian Philosophies).

———— (1996). *Confucian Tradition in East Asian Modernity* (Harvard: Harvard University Press).

———— (2002). "Mutual learning as an agenda for social development," in Dominic Sachsenmaier (ed.), *Reflections on Multiple Modernities: European, Chinese and Other Interpretations* (Leiden: Brill), pp. 129–36.

———— (2008). "Response," *Dao: A Journal of Comparative Philosophy—Special Issue, Tu Weiming and Confucian Humanism* 7.4, pp. 437–47.

Vankeerberghen, Geiet (2001). *The Huainanzi and Liu An's Claim to Moral Authority* (Albany: State University of New York).

Van Norden, Bryan (ed.) (2002a). "Against Confucianism," Y. P. Mei (trans.). Available at http://faculty.vassar.edu/brvannor/Reader/anticonfucianism.html.

———— (ed.) (2002b). *Confucius and the Analects: New Essays* (Oxford: Oxford University Press).

———— (2011). *Introduction to Classical Chinese Philosophy* (Indianapolis: Hackett Publishing).

Watson, Burton (trans.) (1963). *Hsun Tzu: Basic Writings* (New York: Columbia University Press). Kindle Edition (24 February 2012).

———— (trans.) (1964). *Han Fei Tzu: Basic Writings* (New York: Columbia University Press).

———— (trans.) (1968). *The Complete Works of Chuang-Tzu* (New York: Columbia University Press).

———— (trans.) (2002). *The Essential Lotus: Selections from the Lotus Sutra* (New York: Columbia University Press).

Wei, Tat (trans.) (1973). *Ch'eng Wei-shi lun Doctrine of Mere-Consciousness by Husan Tsang* (Hong Kong: The Ch'eng Wei-shi lun Publication Committee).

Whitehead, Alfred North (1979). *Process and Reality* (New York: The Free Press).

Wittgenstein, Ludwig (1922). *Tractatus Logico-Philosophicus*, Frank Ramsey and C. K. Ogden (trans.) (London: Kegan Paul).

——— (1953). *Philosophical Investigations*, G. E. M. Anscombe (trans.) and Rush Rhees (ed.) (Oxford: Basil Blackwell).

——— (1969). *On Certainty*, G. E. M. Anscombe (trans.) and G. H. Von Wright (ed.) (Oxford: Basil Blackwell).

Wood, Alan T. (1995). *Limits to Autocracy—From Song Neo-Confucianism to a Doctrine of Political Rights* (Honolulu: University of Hawaii Press).

Wolf, Susan (1982). "Moral Saints," *The Journal of Philosophy* 79.8, pp. 419–39.

Wong, Yuk (2003). "Legalism," in Antonio S. Cua (ed.), *Encyclopedia of Chinese Philosophy* (New York: Routledge), pp. 361–3.

Wright, Arthur (1959). *Buddhism in Chinese History* (Stanford: Stanford University Press).

Xiao, Gongquan (1945).《中國政治思想史》(*Zhongguo Zhengzhi Sixiang Shi, A History of Chinese Political Thought*), 2 vols (Chongqing: Shangwu yinshuguan). Vol. 1 trans. into English by Frederick W. Mote as *A History of Chinese Political Thought: From the Beginning to the Sixth Century AD* (Princeton: Princeton University Press, 1979).

Xiao, Yang (2002). "Liang Qichao's political and social philosophy," in Chung-ying Cheng and Nicholas Bunnin (eds), *Contemporary Chinese Philosophy* (Oxford: Blackwell Publishing), pp. 17–36.

——— (2006). "When political philosophy meets moral psychology: expressivism in the *Mencius*," *Dao: A Journal of Comparative Philosophy* 5.2, pp. 257–71.

Yan, Fu (1986). *Yan Fu Ji* (*Collected Works of Yan Fu*), 5 vols (Beijing: Zhonghua Shju).

Yap, Key-chong (2003). "Zhang Dongsun (Chang Tung-Sun)," in Antonio S. Cua (ed.), *Encyclopedia of Chinese Philosophy* (New York: Routledge), pp. 857–61.

Yu, Jiyuan (1998). "Virtue: Confucius and Aristotle," *Philosophy East and West* 48, pp. 329–47.

Yu, Yingshi (1984).《中国近代思想史上的胡適》(*Zhongguo jindai sixingshi shan de Hu Shi, Hu Shi in the History of Chinese Modern Thought*) (Taiwan: Lianjing Publishing House).

Zhang, Dainian (2002). *Key Concepts in Chinese Philosophy* (New Haven: Yale University Press).

Zhang, Dongsun (1934). *Renshi Lun* (*Epistemology*) (Shanghai: World's Books).

——— (1939). "A Chinese philosopher's theory of knowledge," *The Yenching Journal of Social Studies*, 1.2, reprinted in S. I. Hayakawa (ed.), *Our Language and Our World: Selections from Etc.: A Review of General Semantics* (New York: Harper, 1959), pp. 299–323.

Zhang, Shuangdi (1997).《淮南子教釋》(*Huainanzi jiaoshi, Interpreting the Huainanzi's Teachings*) (Beijing: Beijing University Press).

Zhou, Guidian (1994). *Xu shi zhi bian: Wang Chong Zhexue de zong zhi* (*The Distinction between Truth and Falsity: The Purpose of Wang Chong's Philosophy*) (Beijing: Renmin Chubanshe).

Zhou, Xiaoliang (2013). "The studies of Western philosophy in China: historical review, present states and prospects," paper presented at the Chinese Academy of Social Sciences (July 2007). Available at http://www.cnki.com.cn/Article/CJFDTOTAL-ZXYJ200707008.htm.

Zuo, Yuhe (1998).《张东荪传》(*Zhang Dongsun Zhuan, Biography of Zhong Dongsun*) (Jinan: Shandong People's Press).

哲学

Index

Analects 112–20, 165, 170, 223, 248
analogical argument, Mencius's use of 82–4
antirationalism 76
archetypes 47–8
Arhat 148
Aristotle 58, 73, 116, 153, 159, 228, 235, 240, 249, 263, 265

bagua 10
Berkeley, George 43, 242, 246
bianshi (debaters) 64, 68–81, 82, 183, 247, 248; Gongsun Longzi (*bianshi*, debater) 74, 79, 240, 248; Hui Shi (*bianshi*, debater) 74–80, 240
Bishop, Donald ix, 253, 257
Bodhidharma 102, 241
Bodhisattva 38–9; in Hua-yan 150
Book of the Early Han (Hanshu) 27, 229
Book of Great Unity 202
Brahmana 149
Buddhism, Chan Buddhism xi; Consciousness-only Buddhism 40–4, 51, 53, 233; Four Noble Truths of 34–5; Five Precepts of 146; Hua-yan Buddhism 150; Mahayana Buddhism 100, 148, 228; Ten Precepts of 146; Tiantai Buddhism 37–40, 97–100, 102,

228; and Wang Yangming 102–3; and way of morality 150–1, 248; way of precepts in 145–6
Bunnin, Nicholas ix, 255, 257, 258

causality 23, 41, 46, 54, 61, 70–1; Mill's methods for determining 71–2
celibacy 148
Chan, Wing-tsit x, 246, 254,
Chan Buddhism x; and Wang Yangming 102–3; and way of morality 150–1, 248
Cheng Chung-ying ix, xi, 8, 55, 245, 254, 255, 257, 258, 260
Chronicles of Zuo (Zuozhuan) 15, 16–17, 223
Classic of Changes (Yijing) 8–11, 15, 224, 263
Classic of History (Shujing) 8, 15, 17–18, 23, 65, 225, 255
Concept of Mind, The 73, 262
Confucius vii–viii, 16; and Mozi 125–8, 140, 160; on rulership 170–3, 186, 193, 195, 211, 215, 217, 220, 223, 225, 226, 239, 245, 250, 253, 254, 261, 262, 264; in *Zhuangzi* 26, 80–1, 82, 85, 112–19
Consciousness-only Buddhism 40–4, 51, 53, 233

correlative cosmology, correlative physics 6, 12, 26, 58, 110
Critical Essays (Lunheng) 90–4, 232

Dai Zhen 46, 55–6, 61; on desire in morality 162–5, 166, 224, 242, 247, 255, 261, 263, 264
Dao 9–11, 13, 19–26, 29–31, 34, 49, 61, 76, 80–1, 90, 117, 119; *dao* of the ruler, 191; Heaven's *dao* 120–2, 129–34, 158, 172, 173, 180–2; in *Masters of Huainan* 193–7, 246
Daodejing 19–25, 75, 76, 129–34; on rulership 180–2, 191, 192, 226–7, 246, 251, 257
de (virtue, charismatic power) 18, 25, 57, 80, 91, 92, 130–2
Dhammapada 148, 162
disputers, rhetoricians, *see bianshi*
Dong Zhongshu 26, 240

effortless action (*wu-wei*) 21, 23, 27, 29, 76, 81, 95, 104, 130–1, 134; in *Masters of Huainan* 194–7, 232; and ruler 181–4, 188, 191
Eight Trigrams (*bagua*) 10
Eightfold Path 35
Elevating the Worthy (in Mozi) 122–3
Enlightened Despotism 207
equilibrium (harmony, *zhonghe*) in Zhu Xi 152–5, 166
Esoteric Meaning of the Lotus Sutra 98–9
Eudaimonia (as highest good in Aristotle) 153
Evidential Study of the Meaning and Terms of the Mencius (by Dai Zhen) 164, 224
Evolution and Ethics (Tianyanlun) 58–9, 198, 203
exemplary person (*junzi*) in Confucius 115–19, 124, 149, 164, 175, 188

fa, Heaven's models, norms, in Mozi 125–7
false analogy 83–4
Fan Ruiping 220–1
Fate (*ming*) in Mozi 64–6, 120–2; belief in criticized by Wang Chong 91–4, 247, 254, 261
fiduciary community 216–19
filial piety in Dai Zhen 57; in Confucius 114–15; in Wang Yangming 105, 161; in Zhu Xi 155–7
Five Elements or Phases (*wuxing*) 6, 9, 16–17; and the "Great Plan" 18–19; in *Masters of Huainan* 30, 32, 42; and Supreme Ultimate 47, 48–50, 54; and Western science 58, 61, 95, 122, 155
Five Precepts 146
Five Relationships (of Confucianism) 113–15; compared with 'inclusive concern' 126, 128, 149, 249
Four Noble Truths of Buddhism 34–5
Four propensities, seeds in human nature in Mencius (*siduan*) 134
Fung Yulan viii–ix; on Principle in Zhu Xi 47–50, 197, 256

Gaozi debate with Mencius on human nature 83–4
Gongsun Longzi (*bianshi*, debater) 74, 79, 240, 248
"Great Commentary" 8–15, 224–5
"Great Plan" (*Hong Fan*) 8, 17–19, 23, 225

Han Fei and Legalist school 184–7; *dao* of the ruler 191; five tactics of government 188–91; reinterpretation of Daoist concepts 191–2, 197, 225, 240 harm principle (of John Stuart Mill) 199–200

heart-mind (*xin*): its moral drives 134–43; 154–7, 165–8, 175–6; in Wang Yangming 104–6, 157–9; in Xunzi 86–90, 93, 102

Heaven (*tian*) 6; the *dao* of Heaven 21–2, 39, 61, 194–5; Heaven's delegated officials 178, 246; in Mozi 64–6, 79, 88; principles and patterns of 10, 17–18, 32, 21; Wang Chong on 91–5, 101, 120–5, 128, 162–5; Xunzi on 89

heaven and earth (*tiandi*) 6, 9–10, 19, 20, 23–4, 26, 27–31, 46, 49, 50–4, 80, 162–5, 191–2

Hu Shi 58–62, 226, 243, 247, 255, 257, 265

Huainanzi (*see Masters of Huainan*)

Hua-yan Buddhism 150

Hui Shi (*bianshi*, debater) 74–80, 240

human nature (*xing*) 12–13, 54–7; Han Fei on 185–6, 225, 262, 263; "inborn nature" in *Daodejing* 133; Mencius and Gaozi 83–4; Mencius on 134–40; Xunzi on 140–3

humane government (*renzheng*) 173–5, 258

humaneness (*ren*): in Confucius 113–15, 137–8; criticized in Daoist materials 77, 129, 133–5; in Later Mohist sections 70; in Mencius 175–83, 192–4, 204, 246; Wang Yangming on 156–7

Idealism 40–4, 51–3

"inclusive concern" (*jian ai*) 126–9, 138, 157, 204, 249

Instructions for Practical Living (by Wang Yangming) 51, 52, 156, 161, 232, 254

Jixia Academy 74, 82, 85, 140, 225, 227, 230, 233

just war (theory of) 179

"justice as harmony" 221

justified true belief 96–7

Kang Xiaoguang 220, 243, 261

Kang Youwei 202, 227, 250

Kant, Immanuel 46; compared with Zhu Xi 50–1, 108, 151; and Mou Zongsan 165–8, 231, 235, 242, 249, 258

karma 146–7

Lai, Karyn x, 68, 246, 248, 249, 259

language instinct 136–7, 262

Lao-Zhuang Daoism 19–27, 75–81, 85, 90, 103, 129–32, 180–4, 226

Later Mohist/Mohism (*bianshi* debaters) 64, 69–78, 247, 256

Legalism 184–7, 227, 265

li (Principle[s]) 6, 9, 10, 17, 45–9, 51, 55–7, 106, 247

li (rites and proprieties of conduct) 114, 115, 116, 133, 135, 137, 140, 141, 142, 143, 144, 145, 165, 171, 173, 175, 192, 218, 259, 263

Liang Qichao 202–3, 210, 227, 243, 250, 255, 258, 259, 265; on new citizenry 203

limiting concept 23

Little Red Book, the (*see Quotations from Chairman Mao*)

Liu, Jeeloo ix, 41, 100, 176, 246, 250, 260

Lotus Sutra 37, 39, 98, 99, 228

Luohan 148

Luxuriant Dew of the Spring and Autumn Annals 26

Ma Junwu 59, 263

Mahayana Buddhism 100, 148, 228

Mao Zedong 207–14; on democratic dictatorship 212; on new democracy 210–12; on new economy 212–13, 228–9, 243, 251, 255, 259, 260, 263; on politics as dialectics 208–10

Marxism, Sinification of 207–14

Masters of Huainan (*Huainanzi*) 26, 27–33; political views of 192–7

material substance 42

materialism in India 41–3; dialectical materialism and Marxism 208, 263

May Fourth Movement 215, 228, 243

Mencius 51, 85, 102, 128, 140, 156, 158, 160, 165, 177, 224, 227, 230, 233, 235, 240, 247, 249, 250, 254, 255, 259, 261, 263, 265; on analogical reasoning 82–4; four propensities, seeds (*siduan*) 134–9; and Gaozi 83–4; on humane government 174–7; on just war 179; and Xunzi 140–3

meritocracy 122, 170, 186

meta-ethics 111

Mill, John Stuart, *On Liberty* 198, 199–201; Methods for Determining Cause 71, 243, 261

moral experts 144–5, 264

Mou Zongsan 165–8, 231, 261

Mou Bo xi, 239, 252, 254, 256, 260, 263

Mozi 64, 82, 85, 87, 93, 95, 97, 102, 143, 157, 179, 186, 193, 230–1, 239, 247, 258, 260; Elevating the Worthy 81–5; Heaven as agent 120–1; judging between claims 65–8; and "inclusive concern" for all persons 126–9, 138; objective universal morality 124–6

nature (*xing*) 12, 13, 14, 49, 51, 54, 57, 83–5, 95, 98, 105, 108–10; Buddha nature 150, 156, 162, 175; Han Fei on 185–6, 197, 207, 216, 249, 253, 255, 261, 262, 263; inborn nature 133; Mencius on 136–40; Xunzi on 141–3

Neo-Confucianism 45–6, 55, 59, 154, 156, 165–7, 235, 247, 253, 254, 255, 256, 258, 260, 261, 263, 264, 265

New Confucianism 215, 220, 231, 253

New Culture Movement 226

nirvana 34, 35–6, 37–9, 146, 147, 148, 150

normative ethics 111, 125

On Liberty 198, 19; Yan Fu's translation of 200, 261

Origin of Species, Ma Junwu's translation of 59, 260

"perfected person" (*zhenren*) 76, 78, 81, 91, 134, 182, 195, 197, 249

Pinker, Steven 136; against the blank state idea 249, 262

Platform Sutra of the Sixth Patriarch 102

Plato viii, the Forms 47, 50; on knowledge 96–7; the *Republic* 202, 240

Pluralistic Cultural Epistemology 107–10, 234

politicized Confucianism 218

"politics means rectifying" 171

Pragmatism 220, 226, 255, 258

pure knowledge (*liangzhi*) 51–5, 100–6, 156–60

qi (concrete objects) 6, 46, 53, 54

qi (primordial substance, energy) 6, 9, 10, 11, 12, 13, 14, 15, 16, 19, 20, 29, 30, 31, 32, 37, 40, 42, 49, 50,

52, 53, 54, 56, 57, 58, 61, 93, 94–6, 122, 155, 192, 193, 194, 196, 229

Quotations from Chairman Mao (a.k.a. the *Little Red Book*) 207, 255

Records of the Grand Historian (*Shiji*) 68, 82

Reductio ad absurdum 91

ren, humaneness: Confucius 113–15, 137–8; criticized in Daoist materials 77, 129, 133–5; in Later Mohist sections 70; in Mencius 175–83, 192–4, 204, 246; in Wang Yangming on 156–7

rulership: Confucius on 170–3; Hanfei on 186–7, 190, 196, 210, 229, 253; Lao-Zhuang and Yellow Emperor Daoism 182–4; Mencius on 176–8; Mozi on 127

Russell, Bertrand 2, 108, 248, 262

self-cultivation 112, 115, 135, 149, 160, 163, 171, 215; Confucius on 116–18, 109–110; Tu Weiming on 215–19; Zhu Xi on 153–6

selfish desire, selfishness (*siyu*) 104, 105, 106, 140, 153–5, 157–9, 160–2, 172

Shang Yang 176–7, 179, 184, 197, 250

Siddhartha Gautama (the historical Buddha) 34, 98, 228

social contract 205, 217, 218

Social Darwinism 198–9

solipsism 43, 44

state of nature 185, 192

storehouse consciousness 41, 42, 44; in Xuanzang 44, 90

Supreme Ultimate (*taiji*) in Zhu Xi 46–50, 51, 55, 155,

"teaching of complete virtue" 166

"teaching without words" ("wordless teachings") 81, 194, 195

ten paradoxes of Hui Shi 75

Ten Precepts 146

Ten Wings of *Classic of Changes* 9, 165, 224

Threefold Truth Epistemology 97–100, 145

tian (see Heaven)

Tiantai Buddhism 37–40, 97–100, 102, 228

Tu Weiming 214–19, 220, 231, 243, 251, 262, 264

"universal laws of all nations" in Liang Qichao 205

"unmoved mover" 13

utilitarian, utilitarianism 87, 127, 159, 175, 176, 205

virtue (*de*) 18, 25, 57, 80, 91, 92; (charismatic power) 130–2

Wang Chong 90–7; *Critical Essays* (*Lunheng*) 90–4; falsity (*xu*) 91–2, 95–7; method of the four doubts 93

Wang Yangming 46, 51–4, 55, 56, 100–3, 156–61, 162, 163, 166, 232, 242, 248, 255, 258, 254

"way of precepts," Buddhism 145–8

Western Learning (*Xi xue*) 203, 205, 207

wu-wei 21, 23, 27, 29, 76, 81, 95, 104, 130–1, 134; in *Masters of Huainan* 194–7, 232; and ruler 181–4, 188, 191

wuxing 6, 9, 16–17; and the "Great Plan," 18–19; in *Masters of Huainan* 30, 32, 42; and Supreme Ultimate 47, 48–50, 54; and Western science 58, 61, 95, 122, 155

Xuanzang 40–5, 232–3, 241
Xunzi 85–7, 185, 225, 233–4, 240, 248, 256, 257, 259, 260, 262, 263, 264; on *bianshi* debaters 74; on moral experts 144–5; on moral self-cultivation 140–43; on use of reason to gain correct knowledge 86–90

Yan Fu 58–9; on John Stuart Mill 197–201, 203, 234, 243, 250, 263, 265
Yangzi attacked by Mencius 82, 239
Yellow Emperor 5, 23, 55, 122–5, 152
Yellow Emperor Daoism 28, 81; on rulership 182–4, 191, 193, 196, 246
yin and *yang* 10–13, 15, 19, 20, 24, 28, 29, 30, 37, 42, 47, 49, 58, 59, 89, 93, 193, 196, 245

Zhang Dongsun 107, 234, 235, 243, 258, 265, 266; theory of knowledge 107–10
Zhiyi 37, 39, 40, 97–100, 241
Zhongyong 152, 165
Zhouyi 9, 11, 26, 224, 245, 262
Zhu Xi 45, 51, 54, 55, 56, 156, 157, 158, 160, 162, 163, 165, 166, 232, 235, 242, 246, 247, 249, 251, 253, 254, 260, 263; on Principle(s) 46–50; on self-cultivation 153–6
Zhuangzi 19, 23–8, 87, 129, 132–4, 192, 195, 226–7, 240, 248, 254, 256, 259; criticism of reason and Hui Shi 74–81; Lao-Zhuang and Yellow Emperor Daoism 182–4